# OLD WARSAW
# COOKBOOK

# The Hippocrene Cookbook Library

Afghan Food & Cookery
African Cooking, Best of Regional
Albanian Cooking, Best of
Argentina Cooks!, Exp. Ed.
Australia, Good Food From
Austrian Cuisine, Best of, Exp. Ed.
Belgian Cookbook, A
Brazilian Cookery, The Art of
Bulgarian Cooking, Traditional
Burma, Flavors of,
Cajun Women: Cooking With
Caucasus Mountains, Cuisines of the
Croatian Cooking, Best of, Exp. Ed.
Czech Cooking, Best of, Exp. Ed.
Danube, All Along The, Exp. Ed.
Dutch Cooking, Art of, Exp. Ed.
Egyptian Cooking
Eritrea, Taste of
Filipino Food, Fine
Finnish Cooking, Best of
French Caribbean Cuisine
French-English Dictionary of
   Gastronomic Terms
French Fashion, Cooking in the
   (Bilingual)
Greek Cuisine, The Best of, Exp. Ed.
Haiti, Taste of, Exp. Ed.
Havana Cookbook, Old (Bilingual)
Hungarian Cookbook, Exp. Ed.
Hungarian Cooking, Art of, Rev. Ed.
Icelandic Food & Cookery
Indian Spice Kitchen
International Dictionary of
   Gastronomy
Irish-Style, Feasting Galore
Italian Cuisine, Treasury of
   (Bilingual)
Japanese Home Cooking
Korean Cuisine, Best of
Laotian Cooking, Simple
Latvia, Taste of
Lithuanian Cooking, Art of
Mayan Cooking

Mongolian Cooking, Imperial
Norway, Tastes and Tales of
Persian Cooking, Art of
Peru, Tastes of
Poland's Gourmet Cuisine
Polish Cooking, Best of, Exp. Ed.
Polish Country Kitchen Cookbook
Polish Cuisine, Treasury of
   (Bilingual)
Polish Heritage Cookery, Illustrated
   Edition
Polish Holiday Cookery and Customs
Polish Traditions, Old
Portuguese Encounters, Cuisines of
Pyrenees, Tastes of
Quebec, Taste of
Rhine, All Along The
Romania, Taste of, Exp. Ed.
Russian Cooking, Best of, Exp. Ed.
Scandinavian Cooking, Best of
Scotland, Traditional Food From
Scottish-Irish Pub and Hearth
   Cookbook
Sephardic Israeli Cuisine
Sicilian Feasts
Slovak Cooking, Best of, Exp. Ed.
Smorgasbord Cooking, Best of
South African Cookery, Traditional
South American Cookery, Art of
South Indian Cooking, Healthy
Spanish Family Cookbook, Rev. Ed.
Sri Lanka, Exotic Tastes of
Swiss Cookbook, The
Syria, Taste of
Taiwanese Cuisine, Best of
Thai Cuisine, Best of, Regional
Turkish Cooking, Art of
Turkish Cuisine, Taste of
Ukrainian Cuisine, Best of, Exp. Ed.
Uzbek Cooking, Art of
Wales, Traditional Food From
Warsaw Cookbook, Old

# OLD WARSAW

# COOKBOOK

## Rysia

HIPPOCRENE BOOKS
New York

This paperback edition published in 1990 by
HIPPOCRENE BOOKS, INC.
171 Madison Avenue
New York, NY 10016

*Fourth printing, 2003*

ISBN 0-87052-932-3

*Illustrated by*
Irena Lorentowicz

Original Library of Congress Card No. 56-8468
Original copyright © 1958 by Roy Publishers, A.N., New York.

Printed in the United States of America.

## ACKNOWLEDGMENT

I wish to thank Mrs. Elizabeth Clark, Mrs. Phyllis Coons, and Mrs. Barbara Wells for helping me in adapting the original Polish recipes to standard American measures. I also want to thank all the many friends who contributed to the "International Gourmet Dishes" section, and with whom I had much enjoyment in trying them out.

RYSIA

# ABBREVIATIONS

| | |
|---|---|
| c. | cup |
| lb. | pound |
| pt. | pint |
| qt. | quart |
| gal. | gallon |
| t. | teaspoon |
| T. | tablespoon |
| oz. | ounce |
| pkg. | package |

# CONTENTS

# INTRODUCTION

*We may live without poetry, music and art;*
*We may live without conscience and live without heart;*
*We may live without friends; we may live without books;*
*But a civilized man cannot live without cooks*

BULWER LYTTON, EDWARD ROBERT

THE gathering of people around a well-laden and nicely decorated table, to pass some time in eating and in friendly conversation, is surely one of the most ancient and still one of the most pleasant social activities.

Epicure teaches us that the fundamental physical needs of a living being can be reduced to just three; the need to eat and drink, to sleep and to procreate.

Survival though is not the only aim in our fulfilment of biological necessities. So far as sleeping goes as an essential to living beings, it can truly be said that it is being fulfilled nowadays more or less in the same manner as many thousands of years ago. How meaningless the remaining two "needs" would be if narrowed to the sole aim of survival! The sources of poetry, music and art have been nourished through the ages by the infinite variations and challenge of satisfying the other two "needs."

Since the time of our early ancestors, who satisfied their hunger with the raw meat of captured animals or with the vegetables and fruit offered by nature, "cooking is become an art, a noble science" —as Robert Burton observed in his *Anatomy of Melancholy*.

As in many other aspects of so called technological progress, however, even in the fulfilment of hunger, there is the danger of sacrificing to efficiency, speed and caloric count—the intangibles of humanity. . . . And in the speeded up tempo of our times we are sometimes apt to forget the values that should rule even such "biological activity" as eating or drinking: such as friendliness, relaxation and generous hospitality and the ability to share the common table with humour and warmth.

The great pressures brought upon us by the machine age have often tended to discourage such leisurely traditions as hospitality and local customs, while encouraging a tendency to uniformity and a neglect of such social activity as the art of good and original cooking. On the other hand the potential speed of communication between various countries of the world, has made it possible for all to know more of other people's customs, and no one nowadays hesitates to eat a Chinese dinner in Chicago or a French dinner in Calcutta or a sandwich and a Coca-Cola in Rome.

This interchange of customs between countries through the exchange of recipes is certainly not new, although greatly accelerated. The same occurred in the past when exchange of cooking arts and of cooks was almost as important as the exchange of diplomatic notes and of ambassadors.

It was not different in Poland in the past.

In ancient Poland the social character prevailed in everyday life, whenever men gathered, the standing motto was: eat a lot. Do it before a battle, a hunt or a celebration, do it for amusement, do it for company or even do it for show. One believed that a healthy person can eat a lot: the more he eats the heartier he will be. Few rules of etiquette were observed among them, one law always prevailed: each newcomer had to be welcomed with open arms. The *credo* of the host was to perform his duty with the utmost generosity.

The traditional Polish cooking was basically simple, though ample; always turning to the wealth of the earth and forest for its staples. With the trips abroad of the Polish nobility and the influx of foreign influence, taste conformed slowly to the rules of the West. In the beginning the "French" or the "Italian" ways of eating were laughed at, the small servings of different courses were looked upon with scorn, but progressively the Polish cooking blended many elements of Western *comme il faut* together with its own basic substratum. Nevertheless Polish cooking remained original and an entity in itself. All the herbs and spices were used without discrimnation: they arrived in Poland from the Far East and were quite expensive . . . thus a Polish nobleman to be a true host, felt that in order to show all his generosity he had to add as much as possible of pepper and cloves, raisins and cinnamon, saffron and paprika, the more the better! The proverb said: *Drozsza przyprawa niz potrawa* (more expensive the seasoning than the food). But this was the custom only of the upper-upper classes in Poland. The poor people didn't know the taste of fancy spices and ate exculsively of the products given by the earth and the dairy. Potatoes, which later became so popular, did not exist for Polish peasants before the nineteenth century. Another paradox in food fashions was that mushrooms, almost unknown to Polish society, were widely used by the lower classes.

Until the sixteenth century the habit of drinking was still a sober one. Beer was the only drink served during a meal. There were 486 different qualities of beer. English beer was the "proper" one to drink. Wines were served after dinner, and glasses were broken as a sign of great respect to the guest who used them: there could be no worthier follower. . . . Water was brought to the table only during the reign of August III and it was commonly said that its only use was for washing. At the end of the sixteenth century wine started to be more popular. First it was imported from Hungary. In the seventeenth century the wine of Burgundy was acclaimed, in the nineteenth century, Champagne. Vodka, traditionally associated with Poland, was practically unknown until the twentieth century, except to the peasants. Coffee arrived in Poland from the East at the end of the eighteenth century, tea from England at the same time. So we see how things have not really changed much after all, apart from their tempo, and to-day as in the Old Warsaw it is often considered more elegant to serve unusual dishes to guests.

The hostess of to-day, like her great-grandmother, takes pride in drawing on the secrets of the cuisine of other countries. Unlike her forbears she cannot have in her kitchen a French pastry cook and an Italian chef, so she has developed her own skills. She has the source books of a thousand good cooks instead of the services of several and she can become in her own kitchen a citizen of the world.

# APPETIZERS

Appetizers have a great tradition in making a Polish meal. Poles have always liked to eat a lot; be it from need or habit, but much more for company and amusement. Appetizers thus served with a drink of vodka were always a good way to start an easy-going and happy dinner, where "feasting" was above all understood as passing time in community, and sharing the pleasures of life. Each newcomer was always accepted with open arms. This was the main principle of Polish etiquette.

Appetizers depend more on imagination and good taste than on any formal recipes. Their preparation should consider the specialities of the season, decorative effects and their relation to the dinner that follows. So we are providing a few suggestions, a few scattered recipes, leaving the rest to the whimsy of the lady of the house.

## 1. SUGGESTIONS: READY-MADE

*Marinated herring* served on pumpernickel bread. To give that finished look, cut bread into squares or circular shapes and trim away the crusts.

*Herring in sour cream* served on round Melba toast or as above.

*Caviar,* red or black, served on round Melba toast or soya-bean crackers.

*Kielbasa,* Polish sausage cut in small pieces and served on toothpicks with a drink of vodka.

*Fillets of Anchovies* on round Melba toast or pumpernickel bread squares.

*Olives* black or green in a bowl or dish.

*Marinated Mushrooms,* marinated hearts of artichokes, or any marinated vegetable, for example: green tomatoes, cauliflower, red peppers, make a colourful beginning to a meal.

## 2. RECIPES

### Chicken Livers

| | |
|---|---|
| 4 chicken livers | 2 hard-boiled eggs |
| ½ c. of milk | ½ lb. ham |
| 2 T. chicken fat or butter | 3 T. peanut oil |
| 1 onion | Salt and pepper |

Take 3 or 4 chicken livers. Soak them in milk for 2 hours. Drain and fry until they are hard (or cooked through). Fry them in chicken fat for the best result, but butter will do. Then mince the liver in a mincer together with a medium-sized onion (if you do not have a mincer, chop them very finely) and two hard-boiled eggs, plus ½ lb. of ham or broiled pork chops—a touch that will delight your friends. Add salt and pepper and 3 T. of peanut oil. Use as a spread on bread, crackers or toast.

### Anchovy Paste

| | |
|---|---|
| 2 t. anchovy paste | 2 T. soft butter |

Take 2 t. of anchovy paste, add 2 T. of butter and work into a smooth paste. Serve on white sandwich bread and cut into cookie shapes. Soya-bean crackers are preferred by some.

### Roquefort Cheese Spread

4 oz. Roquefort cheese          3 oz. cream cheese
4 T. sour cream

A medium-sized piece of Roquefort cheese (4 oz.) passed through
the sieve and mixed with a small 3 oz. package of cream cheese and
4 T. of sour cream is undoubtedly food for the Gods. Serve on oyster
crackers. Cover with another cracker, giving it a well-tailored
look.

### Cottage Cheese Spread

¼ lb. cottage cheese          Salt
3 sections garlic             Paprika
4 T. sour cream               1 t. Worcestershire sauce

Take a ¼ lb. of cottage cheese, (or cream cheese) add 3 sections of
garlic and let it stand for 3 hours. Then, take out the garlic and add
4 T. of sour cream, a dash of salt and paprika and a t. of Worcestershire sauce. Serve as a dip with potato chips.
If you have a late evening engagement or an opera ticket, you can
use instead of garlic, 2 bouillon cubes dissolved in 2 t. of water. Add,
as a colour touch, chopped parsley, dill or chive.

### Mozzarella Cheese Toasted Canapés

Mozzarella (or any easy melting     Salt
  cheese)                           Paprika
White sandwich bread

Cut thin white sandwich bread into four-square pieces. Cover with
a piece of Mozzarella. Add a dash of salt for flavour and paprika for
colour. Broil until the cheese melts and begins to get a healthy rosy
hue.

### 'Vol au vent' with Mushrooms

Crawford's "Ufillit" biscuits.    1 can mushrooms
1 c. milk                         1 small onion
1 T. flour                        1 T. butter

Prepare a white sauce with 1 T. of butter, 1 T. of flour and one cup
of milk. The consistency should be fairly thick. Brown finely chopped onion in butter. Add a small can of sliced mushrooms. Simmer
for 5 minutes. Combine with white sauce. Serve in Crawford's
"Ufillit" biscuits. The Crawford biscuits are delicious, but any un-
filled biscuits from the corner bakery shop will do nicely. Place the
filled biscuits in the oven (250°) for 15 minutes. Chopped ham or
smoked bacon may be used in place of mushrooms.

## Eggs in Mustard Sauce

Hard-boiled eggs                              Mustard Sauce

Cover peeled hard-boiled eggs with mustard sauce (see p. 101) and serve on a plate. It makes a good Lenten appetizer.

## Triscuit à la Italienne

Triscuits (or white bread, cut          Tomatoes
   to cookie shapes)          Fillets of anchovies
Grated cheese (Parmesan)                 Garlic salt
Salt and pepper

Slice tomato. Place on buttered triscuit crackers. Put a fillet of anchovy or a piece of ham in the middle, and sprinkle abundantly with grated Parmesan cheese. Add a dash of pepper, salt and garlic salt. Put in oven for 15 minutes (250°).

## Lobster Avocado Canapés

¼ lb. cooked lobster                     1 avocado pear
3 T. olive oil                            Juice of 1 lemon
2 sections garlic                         Salt and pepper

Chop cooked lobster meat. Mix with mashed avocado. Add pressed garlic or garlic salt, salt and pepper to taste, olive oil, and the juice of part, or all of 1 lemon if needed. Spread on white bread cut with the cookie cutter.

## Stuffed Celery

Celery                                     7 radishes
¼ lb. cottage cheese                     Salt and pepper
2 T. chopped chives or scallions         Paprika
3 T. sour cream

Mix 3 T. of sour cream with ¼ lb. of cottage cheese. Add chopped radishes and chives or scallions. Sprinkle with salt, pepper, and paprika. Fill pieces of celery and serve.

## 'Saucisson à la Polonaise'

Vienna Sausages (cocktail size)

Use cocktail size frankfurters. Fry them and serve on coloured tooth picks. Stick them in a head of red cabbage for decoration. To keep warm and gay or for toasting, place a candle or an alcohol burner on the platter, or in a hollow place in the centre of the cabbage, and pass the sausages over the flame just before eating.

### Shrimp in Mayonnaise

Shrimp, cooked        Mayonnaise

Frozen, fresh or canned shrimps may be used. Take a fresh eggplant. Cut off both ends and stand on a platter. Fill the top of the eggplant with mayonaise and stick the shrimps into the eggplant with tooth picks in porcupine fashion.

### Bread Sticks in Ham Blankets

Bread sticks        Smoked prosciutto
Italian fresh ham        Butter

Butter the bread sticks, leaving one end unbuttered for holding. Wrap with slices of Italian smoked ham and serve.

### Stuffed Eggs Polish Style

Hard-boiled eggs        Chopped chive
2 T. butter        2 T. sour cream
Bread-crumbs

Chill hard-boiled eggs in cold water. When completely cold, cut them in the shell lengthwise. Take out the half egg carefully without damaging the shell. Chop the egg. Add a dash of salt and pepper, chopped chive or onion browned in butter, and two T. of sour cream. Refill the shells, sprinkle the tops with bread-crumbs and brown again, face down in frying pan, or butter the tops and brown under broiler.

### Sardine Spread

1 can sardines        ¼ lb. cottage cheese or a small
Juice of 1 lemon        package (3 oz.) of cream
3 T. sour cream        cheese
Salt and Paprika

Mix a can of sardines with ¼ lb. of cottage cheese, sour cream, lemon juice, and finally salt and paprika, to taste. Serve on pumpernickel bread.

### Watercress Canapés

Watercress        3 oz. cream cheese
2 T. chopped scallions        2 T. sour cream
Salt and pepper

Chop watercress. Mix with a 3 oz. package of cream cheese. Add sour cream, salt, pepper and chopped scallion or chive. Serve on white bread, from which the crusts have been cut.

### Pimento Cheese Filling

Hard rolls                                              Pimento cheese
Marinated pickle

Take a long, hard-crusted, rectangular roll, not too fresh. Cut off one end and take out the inside, leaving merely the crust. Fill with pimento cheese and stick a marinated pickle in the middle. Chill. Slice to make round rings. The result is better than the seven wonders.

### Cucumber Canapés

Cucumber                                                Bleu cheese
White bread

Slice unpeeled cucumbers and put a thin slice of bleu cheese on top of each. Serve on circular pieces of white bread cut to size of a cucumber slice.

### Egg Salad Canapés

2 hard-boiled eggs                                      3 T. sour cream
1 T. French's mustard                                   2 T. mayonnaise
Salt and pepper

Take two chopped, hard-boiled eggs, mixed with 3 T. of sour cream, 1 T. of French's mustard and 2 T. of mayonnaise. Add salt and pepper to taste. Serve on white bread cut imaginatively. This may be varied by the use of other types of mustard—especially herb-flavoured mustards.

### Five-Decker Sandwiches

Pumpernickel bread                          Watercress spread (see above)
Pimento cheese                              Red caviar

Serve thinly-cut slices of pumpernickle bread, alternating with spreads of watercress (see above), pimento cheese, and red caviar. Slice sandwiches lengthwise into strips about an inch wide. The finished product looks like the rainbow.

### Cheese and Pear Bits

Pear                                        Provolone cheese, or any sharp,
                                                    tasty cheese

Cut a pear into domino-like squares. Cut Provolone cheese in the same shapes. Fasten together with tooth picks. Sprinkling the pear with lemon juice will retard discolouration.

### Melon and Smoked Ham

Cantaloupe                                  Italian smoked ham (prosciutto)

Cut a cantaloupe in wedges, removing rind. Serve on it a thin slice of smoked Italian ham.

## Cheese Sticks

| | |
|---|---|
| 2 packages Snappy cheese (or 12 oz. of any soft melting cheese) | Dash of salt |
| | Pepper |
| | Paprika |
| ¼ lb. butter | 1 c. flour |

Mix cheese and butter together, add flour, a little salt, pepper and paprika. Fill a cookie tube and squeeze out sticks of 2-3 inch lengths. Place on a baking sheet and bake in a hot oven for 12 minutes.

## Pierozki

| | |
|---|---|
| 1 c. flour | 1 package cream cheese (4 oz.) |
| ¼ lb. butter or margarine | |

*Filling:*

| | |
|---|---|
| 2 hard-boiled eggs | 1 onion, chopped |
| 1 c. mushrooms | Salt and pepper and butter |

Mix softened butter with cream cheese in a bowl. Add flour and work it in with a fork. When smooth, place the dough in refrigerator until ready to use, or at least for 1 hour. In the meantime, prepare the filling. Fry finely-cut onion with mushrooms. Chop the hard-boiled eggs and mix with browned mushrooms. Add seasoning. Roll out little squares of dough, fill with mushroom filling and seal the edges, trying to make a walnut-like shape and size. Place on baking sheet and bake in a moderate oven for ½ hour or until lightly coloured. Pierozki can be filled with a large variety of things. Cocktail frankfurters or regular size frankfurters cut in small pieces make a delicious filling. Any strongly flavoured, melting cheese serves as a good filling. In Poland, most cherished were pierozki filled with buckwheat groats. Cook your buckwheat, season and mix with lightly browned onion, then use as filling for pierozki.

# SOUPS

Each nation has its particular or proper food, without which the daily meal would be incomplete. Italians would not go without spaghetti, the Chinese without rice, the Poles without a bowl of hot soup. Mostly Polish soups are made or served with sour cream. Quartered hard-boiled eggs are often used for garnishing. During hot summer days cold soups are eaten, most often they are sweet fruit soups, which are well chilled before serving.

### Meat Stock

| | |
|---|---|
| 8 c. cold water | 1 potato, cut |
| 2 lb. beef | 2 celery stalks, cut |
| 1 marrow bone | Fresh parsley |
| 1 large onion, cut | 2 bay leaves |
| 2 carrots, sliced | 2 bouillon cubes |
| Salt and pepper to taste | |

Bring all the ingredients to a boil. Simmer for two hours. During the cooking, skim the fat from the top. Strain. The meat can be used as boiled meat with any warm or appetizing sauce—also with pickle-relish.

### Consommé

Ingredients the same as for the meat stock. When the soup is ready, strain and add: 4 well-beaten egg yolks with 6 T. of sweet cream and 3 T. of grated cheese. Let it simmer for 2 minutes. Serve very hot.

### Five-Minute Bouillon

| | |
|---|---|
| 4 c. water | 3 T. grated cheese |
| 4 bouillon cubes | 2 T. pastina or alphabet |
| ½ t. basil | macaroni |
| 2 T. butter | Salt and pepper to taste |

Bring water to a boil and add bouillon cubes. When they are dissolved, add the rest of the ingredients. Simmer for 5 minutes before serving.

### Chicken Soup

| | |
|---|---|
| 1 fowl | 2 carrots |
| 8 c. cold water | 2 celery stalks |
| 2 lb. beef | Fresh parsley |
| 1 marrow bone | Bay leaf |
| 1 large onion | 1 potato (whole) |
| 2 bouillon cubes | 1 small can mushrooms |

Make four cuts in the onion, hold on fork and brown over open flame. Then put all ingredients into a soup kettle, bring to the boiling point. Simmer for 2 hours. Serve with dumplings (see p. 27), egg drops (see p. 29), noodles, or cream of wheat squares (see p. 26).

### Duck Soup (or Goose Soup)

| | |
|---|---|
| Duck giblets (or goose) | 1 c. sweet cream |
| 1 lb. spare ribs | ½ t. all-spice |
| 2 stalks celery | 1 c. dried prunes |
| 1 large onion | Salt |
| 3 T. raisins | ½ c. garlic vinegar |
| 1 t. sugar | ¼ c. dried apples |

Put the garlic vinegar in a bowl and catch the blood of a freshly killed duck or goose, stirring to avoid coagulation. Prepare a broth out of the spare ribs and the duck giblets, celery, onion, prunes, apples, raisins. When ready, remove spare ribs and giblets, cool, and mash all the ingredients. Then add the blood-vinegar combination, while beating with an eggbeater to prevent curdling. Bring to a boil and serve immediately.

### Liver Soup

| | |
|---|---|
| 4 c. meat stock | 1 lb. calf's liver |
| 2 onions, chopped | 3 egg yolks |
| 3 slices bacon | 2 carrots, cut |
| Parsley, chopped | 2 celery stalks, cut |
| 2 leeks, cut | |

Sauté calf's liver on bacon with onions and cut vegetables. Pass them through the mincer, together with the vegetables, when they are tender and brown. Combine with meat stock and simmer for 5 minutes. Mix in 3 well-beaten egg yolks just before serving.

### Calf's Brain Soup

| | |
|---|---|
| 4 c. meat stock | 2 carrots |
| 1 calf's brain | 4 T. butter |
| 1 celery stalk | 2 T. flour |
| Parsley | 3 egg yolks |
| Soaked bun | |

Sauté the calf brain with 1 T. of butter. Mash brain with a fork. Add 2 T. of flour and the soaked bun, from which you have previously squeezed the remaining milk. On the side, simmer the chopped vegetables in butter. When soft, add the calf's brain and bun. Strain through a sieve. Combine with meat stock. Simmer together for 5 minutes. When ready to serve, add slowly, 3 beaten egg yolks, stirring constantly.

### Lobster Soup

| | |
|---|---|
| 1 large lobster | 2 c. sour cream |
| 4 c. meat stock | 2 T. fresh dill or parsley |
| 3 T. Butter | 1 T. flour |
| Salt and pepper | |

Cook the lobster for 5 minutes. Change water, cook again in water to cover, for $\frac{1}{2}$ hour. Take out the lobster; reserve the lobster broth. Shell the lobster. Pass the meat through the mincer. Place in a pan with butter and simmer slowly for $\frac{1}{2}$ hour. Combine with the lobster broth and the meat stock. Beat the sour cream well with 1 T. of flour, and slowly pour into the soup. Sprinkle with dill and serve. This recipe should be remembered and used for the "important" evenings.

### Turtle Soup

| | |
|---|---|
| 1 can turtle meat | 2 T. butter |
| 4 c. meat stock | 5 T. sweet wine |
| 2 bouillon cubes | 1 T. butter |
| 5 mushrooms | ½ T. corn starch |

Add bouillon cubes to the meat stock and simmer. Combine with the can of turtle (the meat should be cut into small strips). Add finely chopped mushrooms browned in butter and the wine. On the side prepare a roux of 1 T. of butter with ½ T. of corn starch, and carefully mix with the soup. Serve.

### Fish Soup

| | |
|---|---|
| 1 lb. carp | 4 c. boiling water |
| 1 lb. mackerel | 2 onions |
| 2 stalks celery | Salt and pepper |
| 2 bouillon cubes | Parsley |

*Fish balls:*

| | |
|---|---|
| Remaining fish | 1 onion, grated |
| 2 egg yolks | 2 egg whites |
| 1 T. butter | 2 T. bread-crumbs |

Cook the vegetables with the bouillon cubes in boiling water. When the vegetables are tender, add both carp and mackerel and then cook for 25 minutes. Strain, retaining liquid and fish. Make fish balls as follows: Chop the cooked fish. Add a small grated onion. Mix two egg yolks with 1 T. of butter and add to the chopped fish. Add 2 T. of bread-crumbs. Fold in two whites of egg stiffly beaten. Make round balls and drop in the strained, boiling soup. When they are ready they will float to the surface. Serve at once.

### Barley Soup

| | |
|---|---|
| 8 c. meat stock | 1 c. pearl barley |
| ¼ c. mushrooms, sliced | 2 raw carrots, diced |
| 2 raw potatoes, diced | 3 T. sour cream |
| 3 T. butter | Fresh parsley |
| Salt and pepper to taste | |

Soak the barley, in enough water to cover, overnight. Combine the other ingredients except cream and parsley. Bring to a boil and simmer until tender. Stir in sour cream. Sprinkle chopped parsley on top of the soup and serve immediately.

## Onion Soup

| | |
|---|---|
| 6 onions | 3 T. butter |
| 4 c. meat stock | 4 T. of grated cheese (Parmesan) |
| 1 T. flour | Salt and pepper |
| Bread croûtons | |

Slice onions thinly and sauté in butter until lightly browned. Add to meat stock. Cook until tender and season. Pass through a sieve. Mix browned butter with 1 T. of flour and stir into soup. Shake grated cheese on the soup, or put in a separate dish. Serve with croûtons.

## Bread Soup

| | |
|---|---|
| 4 c. meat stock | 1 slice of toast per person |
| salt and pepper to taste | 2 frankfurters, cut in pieces |
| 1 poached egg per person | |

Place 1 slice of toast, a piece of frankfurter, and a poached egg in each soup bowl, pour in meat stock piping hot, and serve.

## Lemon Soup

| | |
|---|---|
| 4 c. meat stock | $\frac{1}{2}$ c. rice |
| Juice of 2 lemons | 1 c. sweet cream |
| 2 T. butter | |

Cook the rice until it is tender. Drain and mix well with butter and cream. Add lemon juice and hot meat stock. Bring to a quick boil and serve. If you want to add a touch of colour, you may garnish it with chopped fresh parsley and a sprinkle of paprika.

## Hungarian 'Pot au feu'

| | |
|---|---|
| 6 c. meat stock | 2 c. sour cream |
| $\frac{1}{2}$ lb. sauerkraut | 3 slices bacon, cut |
| Seasoning | 1 onion, chopped |

Cook the sauerkraut with the meat stock for 1 hour. Add browned onion and bacon. Mix in the sour cream just before serving. Season to taste. Boiled potatoes may be served with the soup.

## Pea Soup

| | |
|---|---|
| 8 c. water | 1 lb. dried split peas, soaked |
| 1 beef or ham bone | overnight |
| 2 onions, sliced | 2 carrots, sliced |
| 2 bouillon cubes | 3 sections garlic |
| 2 celery stalks, diced | 1 T. butter |
| Salt and pepper to taste | 1 T. flour |

Combine water, bone, vegetables and bouillon cubes. Bring to a boil and simmer until tender. Stir flour into butter, brown, and add slowly to soup. Serve with bread croûtons. (see p. 26). The addition of savoury also will give pea soup a little different flavour.

## Tomato Soup

| | |
|---|---|
| 6 c. meat stock | 1 T. sugar |
| 3 T. butter | 1 lb. tomatoes |
| 5 T. sour cream | 2 c. cooked rice |
| Salt and pepper to taste | |

Sauté the tomatoes in butter. When tender, sieve and combine with meat stock. Simmer for ½ hour. Serve with sour cream stirred in and add rice which has been cooked separately.

## Sauerkraut Soup

| | |
|---|---|
| 2 lbs. smoked pork shanks | 4 c. cold water |
| 1 onion | 2 T. butter |
| 2 T. sugar | ½ c. raisins |
| 1 lb. sauerkraut | Salt and pepper to taste |

Cook the meat until tender. Add onion browned in butter, sauerkraut and raisins. Simmer for one hour. Season and serve.

## Caraway Seed Soup

| | |
|---|---|
| 4 c. meat stock | 1 T. butter |
| 1 T. flour | 1 c. Polish sausage, diced |
| 1 T. caraway seeds | (Jewish salami can be |
| Salt and pepper | substituted) |

Melt butter and stir the flour into it. Add the meat stock warm. Season to taste. Add the rest of the ingredients and simmer for 15 minutes before serving.

## Sorrel Soup

| | |
|---|---|
| 6 c. meat stock | 1 lb. fresh sorrel |
| 3 cooked potatoes | ½ c. sour cream |
| 3 T. butter | 3 hard-boiled eggs |

Scald sorrel. Chop finely and sauté in butter. Strain through sieve. Mash the boiled potatoes and combine with the sorrel. Add the meat stock. Simmer for 15 minutes. Add sour cream. Cut the hard-boiled eggs in quarters, and use to garnish the soup.

## Lentil Soup

| | |
|---|---|
| 1 ham or pork bone | 2 onions, sliced |
| (preferably smoked ham) | 2 bouillon cubes |
| 8 c. water | Dried rosemary |
| 1 lb. lentils, soaked overnight | Salt and pepper |
| 3 sections garlic | 4 T. olive oil |
| 2 carrots, sliced | 2 celery stalks, cut |

Place all the ingredients in water and cook slowly for 3 hours. Remove the bone. The olive oil may be added before serving, not only to make it more nutritious but also to give a continental taste.

## Spring Soup

| | |
|---|---|
| 6 c. meat stock | 1 lb. asparagus, fresh or frozen |
| 4 large carrots | $\frac{1}{4}$ lb. spinach |
| 2 T. margarine or butter | 1 onion |
| 2 T. flour | |

Chop the vegetables and cook in the stock, leaving the spinach until the last, adding it when the other vegetables are almost cooked. Melt butter and stir in flour until smooth. Dilute with a few spoons of stock, then combine with the soup and serve.

## Dill Pickle Soup

| | |
|---|---|
| 4 c. meat stock | 4 dill pickles |
| 1 c. sour cream | 2 T. butter |
| 2 T. flour | Salt and pepper |

Dice pickles. Roll in flour, then sauté in butter. Add the meat stock and simmer for $\frac{1}{2}$ hour. Add the sour cream and serve.

## Vegetable Stock

| | |
|---|---|
| 6 c. cold water | 2 potatoes |
| 2 carrots | 2 stalks celery |
| Parsley | 1 large onion |
| 2 leaves of cabbage | Salt and pepper |

Cut the cleaned vegetables. Cook all the ingredients slowly for $1\frac{1}{2}$ hours. Strain for clear stock.

## Potato Soup

| | |
|---|---|
| 6 c. bouillon | 2 T. butter |
| 2 c. raw potatoes | 1 T. flour |
| 3 slices of bacon | 1 onion, chopped |
| Parsley or dill (fresh) | 2 stalks celery |
| Salt and pepper | 2 carrots |

Chop the bacon and fry it with chopped onion until slightly yellow. Cook the potatoes with the other vegetables. When tender, mash vegetables and combine again with the liquid which may be made with the aid of bouillon cubes, preferably chicken. Then add the bacon and onion. Simmer 10 minutes. In a separate pan, melt the butter and stir the flour into it until smooth, keeping it light coloured. Add slowly to soup. Sprinkle with chopped parsley or fresh dill when ready to serve.

## Mushroom Soup

| | |
|---|---|
| 4 c. vegetable stock | 1 c. fresh mushrooms, chopped |
| 2 T. butter | 2 T. flour |
| 4 T. sour cream | Chopped dill or parsley |
| 1 onion, chopped | |

Sauté the mushrooms with lightly browned onion until they are tender. Add flour and cook for 5 minutes over low flame, stirring constantly. Combine with vegetable stock. Simmer for 10 minutes. Stir in sour cream. Serve immediately with a sprinkle of dill or parsley.

### Cauliflower Soup

| | |
|---|---|
| 2 small cauliflower | 3 egg yolks |
| 2 T. flour | Salt and pepper to taste |
| 3 c. vegetable or meat stock | 3 T. sweet cream |
| 2 T. mushrooms, diced | 2 T. butter |
| 2 T. butter | |

Cook cauliflower in salted water. When tender, drain and mash, leaving a few whole pieces of cauliflower. Add 3 cups of vegetable or meat stock. Melt butter and stir flour into it. Be sure to keep it light coloured. Add it slowly to the soup and simmer for a few minutes. Season. Beat the egg yolk with the sweet cream. Sauté mushrooms in 2 tablespoons of butter and add to soup with eggs and cream. Serve immediately.

### Asparagus Soup

| | |
|---|---|
| 4 c. vegetable stock | 1 lb. asparagus |
| 1 T. butter | 1 T. flour |
| 3 egg yolks | 1 c. sweet cream |

Cook asparagus gently until tender. Drain. Cut off the tips and reserve. Mash the stems. Add the vegetable stock. Melt the butter and stir flour into it, keeping it light coloured. Add slowly to soup. Beat three egg yolks with the sweet cream and combine with the rest of the soup. Season. Simmer for a few minutes. Add the asparagus tops just before serving. The flavour of any asparagus dish is in direct relation to the freshness of the asparagus used.

### Fresh Cabbage Soup

| | |
|---|---|
| 4 carrots, sliced | 5 slices of bacon |
| 2 potatoes, sliced | 2 T. flour |
| ¼ lb. cabbage, cut | 2 T. butter or margarine |
| 2 celery stalks, cut | 6 c. water |

Cook all the ingredients for half an hour. Melt butter, blend in flour and combine with soup. Serve with Danish dumplings. (see p. 27).

### Chestnut Broth

| | |
|---|---|
| 1 lb. chestnuts | Salt |
| 4 c. vegetable broth | toasted croûtons |
| 2 T. butter | 2 egg yolks |

Place the chestnuts (puncture each of them with a sharp knife) in boiling water and let them cook for 10 minutes. Peel them. Scald again with boiling water and take the second skin off. Simmer the chestnuts in butter. When they are tender and soft, pass them through

the sieve and mix with the egg yolks. Stir the chestnut mixture into
the broth and serve with croûtons. (see p. 26).

### Traditional Polish Barshch

Since early days barshch was used in Poland as the traditional feasting dish for Christmas or Easter dinner, or cold for Harvest Festival.
Whenever you had a guest in the house, barshch was the proper
"thing" to serve. The foundation for barshch is a beetroot ferment,
"kwas". Vegetables or meat stock are used alternatively, depending
upon occasion. During summer days cold barshch is served. Usually
it is barshch with sour cream rather than clear barshch.

### Kwas
(kwas is the foundation for barshch)

6 large beets, cut                     10 c. water, lukewarm
1 piece sour rye bread

Place the cut beets in an earthenware container. Cover with lukewarm water, add a piece of rye bread. Cover the container with wax
paper and keep in a warm place (on top of your stove for instance).
When the kwas is sour, store it, strained, in your refrigerator.

### Clear Barshch

4 c. meat stock                        6 large raw beets
4 mushrooms, dried, soaked             3 sections garlic
   overnight                           Salt and pepper
2 c. beet "kwas"

Dice the beets and cook in the meat stock with all the ingredients,
except "kwas." Let it simmer for 1 hour. Add the "kwas," and serve
hot with boiled potatoes which have been garnished with fried bacon
slices and onion, or "ushka" (see p. 27).

### Ukranian Barshch

Clear barshch (see above)              1 c. diced cooked pork meat
1 c. Polish sausage                    1 c. tomatoes, sautéd
1 c. shell beans, cooked or
   canned

Prepared as the clear barshch. When ready add 1 c. of Polish sausage and 1 c. of cooked diced, pork meat, 1 c. of shell beans and a
c. of sautéd tomatoes. Simmer for 10 minutes, then serve.

## Lenten Barshch

| | |
|---|---|
| 8 c. water | 2 stalks celery |
| 2 raw potatoes | 1 large onion |
| 3 sections garlic | ¼ c. dried mushroom, chopped, |
| 1 c. sour cream | soaked overnight or 1 c. fresh |
| 1 T. flour | mushrooms |
| 1 T. butter | 4 hard-boiled eggs |
| 6 large beets | 3 carrots |

Prepare a vegetable stock from the given vegetables. The mushrooms should have been soaked overnight and then diced before cooking. Melt butter and stir in flour. First add 3 T. of vegetable stock gradually. Cook until thick then combine with the vegetable stock. When ready to serve, stir in sour cream and garnish with quartered, hard-boiled eggs.

## Quick Barshch

| | |
|---|---|
| 1¼ lb. beets | Juice of 2 lemons or citric acid |
| 1 large onion | Sugar to taste |
| 2 carrots | 2 T. butter |
| 2 stalks celery | Salt and pepper |
| Parsley and dill | Paprika |
| 2 sections garlic, pressed | |

Clean and wash the vegetables. Place them in a pot with 6 c. of water and let them cook until tender. Add all the seasoning and butter. Sugar and lemon should be added according to taste, but the soup should have its sour-sweet flavour and its deep red colour. If during cooking the beets lose their colour, grate one or two raw beets and add them to the soup.

## Barshch 'a la Minute'

| | |
|---|---|
| 2 jars ready made barshch | Paprika |
| 2 sections garlic | Juice of 1 lemon |
| Pepper | 1 T. sugar |

Open ready made barshch. Place in a pot and warm together with garlic and some additional pepper and paprika. When warm add lemon juice and sugar if needed.

## Zur

| | |
|---|---|
| ½ lb. whole-wheat flour | 1 piece sour rye bread |
| ¼ lb. bacon | 2 c. lukewarm water |
| 2 sections garlic | 1 lb. potatoes |
| 3 c. boiling water | 1 can mushrooms |
| Salt and pepper | |

Cover the flour with lukewarm water. Add a piece of sour rye bread of approximately 2 inches diameter. Leave the mixture in a warm place for 24 hours. When the mixture is well soured, take out the bread, and pass the rest through a sieve. Bring to a boil 3 c. of water, and slowly pour over the mixture, stirring constantly. Leave it on low flame until it boils. On the side chop the bacon and the mushrooms and fry until lightly browned. Squeeze in the garlic and add both to the soup. Serve with boiled potatoes.

### Easter Soup

| | |
|---|---|
| 3 c. oatmeal, uncooked | 1 c. Polish sausage or Jewish |
| Large piece of sour rye bread | salami |
| 4 c. hot water | 1 T. horseradish |
| Salt and pepper | |

Mix oatmeal with crust of rye bread and hot water and let stand for two days until it sours. Sieve. Cook sausage in this liquid for ½ hour. Add seasoning and horseradish. Serve with potatoes or croûtons. (see p. 26).

### Pumpkin Soup

| | |
|---|---|
| 1½ lb. pumpkin | Salt and pepper |
| 6 c. milk | 1 c. cooked rice |
| 2 T. butter | Nutmeg |
| All-spice | |

Sauté the sliced pumpkin in butter. When soft, pass through the sieve. Add milk and simmer for 15 minutes. Season well. Add rice and serve.

### Beer Soup

| | |
|---|---|
| 2 c. beer | 2 c. sour cream |
| 1 T. flour | 3 T. sugar |

Cover the beer and bring to a boil. Beat sour-cream with flour and sugar and combine with hot beer. Bring to a boil and serve immediately.

### Rice Soup

| | |
|---|---|
| 4 bouillon cubes | 4 c. boiling water |
| 3 T. butter | 2 onions, sliced |
| 1 c. rice, uncooked | Salt. and pepper |

Dissolve the bouillon cubes in the water. Cook rice and onions in it. When the rice is soft, add butter. Season and serve.

### Health Soup

| | |
|---|---|
| ¼ lb. rice | Salt |
| 6 c. vegetable broth | 3 egg yolks |

Cook the rice in vegetable broth. When soft, pass it through the sieve together with the broth. Season. Beat in the egg yolks just before serving.

### Cream of Wheat Soup

| | |
|---|---|
| 4 c. milk | 2 T. butter |
| 1 T. soya sauce | Salt |
| 8 T. cream of wheat | 1 bouillon cube |
| 2 T. grated cheese | |

Sprinkle the cream of wheat on boiling milk. Let simmer for 5 minutes. Add the rest of the ingredients and simmer for 5 minutes more. Serve.

### French Drops on Milk

| | |
|---|---|
| 4 c. milk | Salt |
| 2 eggs | Grated cheese (if desired) |
| 4 T. flour | |

Place the eggs in a bowl, add flour and mix, forming a moderately hard dough. Bring the milk to a boil and drop the dough with a tea spoon on the milk. Season. Simmer for 3 minutes and serve.

### Tapioca on Milk

| | |
|---|---|
| 6 c. milk | ½ c. tapioca |
| Dash of salt | |

Bring milk to the boil. Sprinkle tapioca on the milk, add a dash of salt and cook on very low flame for 5 minutes. Serve hot.

# COLD SOUPS

### Chlodnik

4 c. home-made or canned
    barshch (see page 17)
4 c. buttermilk
½ c. sour cream
½ c. shrimps, cooked and cut up
1 garden-fresh cucumber

Scallions, sliced
radishes, thinly cut
7 hard-boiled eggs, sliced
1 c. beet greens, thinly shredded
2 cucumber pickles, dill if
    possible, cut

Mix all ingredients and store in refrigerator. Serve on hot summer days.

### Litvian Cholodziec

¼ lb. veal
1 cucumber
1 T. chive
1 T. dill
1 T. sorrel (if available)
5 beets with the beet greens
1 T. gelatine
Salt

2 mushrooms
1 onion
4 hard-boiled eggs
1 c. sour cream
1 c. juice of dill pickles
1 lb. cooked shrimps
¼ lb. cooked salmon

Cook veal in water to cover, with onion and mushrooms. When tender take out meat, strain the broth and dissolve in it 1 tablespoon of gelatine. On the side cook slowly finely cut, peeled beets and sorrell. When ready, sieve, and bring to a boil, with the pickle juice. Place in the bowl the strained beets with sorrel, cooled pickle juice, chopped dill and chive. Beat well sour cream and add to the beet mixture. Dice the meat, shrimps, salmon, cucumber and the eggs, and add to the rest. Combine this mixture with the jellied soup and place in the refrigerator. Before serving, chop some ice and sprinkle on top of the serving dish.

### Ice-cold Soup for a Warm Summer Day

| | |
|---|---|
| 6 c. meat stock | ¼ t. red pepper |
| 1½ lb. tomatoes | Salt |
| 1 T. sugar | 1 t. basil |

Cook the meat stock the day before and skim off the fat. Peel tomatoes and add to the broth. Cook for 5 minutes on a strong fire, then simmer on a low flame for 45 minutes. Ten minutes before taking off the fire, add finely chopped pepper, salt, basil, and sugar to taste. Chill and serve cold.

### Cold Beet and Cucumber Soup

| | |
|---|---|
| 8 c. home-made or canned barshch (see page 17) | 1 c. ham, diced (optional) |
| | 1 qt. sour cream |
| 8 c. buttermilk | 1 bunch radishes, sliced |
| 4 scallions, sliced | 1 c. pickles, diced |
| 2 c. cucumbers, diced | 1 c. cottage cheese |
| 4 hard-boiled eggs, diced | Salt, pepper, dill |

Mix the butter-milk and sour cream with the cottage-cheese in a large bowl. Add all the chopped vegetables, pickle, meat and eggs. Chill and serve with pumpernickel bread.

### Consommé Madrilene

| | |
|---|---|
| 4 c. consommé | Parsley, fresh |
| 2 envelopes gelatine | 1 lemon, quartered |

Use recipe for quick consommé (see p.10). Add 2 envelopes of gelatine to 4 c. of warm consommé. Chill and serve with quarters of lemon. Garnish with fresh parsley.

### Consommé Madrilene à la Provencale

| | |
|---|---|
| 1 poached egg per person | Consommé Madrilene |

Use the recipe for Consommé Madrilene. When the broth is cooled but not jellied, put a poached egg in individual cups and pour the consommé over it, then put in the refrigerator to chill. Serve cold.

### Blackberry Soup

Poland is known for its fruit soups. They make a wonderful change during hot summer days when you really do not feel like eating much. They are refreshing and thirst-quenching.

| | |
|---|---|
| 3 c. water | 2 pt. blackberries |
| 1 c. sugar | Juice of 1 lemon |
| ¼ t. cinnamon | 1 c. sour cream |

Cook the blackberries in the water for 15 minutes, adding sugar and cinnamon. Chill. When cold, stir in sour cream and serve.

## Apple Soup

| | |
|---|---|
| 4 c. water | 6 large apples or 1 can |
| 1 c. sweet cream | apple sauce |
| 1 c. sugar | ¼ t. cinnamon (optional) |

Make a thin pureé from the apples, cooked in 4 cups of water or use apple sauce and 1 cup of water. When cool, add sweet cream and serve. Add sugar and cinnamon if desired.

## *"Nothing but"* Soup

| | |
|---|---|
| 6 c. milk | ¼ t. vanilla extract |
| 5 eggs, separated | 5 T. sugar |

Beat the egg yolks with sugar until they become light-coloured. Put on a slow flame, adding milk gradually and stirring constantly until it begins to thicken. Then add vanilla and chill. Beat the egg whites until they are stiff and throw large spoonfuls on the surface of the custard letting them fall as they will. Serve cold.

## Raspberry Soup

| | |
|---|---|
| 4 c. raspberries | 1 c. sweet cream (if desired) |
| ½ c. sugar | 4 c. water |

Bring berries and the water to a boil, adding sugar. Chill and stir in sweet cream. Serve cold with croûtons. (see p. 26).

## Fruit Soup

| | |
|---|---|
| Any fruit in season | 4 c. milk |
| 5 egg yolks | ¼ c. sugar |

Beat the egg yolks with sugar until light. Put on low flame and pour in the milk gradually. When the consistency is thick, chill. When cold, add diced fruit and serve. With this recipe almost any fruit may be used, but particularly good are plums, apricots and sliced peaches.

## Raspberry Soup with Wine

| | |
|---|---|
| 4 c. boiling water | Juice of ¼ lemon |
| 1 c. white wine | Lemon peel, cut |
| 4 c. raspberries | ½ c. sugar |

Reserve ½ c. of raspberries. Crush others and combine with boiling water, wine, lemon juice and several pieces of lemon peel and sugar. Cook for 15 minutes. Chill and when cold, add the ½ c. of whole raspberries. Serve well chilled.

### Plum Soup

1 lb. plums                          1 c. sour cream
4 c. water                           ½ c. sugar
Juice of 1 lemon

Cook the plums in water, lemon juice and sugar until tender. Sieve.
Chill and stir in sour cream. Serve very cold.

### Plum Preserve Soup

½ c. plum preserve                   2 T. flour
¼ lb. dry apricots                   2 cloves
½ c. sugar                           4 c. water
1 c. sour cream                      Bread croûtons

Cook plum preserve, apricots and cloves in water for ½ hour, sieve.
Beat the sour cream with flour, adding sugar according to taste.
Pour into the soup. Chill and serve with croûtons (see p. 26).

### Cold Almond Soup

1 c. almonds                         4 egg yolks
6 c. milk                            1 T. flour
½ c. sugar

The almonds should be blanched and peeled, then well dried. Grind
until they are fine. Mix with flour and sugar. Bring the milk to the
boiling point. Add almonds and egg yolks one by one, stirring constantly. Cool in the refrigerator and serve cold with biscuits. Almond
soup may be served hot, traditionally when served for Christmas
dinner.

# ADDITIONS TO SOUPS

A good, large piece of freshly made rye bread is for a Pole as good an addition to soup as any. Throughout the Polish countryside you could see the Polish peasants cherish their daily bread in a particular way. But the lady of the house prefers to be original and she enjoys seeing effect as well as substance. This is why you encounter such a variety of fancy as well as hearty garnishes for soups.

## Croûtons

Dry bread                                         Butter

Cut the bread into cubes, put in flat pan or cookie sheet and brown in the oven. Then sauté in butter and drain on absorbent paper.

## Buckwheat Groats

1 c. buckwheat groats                  1 egg, beaten
2 c. boiling water                           Salt
3 T. butter

Add beaten egg to groats in a frying pan, over low heat, stirring constantly. Mix thoroughly, being careful not to form lumps. When each grain is separated, add slowly to the boiling salted water, again stirring constantly until smooth. Add butter. Simmer for 15 minutes, then add to boiling soup. This is a substitute for rice as a soup thickener.

## Potato Dumplings

3 large raw potatoes                     2 eggs, beaten
1 c. flour                                        $\frac{1}{4}$ c. bread crumbs
Salt and pepper

Grate the potatoes, add salt and pepper and two beaten eggs. Then mix with flour and bread crumbs. Make dumplings with two teaspoons and drop into salted boiling water to cook until they float. Then transfer to hot soup.

## Cream of Wheat Squares

4 c. boiling water                          3 T. grated cheese
3 T. butter                                     $\frac{1}{4}$ c. cream of wheat
Salt and pepper

Pour cream of wheat gradually into boiling water. Season. Add cheese and butter. When cooked, spread on a wet surface, such as marble or a platter, $\frac{1}{2}$ inch thick. When completely cold, cut into squares with a sharp knife and place in individual soup bowls and pour in hot soup. This is usually used with a clear soup.

## French Noodles

1 T. soft butter                             2 eggs, separated
1 T. flour                                       Dash of salt

Beat butter and salt thoroughly, adding gradually 2 egg yolks. On the side, beat the egg whites stiff and fold into the egg yolk mixture.

Sprinkle 1 T. of flour, adding a little more if the eggs are large. Make dumplings with a small spoon and drop into rapidly boiling soup. When they are ready, they will float to the top of the soup. Serve.

### French Noodles with Mushrooms

| | |
|---|---|
| 2 eggs, separated | 1 T. flour |
| 2 T. mushrooms, chopped | Dash of salt |
| 1 T. butter | Butter |

Follow recipe as in French noodles, adding 2 T. of finely chopped, slightly browned, mushrooms with the egg yolk mixture.

### Egg Barley

| | |
|---|---|
| 1 egg | 3 T. grated cheese (Parmesan) |
| Flour | Dash of salt |

Beat the egg with the grated cheese, adding enough flour so that the consistency will be thick enough to be grated on a coarse grater. Add to hot soup and boil for a few minutes before serving.

### Danish Dumplings

| | |
|---|---|
| $\frac{1}{4}$ lb. butter | $\frac{1}{4}$ c. water |
| 2 eggs, beaten | Dash of salt |
| $\frac{3}{4}$ c. flour | |

Melt the butter, adding water. Slowly stir in the flour and mix until the paste has hardened. Remove from the fire, stirring constantly, until the paste is cold. Add eggs gradually. Make dumplings with two t. and drop into boiling soup. When they float, serve.

### Poached Eggs

Poached Eggs can be served with bouillon or any consommé. Carefully drop a raw egg over boiling soup and serve. If you serve bouillon, you may place the egg in the soup bowl and pour the boiling bouillon over it.

### Ushka

| | |
|---|---|
| 2 c. flour | 1 egg |
| $\frac{1}{4}$ c. water | Dash of salt |

Put flour in a big pile on a kneading board. Mix in egg and water in the middle, kneading constantly. When the dough is ready, roll out very thinly and cut two-inch squares. Put a spoonful of filling,

in centre (see below). Fold so that the corners meet in the middle.
Press together with the fingers, then drop into boiling soup. Cook
until they float. Serve very hot.

### Filling for Ushka

| | |
|---|---|
| Left-over meat | 1 bun, soaked |
| 2 onions, chopped | Milk |
| 2 T. butter | Salt and pepper |

Mince left over meat with a roll or day-old bread soaked in milk
(the milk should be squeezed out). Add two browned onions and
mix thoroughly. Fill ushka.

### Meat Filling for Ushka

| | |
|---|---|
| Left-over cooked meat, minced | 2 T. butter |
| 1 onion, chopped | 4 dried mushrooms, soaked and |
| Salt and pepper | chopped |
| Paprika | |

Brown onion in butter, add meat and mushrooms. Simmer together
for a few minutes. Season. Use as filling for ushka, being careful not
to use too abundantly.

### Meatless Filling for Ushka

| | |
|---|---|
| 3 hard-boiled eggs, chopped | 3 T. butter |
| 1½ c. mushrooms, chopped | Salt and pepper |
| 1 onion, chopped | |

Brown onion in butter. Add chopped mushrooms and simmer until
tender. Season. Combine with chopped eggs. Cool before using.

### Mushroom Filling for Ushka

| | |
|---|---|
| 2 onions, chopped | 2 T. bread crumbs |
| 1 can mushroom or 6 dried | Salt and pepper |
| mushrooms | Butter |

Soak the dried mushrooms for one hour in warm water. Chop fine.
Fry with diced browned onions. Add salt and pepper and 2 tablespoons of bread crumbs. Fill ushka.

### Crôquettes for Soup

| | |
|---|---|
| 2 c. mashed potatoes | 2 eggs |
| 1 large onion, chopped and | Butter or margarine |
| browned | Salt and pepper |
| 2 T. bread crumbs | |

Mix all the ingredients except butter and breadcrumbs. Shape into
egg ovals, roll in bread-crumbs and fry in butter. Serve with soup.

## Egg Balls

2 hard-boiled egg yolks
2 raw egg yolks
1 T. sour cream

1 T. grated cheese (Parmesan or
   Romano)
Salt and pepper

Mash the hard-boiled egg yolk with a fork and mix with all the other ingredients. Shape into balls with 2 spoons. Drop into soup, and cook for just a moment. Serve hot.

## Egg Drops

2 eggs
Salt

3 T. flour
1 T. water

Combine all the ingredients and mix into a smooth paste. Drop gradually from a large spoon into the soup and cook for a few minutes.

## Knelki

1 c. cooked meat, minced
1½ slices of dry bread
   or buns, soaked and squeezed

¾ c. sweet cream
Salt

Take finely chopped meat and add moistened bread and salt. Add sweet cream gradually. Beat until the mixture is light. Drop in 1 inch lengths from the side of a t. into boiling water. Cook until they bob up to the surface. Take out carefully and serve with soup.

## Liver Pudding

¼ lb. calf's liver
3 T. butter
2 eggs, separated
1 onion

Parsley, chopped
½ c. flour
Salt and pepper

Grate the onion, brown in butter for one moment. Take it off the fire, add the egg yolks and mix well. Mince the liver. Beat the egg whites until stiff and fold them and the meat into the other mixture. Add salt and pepper and chopped parsley. Sprinkle with flour. Place in a buttered pudding bowl and cook in a pot of boiling water for 1 hour. Cut in small strips and let float in chicken broth.

## Dumplings of Calf's Brain

1 lb. calf brain
1 egg
1 onion
Juice of ¼ lemon
Parsley

2 T. butter
1 mushroom
2 T. bread-crumbs
Salt

Bring salted water to a boil. Add lemon juice. Take the skin off the calf's brain and place in the boiling water. Cook for 5 minutes. Remove and chop fine. Brown chopped onion in butter and, when slightly brown, add chopped mushrooms for a few moments. Pass through a sieve together with chopped calf's brain. Make small round dumplings and boil in water or soup for a few minutes, until they float. In this same way you can make dumplings of fish roe, substituting the roe for brain.

### Stuffed Cucumbers

| | |
|---|---|
| 4 cucumbers | Meat filling (see page 28) |
| Salt | as for ushka |

Peel the cucumbers. Cut them in half and take out the seeds, like taking the core from an apple. Shake salt over the cucumber and leave until the salt draws out the water. Dry the cucumbers and fill with the meat stuffing. Place in a deep pot and simmer in meat stock until tender. Slice, making round circles, and serve in meat broth.

### Chicken Dumplings

| | |
|---|---|
| ¼ lb. raw white meat chicken | 1 small onion |
| ¼ lb. chicken or goose liver | Milk |
| ¼ c. sweet cream | Salt and pepper |
| 3 T. inside of a bun or day-old bread | Dry basil |
| | 1 T. butter or chicken fat |

Soak the inside of a bun in milk, then squeeze the milk out. Mince the bun, onion and liver with the raw chicken, using the fine blade. Add melted butter or chicken fat. Put in the refrigerator. After half an hour, take it off the ice and add gradually sweet cream, salt, pepper and basil. Make dumplings with a small spoon and cook them in the chicken broth for 5 minutes before serving. The dumplings are very good as a side dish. Left-over chicken may also be used. In this case serve with peas and carrots.

### Dumplings for Fruit Soups

| | |
|---|---|
| 1 bun or day-old bread crust | 3 T. raisins |
| ¼ c. milk | 3 T. sugar |
| 2 eggs, separated | ¼ c. flour |
| Lemon peel, grated | Salt |

Soak the bun or bread crust in milk for ½ hour. Chop it very fine. and place in a bowl. Add egg yolks, sugar, melted butter, grated lemon rind, dash of salt and mix well. Add raisins, stiffly beaten egg whites and flour. Make little round dumplings and cook in boiling water for 6 minutes or until they float and serve with a fruit soup.

### Nice or Polish Meringue

2 whites of egg                    4 T. sugar, powdered

Beat the egg whites until very stiff, adding sugar gradually. Place on top of a steaming pot, so that they get a little thicker. With a spoon, drop small quantities of the mixture on a baking sheet which has been covered with wax paper, and put in a moderate oven. When slightly browned, serve the Nice with "Nothing but" soup (see p. 23). The Nice can be used with vanilla pudding. For colour you can sprinkle them with a few drops of raspberry syrup.

# FISH

Fish is a very common food in Poland. Fresh-water fish are greatly used and their kinds are many. When stewed, sour cream is often used; when boiled they are often served in aspic.

### Carp in Red Cabbage

| | |
|---|---|
| 1 carp | 1 head red cabbage |
| 1 T. butter | 1 T. flour |
| 1 large onion | 1 c. red wine |
| 1 T. sugar | Juice of 1 lemon |
| Salt and pepper | |

Pour boiling water over the shredded red cabbage in a colander.
Chop the onion and brown in butter. Sprinkle flour over it and stir in
a cup of red wine. Salt the cabbage and add the lemon juice to it.
Mix the cabbage with the butter and wine sauce and add sugar.
Cover and cook over a low fire. When it is almost tender, add the
cleaned carp cut in bell-like slices. Mix thoroughly with the cabbage
and stew for another 30 minutes. Serve on a platter, covering the fish
with the cabbage.

### Carp in Grey Sauce

| | |
|---|---|
| 1 medium carp | Vegetable Stock |
| Bay leaf | Nutmeg |
| ½ c. raisins | ½ c. blanched almonds |
| Salt and pepper | Polish grey sauce |

Salt the cleaned carp. Cook either the whole fish or cut it in pieces.
Stew over a moderate heat in vegetable stock to cover, adding a bay
leaf and a dash of nutmeg. After 15 minutes, remove from the heat
and drain, reserving the liquid. Make Polish grey sauce (see p. 104),
using the vegetable-fish water for liquid. Place the half-cooked fish in
it and stew for another 30 minutes or until tender. This is very good
served with noodles which have had browned butter poured over
them.

### Carp, Jewish Style

| | |
|---|---|
| 1 carp | Salt and pepper |
| 2 T. butter | 5 carrots, sliced |
| ½ c. raisins | 5 onions, sliced |

Salt and pepper the cleaned carp. Place, either whole or cut in
sections, in cold water to cover. Add sliced carrots and onions,
raisins, and butter. Cover and simmer until tender.

### Carp in Jelly

If the carp is cooked as above and cooled in the cooking liquid, this
jellies. Serve cold in the gelatine with quartered lemons on the side.

## Carp in Mushroom Sauce

| | |
|---|---|
| 1 medium carp | Salt and pepper |
| Butter | Mushroom sauce |

Salt cleaned carp well. Then place in a baking dish and bake in a moderate oven, basting often with melted butter. After about ½ hour, pour over it a mushroom sauce (see p. 97) and finish baking (20-30 minutes).

## Boiled Pike with Horseradish Sauce

| | |
|---|---|
| 1 pike | Salt |
| Parsley | Some carrots and onions |
| Horseradish sauce | |

Take a cleaned pike and salt well. Cook in water to cover on a slow flame, adding parsley, cut carrots and onions. Simmer until tender, being careful not to overcook. This takes about 25 minutes. Serve with horseradish sauce (see p. 98) abundantly poured over it.

## Baked Pike with Horseradish Sauce

| | |
|---|---|
| Pike | Butter |
| Horseradish sauce | |

Wrap a cleaned pike in a large buttered piece of metal foil and place in a slow oven (300°) in a deep pan or baking dish. After an hour look inside to see if it is tender. Cook until it is done, then take off the paper. Place in a narrow dish and pour over it the horseradish sauce (see p. 98). Garnish with slices of lemon and parsley and serve.

## Boiled Pike with Hard-boiled Eggs

| | |
|---|---|
| 1 pike | Salt and pepper |
| Parsley | A few carrots and onions |
| 3-4 T. butter | Small new potatoes |
| 2 hard-boiled eggs | |

Salt a cleaned pike and boil with vegetables as above (see boiled pike). When it is tender, place pike on a platter with boiled potatoes. This is particularly good with small, new potatoes. Brown chopped hard-boiled eggs in butter and pour over the cooked pike and potatoes. Garnish with dill if desired.

### Pike, Jewish Style

| | |
|---|---|
| 1 large pike (3-4 lb.) | 2 buns or crusts of day-old |
| 2 onions | bread |
| 1 egg | Nutmeg |
| Vegetable stock | 2 T. butter |
| 2 bay leaves | Horseradish sauce (optional) |
| ¼ c. milk | |

Clean and salt pike well. Cut off head, leaving it attached to the skin if possible. Carefully take off skin up to the tail, trying to keep it whole. Scrape the meat off the bones and reserve. Soak the buns or crusts in milk and then squeeze out all the milk. Put the fish meat, soaked buns, and onions through the mincer. Mix in the egg, 1 T. of melted butter, salt, pepper, and a dash of nutmeg. Fill the skin of the pike with this mixture, including the head, to reform the shape of the fish, and fasten with tooth-picks to hold. Put in a pot, adding some water, bay leaves and 1 tablespoon of butter. Cover and simmer for at least an hour over a slow flame. Serve with vegetable stock or horseradish sauce (see p. 98) or in plain melted butter.

### Baked Pike with Anchovies

| | |
|---|---|
| 1 medium pike | 1 can anchovies |
| 4 T. butter | 1 bun or crust of day-old bread |
| 2 eggs | 2 cups sour cream |
| Pike's liver | Pike's roe |
| Salt and pepper | Parsley |

Divide the can of anchovies in half. Chop one half of the anchovies and mix with 2 T. of melted butter reserving this mixture for later use. The remaining anchovies should be inserted, one by one, in slits in the skin of the cleaned, salted pike in the manner in which one lards a lean roast with fat to prepare for roasting. Prepare a stuffing by mixing the remaining two T. of melted butter, yolks of 2 eggs, a bun soaked in milk, well-squeezed and crumbled, the chopped pike liver, pike roe and the whites of 2 eggs beaten stiff. Season and stuff the fish with this mixture. Sew up the stomach and place in a baking dish. Pour over the pike the 2 T. of melted butter mixed with the chopped anchovies. After 45 minutes baking in a moderate oven, pour the sour cream over the fish. Return to the oven and finish baking (about 15 minutes). Chopped parsley may be added either to the stuffing or to the butter and anchovies.

## Broiled Perch with Mushrooms

| | |
|---|---|
| 1 perch | 8 dried mushrooms |
| 2 c. sour cream | 1 T. flour |
| 2 bouillon cubes | 2 egg yolks |

The cleaned perch should be put in a baking dish in a small amount of water. Bake in a moderate oven, basting with water from time to time until almost tender. Prepare a sauce of the remaining ingredients in the following manner: cook the dried mushrooms and then chop them fine. Mix them with the sour cream, adding 2 T. of the water in which they were cooked. Dissolve and add bouillon cubes, flour, and egg yolk. Beat well. Pour over the nearly-cooked fish and broil for 20 minutes. Serve immediately.

## Perch à la Radziwill

| | |
|---|---|
| 1 perch | $\frac{3}{4}$ c. white wine |
| 3 T. butter | 5 mushrooms |
| Bread | 1 T. flour |
| 2 Bouillon cubes | 4 egg yolks |
| Salt and pepper | 2 truffles |
| Vegetable stock | |

Clean and skin the perch and remove the meat from the bones. Cook the head of the perch in 1 c. of vegetable stock. Strain and add the mushrooms, bouillon cubes, $\frac{1}{4}$ c. of white wine and 2 truffles. Melt and stir together 1 T. of butter and 1 T. of flour. Add to stock, stirring constantly. When well blended, stir in 4 egg yolks and keep warm to pour over fish when ready to serve. Cut the fish meat into squares, as uniform in size as possible. Salt and put into a pot, adding $\frac{1}{2}$ c. of white wine and a little butter. Simmer for ten minutes or until tender and be prepared to serve immediately. Cut and toast bread cubes the size of the fish squares. Brown in butter. When the fish is cooked, place each piece on a square of the browned toast. Pour the sauce over all and serve.

## Perch with Hard-boiled Eggs

| | |
|---|---|
| 1 perch | Vegetable stock |
| 1 T. butter | 4 hard-boiled eggs |

Clean and salt perch well, One large or several small perch or bass may be used. Cook either whole or cut pieces in vegetable stock to cover until the fish is tender. Chop the hard-boiled eggs fine and brown lightly in butter. Add a few spoons of vegetable-fish stock to the sauce and pour it over the fish when ready to serve.

## Stewed Eel in Wine

2 lb. eel
½ c. white wine
1 onion
1 c. vegetable stock
3 egg yolks

Vinegar
2 T. butter
4 mushrooms
Salt and pepper

Skin the eel, salt and scald in boiling vinegar. Drain. Brown onion in butter. Add wine, sliced mushrooms, stock, a dash of pepper and eel. Stew for 30 minutes on a low flame. Remove the fish. Stir egg yolks, adding one by one, to the stock. Pour over the cooked eel and serve with fish knelki (see p. 29) if desired.

## Eel Roulade

2 lb. eel
2 dill pickles
1 egg
4 c. vegetable stock

3 hard-boiled eggs
4 sliced mushrooms
½ c. vinegar
Salt and pepper

Skin the eel. Split in half and take out the bones. Chop the hard-boiled eggs and add chopped pickles, mushrooms, salt and pepper and mix with the raw egg. Spread the mixture on the inside of half the eel. Cover this with the top half and wrap in a muslin cloth. Add the vinegar to the vegetable stock and boil for 30 minutes with the wrapped eel in it. Remove from the flame and allow the eel to cool in the stock. Then take it out of the cloth. Serve on a platter. Garnish with slices of lemon, marinated mushrooms and sliced hard-boiled eggs and serve cold with mustard sauce on the side. (see p. 101).

## Cod Fish Steamed with Vegetables

2 lb. cod-fish in fillets
Onion, sliced
carrots, sliced
1 T. flour
2 bouillon cubes

Tomatoes, peeled
Celery, sliced
Parsley
1 T. butter

Put the pieces of cod fish in a pot with all the vegetables, bouillon cubes, and water to cover. Stew in a covered kettle until tender (about 20 minutes). Make a paste of the butter and flour in a frying pan. When it is rosy brown, add a few spoons of fish stock and stir the mixture into the fish, being careful not to make lumps. Serve with boiled potatoes or cooked corn meal.

## Fish Soufflé

2 lb. of any white fish (perch,
flounder, etc.)
Grated cheese (Parmesan or
Romano)

1 T. butter
6 egg whites
Salt and white pepper
Nutmeg

Chop raw fish meat fine and work 1 T. of soft butter into it. Add salt and pepper and a dash of nutmeg. Fold in egg whites beaten until stiff and mix thoroughly. Place in a well-greased pan and sprinkle with a good quantity of grated cheese. Bake in a moderate oven for 25 minutes. Test with a straw before removing from the oven. Serve immediately when the straw comes out clean. Serve with a light browned butter sauce (see p. 99) or anchovy sauce (see p. 98)

## Creamed Fish

1½ lb. any fish
2 onions
Salt and pepper

4 T. butter
1 c. sour cream
Lemon

Cut the raw fish in slices or fillets. Sauté with finely chopped onion until tender in the butter. Add cream, salt and pepper. Simmer for 5 minutes. Serve with slices of lemon.

## Fish Ring

2 lb. haddock, swordfish, tuna
or any dry-type white fish
½ c. milk
Salt and pepper

2 T. flour
Breadcrumbs
Butter
1 egg

Pass the fish through a mincer several times or use very fine blade. Mix the minced fish with milk, flour, egg, salt and pepper. Place in a buttered mould. Cover with breadcrumbs. Cook in water for 45 minutes. Serve with vegetables or tomato sauce. As given this recipe makes a very bland ring. It should be served with a rich creamed vegetable sauce. To make a spicier ring, add lemon juice, onion or other seasonings.

## Pudding of Raw Fish

2 lb. fish (any white fish)
1 T. butter
3 eggs, separated
Salt and pepper

1 dry bun or crust soaked
in milk
2 T. sweet cream
Nutmeg

Mince the raw fish or chop fine. Add nutmeg, salt and pepper. Crumble soaked and squeezed bun or crust. Mix well with butter, egg-yolks and sweet cream. Add to the fish. Beat egg whites until stiff and fold into the fish mixture and place in a well-greased and floured baking dish. Set the dish in a pan of warm water and bake in a moderate oven for about 1 hour. Serve with mushroom sauce (see p. 97) or caper sauce (see p. 96).

### Fish Crôquettes

| | |
|---|---|
| 1 lb. cooked fish | 2 truffles or 6 cooked |
| 2 eggs, separated | mushrooms |
| 1 egg, beaten | Breadcrumbs |
| Butter | Flour |
| Salt and white pepper | Fresh parsley |
| 1 T. butter | |

Mix 1 T. of butter with 2 egg yolks. Add chopped, cooked mushrooms, chopped, cooked fish, parsley, salt and pepper. Beat the egg whites stiff and combine. Place on a board and form croquettes in pyramid shapes. Roll them in flour; dip in beaten egg and sprinkle with breadcrumbs. Fry in butter. Pour over them tomato sauce (see p. 99), or Bordelaise sauce (see p. 100). Serve with a green salad.

### Sole in White Wine

| | |
|---|---|
| Fillet of sole | 2 T. butter |
| 1 c. vegetable stock | 1 c. white wine |
| ¼ c. mushrooms, sliced | 1 T. flour |
| 2 egg yolks | Salt and pepper |

Place the sole in a pot with 1 T. of butter, the vegetable stock, mushrooms and white wine. Season and stew under cover for 20 to 30 minutes. On the side melt 1 T. of butter. Stir in flour and dilute with 3 T. of fish stock, being careful not to form lumps. When the fish is tender, place it on a platter and add the remaining fish stock to the sauce. When smooth add egg yolks. Cover the fish with the sauce.

### Stewed Sole with Tomatoes

| | |
|---|---|
| Fillet of sole | 2 T. butter |
| 3 large onions, sliced | 1 c. vegetable stock |
| 1 c. white wine | ½ can tomato paste or 4 peeled |
| 2 bouillon cubes | tomatoes |
| 1 T. flour | Salt and pepper |

Brown onion in 1 T. of butter. Cut the fillet into serving pieces and add to the browned onion in a stewing pan. Add the vegetable stock, white wine, tomato paste or tomatoes and bouillon cubes. Cover and stew for 20 to 30 minutes. When tender, remove the fish from the pan. Melt and mix 1 T. of butter and flour. Stir into fish stock mixture and pour this over the pieces of fish to serve.

### Trout or Sole in Blue

| | |
|---|---|
| Trout or sole | 1 c. white vinegar |
| Butter | Parsley |

Soak the cleaned fish in vinegar for an hour, turning it over a few times. Put it in boiling salted water which should barely cover. Cook on a slow flame for 25 minutes or until tender. Serve on a platter sticking pieces of parsley into the mouth of the fish. Pour melted butter over it.

## Crappies with Horseradish

| | |
|---|---|
| 5 crappies | Salt and pepper |
| ¼ c. butter | 2 T. horseradish |
| ¼ c. sour cream | |

Put the cleaned fish in a baking dish. On the side mix the horse-radish with the sour cream, salt and pepper. Cover the fish with it. Top with pieces of butter and bake in a moderate oven for 30 minutes.

## Fricassee of Left-over Fish

| | |
|---|---|
| Left-over fish | 6 boiled potatoes |
| 3 hard-boiled eggs | 4 T. grated cheese, Parmesan |
| 1 c. sour cream | Salt and pepper |
| 3 T. butter | 3 T. breadcrumbs |

Cut up fish and slice potatoes and eggs. Grease a baking dish and arrange layers of potatoes, eggs and fish, sprinkling each layer with Parmesan cheese. Make sure the first and last layers are potatoes. Cover with sour cream. Melt 1 T. of butter with the breadcrumbs and sprinkle on top of the casserole. Dot with remaining butter and cheese. Put in a moderate oven for 30 minutes.

## Fillet of Haddock in Batter

| | |
|---|---|
| Haddock fillets | 1½ c. flour |
| Fat | 1 egg |
| *Batter:* | 1 T. butter or margarine |
| 1 c. milk | Salt and pepper |
| 2 t. baking powder | |
| ¼ t. salt | |

Mix the flour with the baking powder and the salt. Stir in the milk slowly. Add melted butter and the egg. Season the fish. Dip in the batter and fry in hot fat. Brown well.

## Fillet of Flounder or Sole au Gratin

| | |
|---|---|
| Fillet of flounder or sole | ½ c. white wine |
| 3 T. breadcrumbs | Grated cheese, Parmesan |
| Flour | |

Cut the fish into serving pieces. Roll in flour. Place in a greased baking dish. Sprinkle with white wine, breadcrumbs and grated cheese. Bake in a hot oven for 20 minutes.

## Sole in Sour Cream

| | |
|---|---|
| 1 lb. fillets of sole | Grated cheese, Parmesan or |
| 2 c. sour cream | Romano |
| Butter | 1 T. flour |
| Salt and pepper | Breadcrumbs |

Salt fish. Sprinkle with flour and brown lightly in a frying pan. Place in a greased baking dish. Sprinkle with a good quantity of cheese. Pour over it the sour cream mixed with flour. On top, spread with breadcrumbs and dot with butter. Bake for about 20 minutes in a very hot oven.

## Stuffed Herring

| | |
|---|---|
| 6 large herring | Juice of 2 lemons |
| Butter or fat | 1 small onion |
| Breadcrumbs | 1 hard-boiled egg |
| Flour | 1 raw egg |
| Salt and pepper | Milk |

Soak the herring first in water, changing the water frequently. Then soak in milk. Split and bone. Sprinkle the meat with lemon juice. On the side chop and brown the onion with 2 T. of breadcrumbs. Add 1 hard-boiled egg which has been chopped, the raw egg and salt and pepper. Stuff the herring with this mixture. Roll the herring in flour, then in a raw egg, and sprinkle with breadcrumbs. Fry in deep hot fat. Serve with salad and pickle sauce (see p. 98) or mustard sauce (see p. 101).

## Baked Herring

Prepared in the same manner as for stuffed herring. Pass through flour and wrap each herring in metal foil or white paper greased with butter. Then place in a very hot oven for 15 to 20 minutes. After the baking is completed, remove from the wrapping. Garnish with slices of lemon and pour over melted butter with fresh chopped parsley. Separately serve one of the tangy sauces. (see p. 100).

## Herring Cakes

| | |
|---|---|
| 4-5 herring | 1½ buns or crusts |
| ½ onion | Salt and pepper |
| 1 hard-boiled egg | Milk |
| Butter | Bread crumbs |

Soak herring in water and milk as specified for stuffed herring. Skin and bone the fish and chop fine or put through a mincer. Add bun or crusts soaked in milk and squeezed, counting one bun for every 3 herring. On the side, brown a chopped onion, chopped hard-boiled egg, salt and pepper in butter. Add ground fish and buns and mix

well. Form oblong cutlets. Roll in breadcrumbs. Fry in deep fat.
Serve with a hot sauce (see p. 100).

## Cream of Herring

| | |
|---|---|
| 4 large herring | 2 egg yolks |
| 1 T. butter | 2 buns, soaked in milk |
| Salt and pepper | Nutmeg |
| 1 onion, grated | 3 T. grated cheese, Parmesan |
| 2 egg whites | 3 T. sour cream |

Soak as specified for the stuffed herring. Skin and remove bones.
Chop fine or pass through a mincer with the soaked buns. Mix 2
egg yolks with butter and add to the herring and bread mixture.
Add also salt and pepper, a dash of nutmeg, a grated onion, grated
Parmesan cheese and sour cream. Beat egg whites until stiff and add
to the fish mixture. Form a pyramid in a greased baking dish.
Sprinkle with breadcrumbs and bake in a hot oven for about 30
minutes. Separately serve melted butter.

## Rolled Herring

| | |
|---|---|
| Herring | Mustard |
| 1 onion, chopped | Olive oil |
| 1 lemon, sliced | Bay leaves |
| Salt | Whole peppercorns |

Soak and skin as specified above. Cut the herring in half and cut off
the heads and tails. Cover each herring with mustard. Sprinkle with
chopped onion. Roll the herring into a cornucopia and garnish with
slices of lemon. Throw some peppercorns on top, also a few bay
leaves, and cover the whole dish with olive oil. Put in refrigerator.
Let it stand for a few days before using.

## Fish Crôquettes

| | |
|---|---|
| 1 lb. cod-fish, cooked | 2 c. mashed potatoes |
| Butter | Salt and pepper |
| 1 onion | Parsley |
| 2 eggs, beaten | Breadcrumbs |

Make a smooth paste from the cod fish with the mashed potatoes.
Add salt and pepper, finely chopped parsley, onion chopped and
browned in butter, and the 2 beaten eggs. Form in oval shapes with
two T. or with hands. Roll in breadcrumbs and fry.

### Baked Stuffed Fish

| | |
|---|---|
| Mackerel or pike | 1 t. all-spice |
| *Stuffing:* | 2 stalks celery |
| 2 large onions | 6 T. breadcrumbs |
| 4 T. butter | Milk |
| 2 eggs | ½ c. dried mushrooms |

Chop an onion fine with celery and sauté in butter. Moisten breadcrumbs with milk and combine with onion and celery mixture, allspice and mushroom. Stuff the fish. Place it in a baking dish. Slice the second onion over it. Dot with butter and bake in a moderate oven for about 45 minutes.

### Tuna Fish Roll

| | |
|---|---|
| 3 cans tuna fish | 3 T. vinegar |
| 4 T. grated cheese, Parmesan | 6 T. breadcrumbs |
| ½ c. vinegar | 3 eggs |
| *Sauce:* | 1 can tuna fish |
| 1 c. mayonnaise (see page 105) | 3 T. capers |
| 1 can fillets of anchovy | 4 T. olive oil |

Pass the 3 cans of tuna fish through a sieve. Add the breadcrumbs, grated cheese, salt and pepper. Work it into a smooth paste. Add well-beaten eggs. Mix again. Shape it into a roll. Wrap in gauze. or cheesecloth. Cover with cold water and ½ c. vinegar. Cook for 45 minutes. Remove and chill the tuna fish roll. When cold, slice and cover with the sauce. Garnish with parsley and more capers. To prepare the sauce, sieve 1 can of tuna fish. Mix well with the mayonnaise, chopped anchovy fillets, capers, vinegar, and oil. Serve cold.

### Tuna Fish Casserole

| | |
|---|---|
| 2 cans tuna fish | 2 c. white sauce (see page 96) |
| 4 slices American-type cheese | 4 T. grated cheese, Parmesan |
| 2 eggs | Salt and pepper |

Make white sauce in a double-boiler. Add American cheese, mixing constantly until dissolved. Add tuna fish which has been put through a sieve. Add two well-beaten eggs, salt and pepper. Place the mixture in a greased baking dish. Sprinkle with grated cheese. Bake in a moderate oven for 30 minutes.

### Haddock au Gratin

| | |
|---|---|
| Haddock | 1 large onion |
| 4 T. butter | ½ c. chopped mushrooms |
| 3 T. breadcrumbs | 3 T. grated cheese, Parmesan |
| 1 c. cream or milk | Salt and pepper |

Brown the chopped onion with mushrooms in butter. Place the fish in a greased baking dish with all the other ingredients, including the onion and mushrooms sprinkled over the top. Bake in a moderate oven for 45 minutes, basting with cream from time to time. Place chunks on top before serving. If fillets of haddock are small, the cooking time would be about 20 minutes.

## Gefillte Fish

About 3 lb. of any fish carp, pike, haddock, etc.
4 c. vegetable stock
¼ c. almonds
1 c. bread-crumbs
Salt
¼ c. raisins
Bay leaf
2 large onions, chopped
3 eggs
4 peppercorns
2 T. sugar

Cut off the head of the fish and cook it in vegetable stock with raisins, 2 T. of sugar and bay leaf. In the meantime skin and bone cleaned fish. Mince the meat with blanched almonds. Mix with chopped onions and bread-crumbs. Season. Add 2 T. of sugar and 3 well-beaten eggs. Make balls of this mixture. Remove head from boiling stock and drop fish balls into the liquid, continuing to boil until the balls float. Chill and serve in the jellied stock.

## Boiled Salmon with Hollandaise Sauce

Salmon
¼ c. vinegar
Salt
Melted butter

Cook the salmon in water to which vinegar has been added. When tender, pour melted butter over the pieces of fish and serve with Hollandaise sauce on the side (see p. 100).

## Salmon in Jelly

Salmon
Parsley
1 large onion
2 c. white wine
Bay leaves
Salt and pepper
2 carrots
2 stalks celery
Juice of 1 lemon
3 T. olive oil
Nutmeg
1 pkg. gelatine (1 T.)

Slice the vegetables and cook with the salmon, adding lemon juice, white wine, olive oil, a bay leaf, nutmeg, salt and pepper and stew until the salmon is tender. Slice the salmon into bell-like slices. Place it on a deep platter and garnish it with the vegetables. Dissolve the gelatine in part of the fish stock and pour this over the fish and vegetables. Chill, and serve cold.

### Salmon with Stuffing

| | |
|---|---|
| 3 lb. salmon, in slices | Salmon liver |
| 4 mushrooms | 1 dill pickle |
| 2 fillets of anchovy | 4 T. breadcrumbs |
| 1 T. melted butter | 1 egg |
| 1 bouillon cube | 1 c. water |
| Salt and pepper | |

Chop fine the salmon liver, mushrooms, dill pickle and anchovies. Mix butter with the beaten egg, salt and pepper. Combine the 2 mixtures. Dip salmon slices in it, coating them, and place them in a saucepan with a small amount of the bouillon broth made from one bouillon cube and 1 c. of water. Cover pan and simmer, adding bouillon broth when necessary. Serve when tender.

### Salmon

| | |
|---|---|
| 2 lb. fresh salmon | 3 slices bacon |
| Truffles (optional) | Melted butter |
| Juice of 1 lemon | ¼ c. white wine |

Cut the bacon in small pieces and insert in slits which should be cut in the salmon skin at intervals. If truffles are used, slice them lengthwise and place on top of the fish with butter in a greased baking dish. Bake in a moderate oven, basting from time to time with butter. After 15 minutes, pour lemon juice and white wine over the salmon and continue baking until tender.

### Sturgeon with Sour Cream

| | |
|---|---|
| 2 lb. Sturgeon (tail pieces are the tastiest) | 3 T. butter |
| | 2 carrots |
| Salt | 2 c. water |
| 1 large onion | 1 T. flour |
| 1 c. sour cream | Parsley |

Pour boiling water over the sturgeon to eliminate odour. Skin and salt, letting it stand for an hour. Stew in butter, adding sliced vegetables and two c. of water and cover. When tender, add 1 c. of sour cream which has been mixed with 1 T. of flour. Sprinkle with parsley. Serve with potatoes which have been garnished with fresh dill.

### Oyster Cakes

| | |
|---|---|
| 12 oysters | ¾ c. mushrooms |
| Butter | Salt and pepper |
| 3-4 tomatoes | 3 T. grated cheese, Parmesan |
| Bread-crumbs | |

Boil the oysters until they open. Take them out of the shells. Cook in salted water until tender and chop into small pieces. On the side chop the mushrooms and brown in butter. Combine with the oysters. Add pepper and put the mixture back into the oyster shells. Separately stew three or four tomatoes in butter. Sprinkle with Parmesan cheese. Strain the tomatoes through a sieve and pour over the oysters. Place the filled shells in a baking dish. Top with breadcrumbs and a pat of butter on each. Put into a hot oven for 10 minutes. Serve immediately.

### Shrimp in Soya Sauce

| | |
|---|---|
| 2 lb. raw shrimp | $\frac{1}{2}$ c. wine vinegar |
| 2 large onions | 3 T. butter |
| 1 c. sweet cream | 4 eggs |
| 4 T. soya sauce | |

Cook the shrimps in boiling salted water with $\frac{1}{2}$ c. of wine vinegar. When pink and tender, cool and clean, removing shell. Brown the sliced onion in butter. Add shrimps and sauté for a moment. Add cream and soya sauce and continue cooking for 5 minutes on a low flame. Just before serving stir in 4 well-beaten eggs and serve with rice.

### Lobster in Tartare Sauce

| | |
|---|---|
| 1 lobster | 2 onions |
| Fresh dill | 2 stalks celery |
| Parsley | Olive oil |

Cook lobster for 20 minutes with vegetables in salted water to cover. Take the lobster out of the vegetable stock. Sprinkle shell with oil and wipe it to make the shell shine. Cut in half by slitting end to end. Remove meat, clean, and slice it replacing carefully in the halved shell. Cut the claws and remove meat in the same manner, later replacing it. Put the lobster on a platter. Garnish with salad and greens. Serve tartare sauce (see p. 106) in a separate dish.

### Lobster with Sour Cream

| | |
|---|---|
| 3-5 lobsters | 3 T. butter |
| Salt | 2 c. sour cream |
| 3 T. bread-crumbs | Dill |

Drop lobsters in boiling water for two minutes and then take out. Cut open and remove lobster meat. Melt 3 T. of butter in a large pot and fry the lobster meat for 10 minutes. When the meat is crimson add a little salt and pour in sour cream. Add breadcrumbs, a few sprigs of dill and simmer under cover for 15 minutes. Serve.

## Vol au Vent

Left-over fish or any piece of cooked white fish
1 small can lobster meat
1 T. butter
1 c. vegetable or fish stock
½ c. white wine
1 T. butter
1 onion, sliced
1 T. flour

Knelki (dumplings prepared to serve with this recipe (see page 29)
Juice of 1 lemon
3 egg yolks
½ c. sliced mushrooms
1 T. grated cheese, Parmesan
2 bouillon cubes
Salt and pepper

Prepare knelki (see p. 29). Chop cooked white fish and lobster together. Make a white sauce from 1 T. of butter, 1 T. of flour and 1 c. of vegetable or fish stock. Stir in wine, lemon juice, bouillon cubes and 3 egg-yolks. Combine with fish, adding mushrooms and onion which have been browned in butter. Fill individual shells or large baking dish. Sprinkle with grated cheese. Put in the oven just long enough to warm thoroughly the shells or serving dish.

## Lobster Salad with Avocados

Lettuce
2 avocados
Salt and pepper
5 T. olive oil

2 7-oz. cans lobster meat
Garlic salt
3 T. tarragon vinegar

Shred lettuce. Cut up lobster and avocado. Add salt, pepper and garlic salt. On the side mix tarragon vinegar and olive oil. Pour over the salad mixture and serve. Garnish the platter with sliced hard-boiled eggs, red marinated peppers and parsley.

# MEAT

Until the sixteenth century simplicity prevailed over Polish taste; the preferred meat was boiled beef— "sztuka miesa," Polish sausage—"kielbasa," or "bigos." In the sixteenth century, with the incoming of the French court, French cuisine took hold and more complicated and original dishes were made, "To be different" and "Frenchy" was the word of the day. And so it continued.

### Pot Roast of Beef

| | |
|---|---|
| 3-5 lb. beef | Peppercorns |
| 1 lb. asparagus | Salt |
| 1 onion, cut | 1 cauliflower, in pieces |
| Bay leaf | |

Brown roast in kettle. Add enough water to prevent burning. Add onion and cauliflower. Season. Cover tightly and cook over a good flame for 3 hours. Add asparagus and cook until it is tender. Leftover beef cooked in this manner, and minced is often used as a filling for pierogi, ushka, etc.

### Beef with Horseradish Sauce

| | |
|---|---|
| 3-5 lb. pot roast of beef | 2 egg yolks |
| Salt | 3 stalks celery, cut |
| Horseradish sauce (see page 98) | 1 onion, cut |
| 4 T. butter | 2 carrots, cut |
| 1-2 c. water | Bay leaf, Parsley |

Place the meat in a pot with salted water, sliced celery, carrots, onion, parsley and bay leaf. Cover and cook until done, (approximately 3 to 4 hours). Let the meat become cold. Slice and put in a baking dish. Garnish with cooked potatoes and cover with horseradish sauce mixed with 2 egg yolks and butter. Bake 20 to 30 minutes until nicely browned.

### Beef with Béchamel Sauce

| | |
|---|---|
| 3 lb. beef, cooked with vegetables (see above) | Salt and pepper to taste |
| | Béchamel sauce (see page 96) |

Slice the cooked beef and place in a baking dish. Cover with Béchamel sauce and garnish with cooked potatoes. Bake in the oven for 20 to 30 minutes until nicely browned.

### Pot Roast

| | |
|---|---|
| 3-4 lb. beef rump or chuck | 2 onions, cut |
| 3 T. butter | 2 carrots, cut |
| 1 bay leaf | Flour |
| ½ c. stock | Salt and pepper |

Brown the beef in butter. Then, add 1 bay leaf, 2 onions, 2 carrots, salt and pepper, and simmer under cover for about 3 hours, basting with water to prevent burning. Thirty minutes before taking out of the pot, sprinkle flour over the meat and turn it over. Add, if necessary, ½ c. of stock for the sauce. Serve the pot roast with noodles, potatoes or any kind of vegetables.

### Pot Roast with Sour Cream

Prepared in the same way as the pot roast. Thirty minutes before taking out of the pot, cover with 2 c. of sour cream mixed with 1 T. of flour. Serve the meat in the liquid from the pot.

### Pot Roast with Sour Cream and Pickles

| | |
|---|---|
| 3 dill pickles | Other ingredients same as for pot |
| 1 T. flour | roast |
| 2 c. sour cream | |

Prepared in the same way as the pot roast. When the meat is browned, add dill pickles, peeled and diced. Thirty minutes before taking out of the pot, cover with sour cream mixed with flour.

### Pot Roast with Mushrooms

| | |
|---|---|
| ½ c. mushrooms, dried | Other ingredients the same as for |
| 2 c. sour cream | the pot roast |
| 1 T. flour | |

Prepared in the same way as the pot roast with pickles. Instead of adding pickles add ½ c. of sliced dried, soaked and chopped mushrooms. Thirty minutes before taking out of the pot, cover with sour cream mixed with flour.

### Beef à la Mode

| | |
|---|---|
| 3-4 lb. pot roast of beef | 2 bay leaves |
| ¼ c. salt pork | 2 T. bread-crumbs |
| 2 T. butter | ½ c. vinegar |
| ¼ c. white wine | 1 onion |

Dice the salt pork, and with a knife make small incisions in the beef about two inches apart. Stuff these with the pieces of salt pork. Place in an earthenware bowl and scald with vinegar cooked with an onion. Add bay leaves. Cover and let stand overnight in this bowl. Drain. Then place in a baking dish. Bake in a moderate oven, in melted butter, uncovered, and when it is golden brown, add ½ c. of white wine. Cover and continue baking for about 1 hour or until tender. Before taking out of the oven, sprinkle with bread-crumbs, and baste with its sauce. Serve with red cabbage.

### Roast in the Wild

| | |
|---|---|
| 3-4 lb, top round beef | 4 T. butter or margerine |
| ¼ c. mushrooms, diced | Salt and pepper |
| 1 large onion, diced | 1 T. flour |
| Vinegar | 2 c. sour cream |

Pound the meat well and scald with hot vinegar cooked with 1 onion. Let stand for 24 hours. Thirty minutes before cooking, drain and salt. Place in melted butter with 1 diced onion and diced mushrooms and simmer under cover until it is golden brown, occasionally basting with cold water. Thirty minutes before taking out of the pot, cover with sour cream mixed with flour. Serve with this sauce and dumplings, noodles or potatoes.

### Roast à la Bordelaise

| | |
|---|---|
| 3 lb. round steak | 2 large onions, chopped |
| ¼ c. vinegar | Salt |
| 2 T. butter | 2 T. parsley, chopped |
| ¼ c. red wine | 2 T. tomato paste |
| 2 celery stalks, cut | ½ t. Worcestershire sauce |
| 2 carrots, cut | ½ c. stock |
| 1 bouillon cube | |

Scald the beef with hot vinegar cooked with onion. Let stand overnight if possible; if not, allow to stand at least 2 hours. Thirty minutes before cooking, drain and salt. Brown in melted butter and place in the oven, with red wine, chopped parsley, carrots, celery, onion, stock, tomato paste, Worcestershire sauce and bouillon cube, dissolved. Bake under cover until tender. Serve in the natural sauce after straining.

### Roast in Flemish Style

| | |
|---|---|
| 3 lb. pot roast of beef | 1 large onion, sliced |
| 2 carrots, cut | Salt and pepper |
| 2 celery stalks, cut | 2 heads of cabbage, sliced and cut |
| ¼ lb. Polish sausage | ¼ c. stock |
| Flour | Parsley |
| ¼ c. butter | |

Salt and brown the roast in melted butter. Simmer under cover with carrots, onion and celery and the parsley. After one hour, add pepper, Polish sausage and 2 quartered heads of cabbage. Sprinkle with flour. Add stock. Simmer until tender. Place on a platter with sliced pieces of sausage and garnish with cabbage. Cover it with the strained sauce.

### Filet Mignon with Madeira and Mushrooms

| | |
|---|---|
| Beef steak | Olive oil |
| 1 c. Madeira wine | 1¼ c. of small mushrooms |
| Salt and pepper | ¼ t. Worcestershire sauce |
| 2 large onions, sliced | Individual portions of toast |

Prepare separately sauce of Madeira wine with mushrooms and Worcestershire sauce. Bring to the boiling point. Before broiling the steak, wipe it with a wet cloth, rub with oil and slash fatty edge. Broil. Cut and place on individual portions of toast. In the meantime, brown onions in butter and place a spoonful on each serving. Pour over the Madeira sauce with mushrooms. Serve with potato croquettes or fried potatoes.

### Filet Mignon with Tomato Sauce

Beef steak  
Olive oil  
Onions  
2 bouillon cubes  
Salt and pepper  

Parsley  
Tomato sauce  
½ t. Worcestershire sauce  
Butter  

Before broiling, wipe the steak with a wet cloth, rub with oil and slash the fatty edge. Then, brown steak on both sides in melted butter with onions. Broil. Add to the tomato sauce (see p. 99), 1 bouillon cube and Worcestershire sauce. The tomato sauce should be thick. Place the steak on individual portions of toast. Pour over half of the sauce and garnish with parsley. The rest of the sauce serve separately.

### English Beef Steak

Beef steak  
2 T. butter  
Salt and pepper  

Flour  
Horseradish  

Salt and pepper and sprinkle the steak with flour just before cooking. Fry on both sides in 1 T. of butter on a very hot flame. On the side, brown some grated horseradish in butter and pour over the steak. Ready-made horseradish may be used.

### Beef Steak with Egg

Prepare the beef steak as the English beef steak. With each steak serve one egg, sunny side up.

### Beef Rolls

2 lb. top round steak  
½ c. butter  
Flour  
Salt and pepper  

1 large onion, grated  
2 T. bread-crumbs  
2½ c. meat stock  

Cut the steak in oblong slices about 4 inches by 2 inches, salt and pepper and rub with the following sauce: grated onion, browned in 1 T. of butter and mixed with bread-crumbs. Roll up each piece of meat, fasten with tooth-picks and roll in flour. Brown in butter, adding the meat stock. Simmer for an hour. Take out the tooth-picks and pour over the sauce. Serve with buckwheat groats (see p. 26).

### Beef Cutlets

| | |
|---|---|
| 2 lb. top round steak | 2 T. butter |
| Flour | 2 c. cold water |
| ¼ onion, chopped | Salt and pepper |
| 4 dried mushrooms | Rosemary |

Cut the meat into thin pieces, pound and salt. Add pepper and rosemary; sprinkle with flour. Brown the pieces in melted butter with onion. Combine with soaked and chopped dried mushrooms, basting with cold water while simmering on a low flame for 45 minutes. In case the sauce should be too thin, add more flour. Separately cook buckwheat groats (see p. 26) and serve together.

### Ground Burgers

| | |
|---|---|
| 2 lb. beef, ground | 2 soaked buns |
| Marrow (optional) | 2 eggs, beaten |
| Butter | 1 grated onion |
| Salt and pepper | Flour |
| 1½ c. stock | |

Combine the meat with marrow, the beaten eggs, salt and pepper, onion, browned in butter, and squeezed buns. Mix thoroughly, then form in oblong patties and roll in flour. Brown in melted butter, then sprinkle with more flour and stock. Simmer for 15 minutes under cover.

### Beef Cutlets with Sour Cream

| | |
|---|---|
| 2 lb. top round steak | Butter |
| 1 T. flour | Salt and pepper |
| 6 dried mushrooms | Paprika |
| 2 c. sour cream | 4-6 potatoes |
| 1 onion, chopped | 1 T. flour |

Cut the meat in pieces. Pound and salt. Sprinkle with flour and brown in butter. Cook the mushrooms in butter on the side and combine with beef when tender, adding the pan drippings too. Add enough water to prevent burning. Simmer for 30 minutes and add potatoes sliced. When potatoes are almost tender, add sour cream, mixed with flour. Simmer for 5 minutes and serve.

### Beef à la Radecki

| | |
|---|---|
| 3 lb. top round steak | Flour |
| 2 large onions, chopped | 2 c. bouillon stock |
| 2 T. bread-crumbs | 3-4 mushrooms |
| 4 T. butter | Salt and pepper |
| Dill, chopped | ¼ c. red wine |

Cut the meat in 4 x 2 inch pieces and coat with the following sauce: browned chopped onion with chopped fresh mushrooms and chopped dill. Roll the meat. Tie lightly with strings and brown in melted butter. Sprinkle with flour. Add bouillon broth and red wine. Cover and simmer on a low flame until they are tender.

## Bitki in Sour Cream

| | |
|---|---|
| 2-3 lb. ground beef | 2 rolls buns or breadcrusts soaked |
| 1 grated onion | in milk |
| 2 c. sour cream | 1 egg |
| Salt and pepper | 1 T. flour |
| Butter | Mushrooms (optional) |
| 2 c. bouillon stock | |

Mince the meat twice with 2 soaked and squeezed buns. Add onion, grated and browned in butter. Mix with 1 egg, salt and pepper and make into round balls. Roll them in flour and brown in melted butter. Add stock and sour cream mixed with flour and mushrooms. Simmer for 30 minutes.

## Chopped Beef Patties

| | |
|---|---|
| 2 lb. lean minced meat | Salt and pepper |
| 1 egg | Bread-crumbs |
| 1 onion, grated | Fat |
| 2 buns, soaked in milk | |

Mix the minced meat with 2 squeezed buns, browned onion, salt and pepper. Form into oblong cakes. Roll in egg and dip in bread-crumbs. Fry in fat on a hot fire. Serve with one of the strong sauces.

## Baked Chopped Beef Cutlets

| | |
|---|---|
| Chopped beef | 2 c. sour cream |
| 2 c. cooked rice | Grated Parmesan cheese |

Prepare as above. Fry in fat and then place in pan with cooked rice. Pour over sour cream and sprinkle with grated Parmesan cheese. Bake in the oven for 20 minutes.

## Goulash

| | |
|---|---|
| 3-4 lb. beef or pork stew meat | Flour |
| 2-3 large onions | Parsley |
| Stock | Salt and pepper |
| 8 potatoes | Fat |
| 1 T. tomato paste | $\frac{1}{4}$ t. paprika |

Cut the meat into small cubes. Chop the onions. Salt the meat and place with onions, paprika and some fat in a pot. Stew on a slow fire until the meat is browned. Then, sprinkle with flour, adding some stock, tomato paste and cut potatoes. Simmer until the potatoes are tender.

## Hungarian Goulash

Prepare in the same way as the goulash. Instead of adding potatoes use sauerkraut, adding 2 T. more of tomato paste. Stew until tender.

## Meat Loaf

| | |
|---|---|
| 2 lb. lean minced meat | ½ onion, grated |
| ½ lb. sausage meat | 2 eggs |
| 2 buns soaked in milk | 2 hard-boiled eggs |
| Salt and pepper | 2 large dill pickles |
| 4 dried mushrooms, soaked | 2 c. sour cream |
| 1 c. mushroom broth | 1 T. flour |

Fry the grated onion. Cook the mushrooms. Reserve the broth. Mix all the minced meat with eggs, squeezed-out buns, onion, chopped mushrooms, salt and pepper. Press the meat flat on a board and in the middle place alternately hard-boiled eggs and pickles. Make a meat roll and place in a baking dish. Bake in a moderate oven for 1 hour. Before taking out, pour over the sour cream mixed with flour and mushroom broth and bake together for 10 minutes.

## Beef Tongue

| | |
|---|---|
| 1 beef tongue | Salt and pepper |
| 2 carrots, cut | Rosemary |
| 1 onion, cut | Bay leaf |
| Water, to cover | |

Cook tongue with all the ingredients until it is tender. When it is cold remove the skin and slice thinly. Broth can be used for soup—lentil soup is extremely good. Serve the tongue with a raisin sauce (see p. 101), or with Sauce à la Diable (see p. 103), or with horseradish sauce. (see p. 98).

## Fried Tongue

| | |
|---|---|
| 1 beef tongue | Bread-crumbs |
| 2 carrots, cut | Butter |
| 1 onion, cut | Bay leaf |
| 1 egg | Salt and pepper |

Cook the beef tongue as in the previous recipe. Take off the skin and slice in thin slices. Dip in egg and sprinkle with bread-crumbs. Fry in melted butter. Serve with Sauce à la Diable (see p. 103).

## Veal with Paprika

| | |
|---|---|
| 2 lb. breast of veal | 2 T. floor |
| 1 T. paprika | 2 T. butter |
| 2 onions, chopped | 2 c. sour cream |
| 3 carrots, cut | 2 c. water |
| 3 green peppers, cut | |

Blanch veal with boiling water. Leave for a moment, then rinse in cold water. Brown the chopped onions with green peppers and carrots in melted butter. Add to the meat and pour in 2 c. of warm water. Cover and simmer for 2 hours. When the meat is tender, salt and pepper. Add sour cream mixed with flour. Stir and warm through. Serve with paprika.

## Veal Cutlets in White Wine

| | |
|---|---|
| 2 lb. thin veal cutlets | 8 dried mushrooms |
| Flour | Salt and pepper |
| ¼ c. white wine | Butter |
| Rosemary | 2 onions, sliced |
| 1 lemon, quartered | |

Pound the meat well. Roll each piece in salted flour. Brown the sliced onions. Add soaked, sliced mushrooms and floured meat. Add wine and additional seasoning if desired (rosemary and pepper). Simmer on low fire for a few minutes until tender. Serve with quarters of lemons.

## Viennese Veal Cutlets

| | |
|---|---|
| 6 veal cutlets | Flour |
| 1 egg | Butter |
| Bread-crumbs | Salt and pepper |

Pound the meat well. Salt and pepper and roll in flour, and then the egg. Sprinkle with bread-crumbs. Fry slowly in butter until golden brown and tender. Do not let the bread-crumbs burn. Serve with potatoes and green salad. Mushroom sauce is nice to pour over the cutlets.

## Cutlets à la Imperial

| | |
|---|---|
| 6 veal chops | Salt and pepper |
| 6 eggs | Paprika |
| Flour | 3 T. grated cheese |
| Butter | |

Pound the meat well. Sprinkle with flour and brown in melted butter. Beat the eggs. Add salt, pepper and paprika. Pour by the T. into a separate frying pan with melted butter. When the egg turns into omelet, place on each cutlet. Sprinkle with grated cheese. Serve with tomato sauce. (see p. 99).

## Stuffed Veal Cutlets

| | |
|---|---|
| 2 lb. thin veal cutlets | 2 eggs |
| 1 c. Bechamel sauce | Bread-crumbs |
| ¼ lb. ham | ¼ lb. Canadian or country smoked |
| American cheese | bacon |
| Salt and pepper | Fat |

Veal should be well pounded and cut in small slices. Place on the top of each cutlet a t. of Béchamel, ½ slice of American cheese, a small piece of ham, and a small piece of bacon. Season. Cover with another veal cutlet. Roll in egg and bread-crumbs and fry in hot fat until veal is cooked.

## Veal Rolls

| | |
|---|---|
| 2 lb. veal cutlets | Parsley |
| 3 T. butter | Garlic, 2 sections, pressed |
| Flour | Rosemary |
| Salt and pepper | Basil, dried or oregano |
| ¼ c. white wine | Béchamel sauce (see page 96) |
| 5 onions, chopped | |

Pound the cutlet well. Season each of the pieces. Sprinkle with herbs, garlic and add 1 t. of Béchamel sauce to each piece. Roll each piece and pin with a tooth pick. Coat with flour and stew under cover in butter with onions and wine. When nearly tender, add sauce to cover and continue cooking until done.

## Zrazy-English Style

| | |
|---|---|
| 2 lb. veal or beef steak | ½ c. white wine |
| 4 onions, grated | Salt and pepper |
| Fat | 1 bouillon cube |
| 1 T. Worcestershire sauce | 4 T. bread-crumbs |
| Dill | |

Slice the meat in thin slices. Pound well. Salt and pepper. Grate the onions and add to these the bread-crumbs, a handful of chopped dill and a dash of pepper. Roll the meat in the prepared mixture and fry in fat. Pour over wine, Worcestershire sauce, dissolve bouillon cube and seasoning. Cover and cook on a very hot flame. Bring to the boiling point and then stew for 30 minutes on a low flame or until tender, adding more broth if necessary.

## Zrazy à la Nelson

| | |
|---|---|
| 8-10 veal cutlets | ¼ lb. butter |
| 1 lb. fresh mushrooms | 2 T. Flour |
| 1 pkg. dried mushrooms | 6 medium-sized potatoes, cooked |
| 3 bouillon cubes | 1 qt. milk |
| ½ pt. sour cream | 4 large onions, chopped |
| 3 slices bacon | Salt and pepper |

Soak dried mushrooms in cold milk for about 3 hours before starting to prepare dish. Drain off milk. Chop mushrooms. Fry fresh mushrooms, onions and bacon (cut in small pieces) together until lightly browned in half the butter (reserving the balance to make a roux with the flour). Take mushrooms, onion and bacon from the fat and add to set-aside milk (to which you have returned the cut-up dried mushrooms). Add veal to fat in skillet and fry lightly on both sides. Add bouillon cubes and milk with its additions. Simmer slowly for about 1 hour. Melt the 2 T. of butter in small skillet. Blend in flour to make roux. Pour a little of the milk (taken from the skillet in which the veal is simmering) in to the flour-butter mixture. Stir until smooth and then add gradually to the larger skillet, stirring constantly to prevent sauce from lumping. This is done 15 minutes before serving. When sauce is thickened, add cooked, drained potatoes and sour cream.

## Zrazy à la Nelson II

| | |
|---|---|
| 2 lb. veal or beef steak | 1 pkg. dried mushrooms, soaked |
| 1 glass red wine | and chopped |
| 4 fresh mushrooms, chopped | 2 lb. potatoes |
| Butter | 1 onion, chopped |
| 1 c. bouillon broth | 2 T. sour cream |

Melt 1 T. of butter and brown in it a finely chopped onion. When the onion gets rosy-coloured, add bouillon broth and chopped mush-

rooms. Pour over a glass of red wine and 1 c. of mushroom broth. Simmer. Cook the potatoes separately. Slice the meat into thin cutlets, pound it. Salt and pepper and sauté on a very hot flame. Then combine with diced potatoes, cover with the onion sauce, adding 2 T. of sour cream and cook for a few minutes more.

### Zrazy à la Strogonow

2 lb. veal or beef steak                    Strogonow sauce

Prepare in the same way as the Zrazy à la Nelson (see p. 59) adding the Strogonow sauce (see p. 102) instead of the sour cream.

### Zrazy with Onion

| | |
|---|---|
| 2 lb. veal or beef steak | 1 c. bouillon broth |
| Salt and pepper | Vinegar |
| 2 large onions | Rosemary |
| Butter | Flour |

Cut the meat into thin cutlets and pound well. Sprinkle with vinegar, salt and pepper and rosemary and coat with flour. Brown lightly on both sides and sprinkle with chopped onions. Separately melt 1 T. of butter and blend in 1 T. of flour. Dilute with bouillon. Stew the Zrazy in this sauce until tender. Serve with buckwheat groats (see p. 26).

### Veal Patties

| | |
|---|---|
| 2 lb. veal | Salt and pepper to taste |
| 1 c. bread-crumbs | 1 T. butter |
| Flour | 3 T. sweet cream |
| 2 T. parsley, chopped | Fat |
| 1 egg, beaten | |

Mince or chop the veal coarsely and combine with melted butter, parsley, seasoning, egg, cream and bread-crumbs. Form cakes or patties. Roll in flour. Fry until cooked through.

### Chopped Veal Patties with Sour Cream

| | |
|---|---|
| 2 lb. veal, chopped or minced | Flour |
| 1 onion, grated | Fat |
| 1 bun, soaked in milk | 1 c. sour cream |
| Salt and pepper | 2 eggs |

Mix the chopped meat with grated onion. Add eggs, soaked bun, salt and pepper. Make small patties. Place in frying pan in hot fat. Brown lightly on both sides. Add sour cream and stew under cover for 15 minutes. Serve with mashed potatoes.

## Hunting Pie

| | |
|---|---|
| 3 lb. veal, cooked | 2 celery stalks |
| 2 carrots | 1 large onion |
| Parsley | ½ c. white wine |
| 1 T. butter | Salt and pepper |
| 1 prepared pie crust | |

Chop all the ingredients, except the meat. Season to taste. Melt 1 T. of butter in a deep baking dish and place all the vegetables and meat inside. Pour over the white wine. Place the pie crust on top and on the side, and put in the oven for an hour.

## Lamb Roast with Garlic

| | |
|---|---|
| 5-6 lb. leg of lamb | 1 T. flour |
| Salt and pepper | Fat |
| Garlic | 1 onion, chopped |
| Bay leaf | Rosemary |
| Basil | Ginger |

Rub the meat with salt and garlic. Cut slits in the skin and fill with garlic pieces. Leave standing for an hour, then brown lightly on all sides. Add the herbs, onion and roast in a moderate oven for 3 hours, basting with cold water occasionally. In the end sprinkle with flour and serve in its own juice.

## Lamb Roast in Sour Cream

| | |
|---|---|
| 4-5 lb. rolled lamb shoulder | 1 onion |
| Garlic, squeezed | Salt and pepper |
| Flour | Bay leaf |
| Rosemary | Basil |
| 2 c. sour cream | |

Prepare and roast as above. When tender pour over sour cream,. mixed with 1 T. of flour and stew for another 15 minutes.

## English Lamb Roast

| | |
|---|---|
| 5-6 lb. lamb roast | Olive oil |
| Pepper and salt | Garlic |
| 1 onion, sliced | |

Rub the meat with salt, pepper, garlic and olive oil. Place slices of onion on it. Put in the refrigerator for 12 hours. Then remove the onion and place in a very hot oven so that it will brown quickly. Reduce heat and roast until tender.

## Roast Lamb Shoulder

| | |
|---|---|
| 4-5 lb. lamb shoulder | 6 fillets of anchovy |
| 2 large onions | 1 egg |
| Thyme | Rosemary |
| Basil | 3 sections garlic |
| 4 T. Parmesan cheese | 1 T. tomato paste |
| 2 T. capers | Salt and pepper |
| 1 bun, soaked in milk | Broth |
| Nutmeg | 1 t. Worcestershire sauce |
| 1 t. soya sauce | |

Have the roast boned and skinned. Cut a little piece off, and chop it with 6 anchovies, capers and onion. Add squeezed bun, salt and pepper, nutmeg and mix well. Then, spread the mixture on the inside of the roast. Roll and tie with a string, placing it in a pan with herbs, onion and fat. Bake in a moderate oven for 1 hour, basting occasionally. Sprinkle with Parmesan cheese. Return to the oven for another hour and baste when necessary. Take out and slice. To the drippings add 1 T. of tomato paste, soya and Worcestershire sauce, and pour over the roast. Serve, garnished with rice.

## Fillets of Lamb à la Provençale

| | |
|---|---|
| 5 thick lamb chops | $\frac{1}{4}$ lb. ham |
| Bacon | 1 c. strong bouillon |
| 1 jigger of Marsala wine | Flour |
| Fresh or frozen peas | Salt and pepper |

Cut slits in chops to make pockets for stuffing. Salt and pepper. Insert small pieces of bacon and ham in each chop. Roll in flour. Brown on a hot fire. Then, pour over the wine and the bouillon and simmer for 30 minutes. Separately prepare the peas. Serve with the peas in the middle, forming a pyramid with the chops around. Pour over its own juice.

## Fricassee of Lamb

| | |
|---|---|
| 3-4 lb. lamb shoulder, cut into 2-inch squares | 1 T. Flour |
| 1 onion, chopped | 1 large cauliflower |
| 3 mushrooms, chopped | Grated rind of 1 lemon |
| 2 T. butter | Juice of 1 lemon |
| 1½ c. bouillon broth | 1 t. Worcestershire sauce |
| Salt | Parsley, chopped |
| 3 anchovies, chopped | Butter |
| | Garlic, squeezed |

Rub lamb with salt and squeezed garlic. Brown in butter. Then add onion, a handful of chopped parsley, chopped mushrooms, chopped anchovies, grated lemon rind, juice of 1 lemon. Add broth and cover, stewing until tender. Separately cook the cauliflower. When tender

blend 1 T. of butter with 1 T. of flour and add with the cut cauliflower to the lamb. Bring to the boiling point. Serve, pouring over
the liquid. Add the Worcestershire sauce if you like a strong flavour.

### Breast of Lamb Stewed in Wine

*White Sauce:*

| | |
|---|---|
| 4 lb. breast of lamb | 1 T. butter |
| 2 carrots, cut | 1 T. flour |
| 1 onion, chopped | 1 c. stock |
| ¼ c. white wine | 3 egg yolks |

Stew the lamb with vegetables until half-cooked. Then add wine
and continue cooking. When tender remove from the flame and
slice. Prepare white sauce blending butter and flour with broth and
egg yolks. Add to lamb and serve.

### Lamb Roast, Hunting Style

| | |
|---|---|
| 5-6 lb. lamb | Flour |
| Garlic | Salt and pepper |
| 4 T. sour cream | Vinegar |
| 1 small slice salt pork | |

Pour boiling vinegar over the lamb. Rub with garlic, olive oil and
let stand for 2 days. Remove from marinade. Make incisions and fill
with small pieces of salt pork or sliced bacon. Salt and place in a
very hot oven for 30 minutes. Reduce heat and cook through. When
tender sprinkle with flour and sour cream. You might serve it with
a sharp Poivrade sauce (see p. 103).

### Lamb Pot Roast with Shallots

| | |
|---|---|
| 4-5 lb. lamb shoulder | 2 c. bouillon broth |
| 2 lb. shallots | 1 T. tomato paste |
| ¼ c. white wine | 2 T. butter |
| 1 T. Worcestershire sauce | Flour |
| 3 large onions | |

Salt meat and brown lightly in a frying pan. Then, stew with sliced
onions in broth for 2 hours. Add white wine, tomato paste and Worcestershire sauce and stew until tender. Separately, stew the shallots
in broth until soft. Drain and brown in butter. Melt 1 T. of butter
and blend in 1 T. of flour and add to the sauce of the meat. Serve
lamb garnished with shallots and strained sauce.

### Lamb Roast with Tomatoes

| | |
|---|---|
| 5 lb. lamb shoulder | 1 c. red wine |
| 3 carrots | Sugar |
| 3 onions | Flour |
| 1 t. Worcestershire sauce | Vinegar |
| Butter | Salt and pepper |
| 2 T. tomato paste | 1 c. bouillon broth |
| 2 stalks celery | |

Scald meat with vinegar. Brown lightly on all sides. Then, stew with cut vegetables in broth, under cover, adding cold water if necessary. After 2 hours add tomato paste, wine, Worcestershire sauce and stew until tender. If the sauce is too sour, add sugar to taste. Before serving, melt 1 T. of butter and 1 T. of flour and add to the sauce. Serve with noodles.

### Lamb Chops with Rice and Tomatoes

| | |
|---|---|
| Lamb chops | 1 T. butter |
| Salt | ½ t. paprika |
| 2 T. grated Parmesan cheese | 1 small can tomato paste |
| 2 c. rice | 2 c. bouillon broth |
| 1 onion, chopped | |

Salt the lamb chops and fry or boil them until cooked through. Brown the chopped onion in butter and when lightly browned, add the rice. Add enough broth to cover the rice. Add paprika, salt and cook for 30 minutes. Then, add the tomato paste. Place the rice in the middle of an oven-proof platter with the lamb chops around. Sprinkle with Parmesan cheese and pour over 1 c. of bouillon broth. Place in the oven for a few minutes. Lamb chops are delicious with any of the good sauces such as Bordelaise, Poivrade, à la Diable or tomato sauce. (See Hot Sauces p. 103).

### Lamb Chops with Parmesan Cheese

| | |
|---|---|
| 5 lamb chops | Salt and pepper |
| 1 egg | 3 T. bread-crumbs |
| Butter | 5 T. grated Parmesan cheese |

Salt and pepper the lamb chops. Sprinkle with melted butter and roll in Parmesan cheese, then in egg, and finally in bread-crumbs. Fry until cooked through. Serve.

### Lamb Chops

| | |
|---|---|
| Lamb chops | Salt |
| Olive oil or butter | |

Pound the chops lightly. Salt and rub with oil or butter. Broil to the desired degree. Serve with soufflé of spinach or with fried potatoes.

## Lamb Chops à la Jardiniere

5 lamb chops
2 c. peas
2 c. green beans, chopped
Salt and pepper

3 chopped tomatoes
1 c. strong bouillon
1 jigger Madeira wine
Butter

Stew the vegetables in butter for a few minutes. Then, brown the chops and place on top of the vegetables. Pour over Madeira wine and bouillon broth and simmer for 15-20 minutes.

## Lamb Chops in Blankets

5 lamb chops
5 chopped mushrooms
2 T. bread-crumbs
¼ c. bouillon broth
1 onion

Parsley, chopped
Butter
Salt and pepper
5 slices bacon

Pound the lamb chops lightly. Salt and pepper. Separately, fry the chopped mushrooms with 1 chopped onion, adding bread-crumbs, a handful of chopped parsley, and salt and pepper. Roll the chops in this mixture and cover them with slices of bacon. Then, wrap them in buttered paper or metál foil. Place in oven for 45 minutes.

## Lamb with Rice (Szaszlyk)

4 lb. shoulder of lamb, cubed
2 c. rice
¼ t. paprika
1 lb. bacon

Butter
2 T. tomato paste
Salt and pepper
4 c. water

Cut the lamb in 2 inch squares. Cut the bacon into pieces. Place the lamb and the bacon alternatingly on skewers. Salt and pepper. Place in the broiler and turn constantly, broiling quickly. Cook the rice separately, scalding it with water before cooking. Then cook it in a fat broth, adding 2 T. of tomato paste and paprika. Also add the butter. Serve with the lamb on top.

## Lamb with Rice II

5 lb. lamb shoulder,
    cut in squares
½ lb. bacon, cut
1 t. basil
3 sections garlic
Salt and pepper

4 onions, cubed
1 lb. Polish sausage, cut up
¼ c. olive oil
1 t. rosemary
5 tomatoes, cut in wedges

Marinate the lamb in oil with all the herbs and the onions. Let it stand for at least 24 hours. Put on long skewers, alternating pieces of Polish sausage, lamb, tomatoes, onions, bacon. Broil in an open fire or in your oven broiler if the weather does not permit a camp fire.

## Lamb with Cabbage

| | |
|---|---|
| 2 small heads of cabbage | 3 c. bouillon broth |
| 3 lb. lamb breast | 1 T. flour |
| 1 t. rosemary | 1 bay leaf |
| 1 t. basil | 1 onion |
| 1 T. butter | Salt and pepper |

Cook the heads of cabbage in salted water until almost tender. Cook the lamb with herbs and the onion until the lamb is half cooked. Cut the cabbage, add to the lamb, and the broth and stew under cover until the meat is tender. Melt butter with flour and stir into the meat broth.

## Stewed Lamb with Peas

| | |
|---|---|
| 3 lb. lamb breast | 2 heads dill, chopped |
| 1 onion | 1 T. flour |
| 1 t. sugar | 1 c. water |
| 2 T. butter | 3 T. vinegar |
| 2 carrots | Parsley |
| 3 stalks celery | 1 lb. peas, frozen or fresh |

Cook the peas separately with 1 t. of sugar and 1 T. of butter. Cook the meat with the other vegetables and herbs, vinegar and a c. of water. When the meat is tender, cut in chunks. Add to the broth a sauce of 1 T. of butter and 1 T. of flour. Add some chopped dill. Stew for a few minutes in this mixture. Serve.

## Stewed Lamb with Caraway Seeds

| | |
|---|---|
| 4 lb. lamb breast or shoulder | 2 c. sour cream |
| 3 stalks celery | Salt and pepper |
| 1 onion | 2 carrots |
| Garlic | 1 T. flour |
| 1 t. caraway seeds | |

Rub the meat with salt and garlic. Cook it with the vegetables in enough water to cover the meat. When tender remove and slice the meat. Add sour cream mixed with flour and caraway seeds to the broth. Then add the meat and stew for another few minutes. Serve with rice or macaroni.

## Stewed Lamb with Pickles

| | |
|---|---|
| Lamb shoulder, boned and rolled | 3 carrots |
| Onions | 3 diced pickles |
| 1 T. flour | 1 flower of dill, chopped |
| Garlic | Salt and pepper |
| 2 c. sour cream | Sugar |

Cook the lamb rubbed in garlic and salt with the vegetables in enough water to cover the meat. Peel the pickles and dice them. When the lamb is half cooked, take it out, and slice it. Put it and the vegetables back into the pot and cook until the meat is tender. Then, add the sour cream mixed with 1 T. of flour. Add sugar to taste and chopped dill. Stew a few minutes longer. Serve with rice and cranberry sauce.

## Stewed Lamb with Tomatoes

| | |
|---|---|
| Lamb shoulder, boned and rolled | 1 T. flour |
| 4 tomatoes, stewed | 1 t. Worcestershire sauce |
| ½ c. red wine | Salt and pepper |
| 2 lb. shallots | 1 t. rosemary |
| 1 bay leaf | Garlic |
| Sugar | |

Stew the lamb until half cooked. Then, slice and replace in the pot adding the shallots, garlic, strained tomatoes, herbs, red wine, salt and pepper. Stew until tender. Then add flour to the juice, sugar to taste, Worcestershire sauce and strain. Pour over the meat and serve.

## Lamb with Potatoes

| | |
|---|---|
| Lamb shoulder or lamb | 6-8 potatoes |
| left-overs | 1 T. flour |
| Garlic | 2 T. vinegar |
| 1 T. butter | 1 t. Worcestershire sauce |

Rub the lamb with garlic and stew until tender. Slice in thin pieces. Separately cook the potatoes, peeled and sliced, until half-tender. To the meat juice add sauce of 1 T. of butter and 1 T. of flour, also 2 T. of vinegar. Then stew the potatoes and the meat together in it until the potatoes are tender. Add ½ t. Worcestershire sauce to the juice and serve.

## French Lamb Stew

| | |
|---|---|
| Lamb shoulder, cubed | ½ lb. peas, fresh or frozen |
| Garlic | 1 T. tomato paste |
| 1 lb. shallots | 4 potatoes |
| Paprika | ½ lb. spring beans |
| 2 T. butter | 1 T. flour |
| ¼ c. red wine | 1 t. Worcestershire sauce |
| 1 onion, chopped | Salt and pepper |
| 1 c. bouillon broth | |

Cut off the excess fat of the lamb. Rub the meat with salt and garlic. Brown in hot melted butter. When browned, add 1 chopped onion. When the onion gets browned, baste the meat with cold water or some broth. Stew for another hour. Cook potatoes until half-tender. Separately, cut the vegetables and add them to the meat with paprika, bouillon broth and tomato paste. Stew until the vegetables are tender. Add the half-cooked potatoes, sliced. Add the sauce of 1 T. of butter and 1 T. of flour to the meat juice also the red wine and Worcestershire sauce. Stew another 10 minutes.

### Turkish Lamb Stew

| | |
|---|---|
| Lamb shoulder, cut up | 3 large onions, chopped |
| Butter or margarine | 1 T. butter |
| 2 T. tomato paste | Paprika |
| 1 c. bouillon broth | Salt and pepper |
| 2 c. rice | |

Boil the rice for 10 minutes, and strain. Brown the meat slightly. Place it together with slightly browned onions and rice in a baking dish. Add tomato paste, bouillon and 1 T. of butter. Sprinkle with paprika. Cover and bake for 2 hours in a slow oven, making sure the liquid does not evaporate and adding more water if necessary.

### Loin of Pork—Viennese Style

| | |
|---|---|
| 4 lb. pork loin | Butter |
| Hot vinegar | Flour |
| 1 onion, chopped | Salt and pepper |
| Caraway seeds | |

Scald the meat with boiling vinegar and leave standing for 2 hours. Drain. Salt and pepper and sprinkle with caraway seeds. Place in a moderate oven and baste often. When it begins to get rosy sprinkle with chopped onion. The roast should be in the oven for 3 hours. Serve with cabbage and potatoes.

### Roast Loin of Pork

| | |
|---|---|
| 5 lb. pork loin | 5 T. butter or margarine |
| 2 T. flour | Rosemary, optional |
| Garlic, cut, optional | 4 c. milk |
| Salt and pepper | |

Coat the roast with salt, flour and rosemary. Brown in a frying pan with butter. When nicely rosy, place it in a pot and add one quart of milk and season. Baste occasionally. Serve with potatoes and apple sauce.

### Ham Baked in Dough

| | |
|---|---|
| 5 lb. ham | 2 T. butter |
| 4 c. milk | 4 eggs |
| 1 t. salt | 6 c. whole wheat flour |
| 3 t. baking powder | |

Wash and clean the ham. Dry with a cloth. Prepare batter. Mix and sift dry ingredients. Add milk gradually and the beaten eggs. Mix until smooth and add butter. Dip the whole ham in the batter and bake in a hot oven for 3 hours. When the ham is tender take off the dough carefully, and slice the ham in thin slices. Serve with tartare sauce. (See p. 106).

### Cold Ham à la Imperial

| | |
|---|---|
| 1 medium sized boneless ham | ½ t. basil |
| ½ t. rosemary | 1 onion, chopped |
| Salt | 1 bouillon cube |
| 3 mushrooms, diced | ½ lb chicken's liver |
| 2 T. soft butter | 2 envelopes gelatine |
| 2 c. sweet, heavy cream, whipped | 1 t. Worcestershire sauce |
| ¼ c. of Madeira or red table wine | |

Cook the ham with herbs and onion and slice thinly. Pass the liver through a sieve. Cook with chopped mushrooms, butter, Worcester-

shire sauce and the red wine. Fold in the beaten cream. Coat each piece of ham with this mixture and reconstruct the ham shape. Then, dissolve the gelatine in the ham broth and pour over the ham, covering it completely. Chill and garnish with greens, and serve mayonnaise separately.

## Cold Cooked Ham

| | |
|---|---|
| 4 lb. boneless ham | Salt and pepper |
| 1 onion, cut | 1 T. sugar |
| 1 t. rosemary | 1 t. basil |
| 5 cloves | 2 envelopes gelatine |

Soak the ham in water overnight. Then cook in boiling water with herbs, sugar and onion until tender. Slice thinly and cover with gelatine dissolved in the ham broth. Serve oil and vinegar, tartare sauce (see p. 106), or mustard pickle separately.

## Pork Cutlets

| | |
|---|---|
| 2-3 lb. pork cutlets | Bread-crumbs |
| 1 egg | Salt and pepper |
| Fat | Flour |

Pound and salt cutlets. Roll first in flour then egg and finally in bread-crumbs. Fry slowly in hot fat until cooked through. Serve with cabbage, fried potatoes and a strong sauce.

## Pork Chops

| | |
|---|---|
| Pork chops | Lemon juice |
| Salt and pepper | |
| Flour | |

Pound the chops lightly. Sprinkle with lemon juice and leave standing for 1 hour. Salt and sprinkle lightly with flour. Fry in a generous quantity of fat. Serve each chop with a pat of anchovy butter (see p. 102).

## Stewed Pork Chops

| | |
|---|---|
| Pork chops | Flour |
| Salt | ½ c. white wine |
| ½ cup stock or bouillon broth | Lemon juice |
| Caraway seeds | |

Pound the chops lightly and sprinkle with lemon juice. Leave standing for an hour. Salt and sprinkle with caraway seeds. Place in a pan and add broth and stew under cover. When tender, sprinkle the chops with flour, and sauté in fat. Add the wine. Cover and stew for a few minutes. Serve in sauce.

## Pork Chops with Rice

| | |
|---|---|
| 2 lb. pork | Rice |
| 1 onion, chopped | Stock |
| 1 egg | Salt and pepper |
| 2 T. tomato paste | Paprika |
| Bread-crumbs | 1 bun soaked in milk |

Cook the rice in stock, adding the tomato paste, a dash of paprika and cook until tender. Mince the meat with 1 squeezed bun. Add fried onion, salt and pepper, egg and mix well. Make oblong cutlets and roll in bread-crumbs. Fry in hot fat. Serve with rice.

## Royal Bitki

| | |
|---|---|
| 2 lb. lean pork | Butter |
| 2 buns, soaked in milk | ½ onion, grated |
| 1 egg | Salt and pepper |
| Flour | 2 c. sour cream |
| 1 T. capers | 3 T. grated Parmesan cheese |

Pass the meat through a mincer twice with 2 squeezed-out buns. Add ½ grated, browned onion, 1 egg, salt and pepper. Mix well. Make round balls. Roll in flour. Place the meat balls in the centre of an oven-proof platter and surround them with mashed potatoes. Pour over sour cream mixed with 1 T. of flour, add 1 T. of capers. Sprinkle with grated Parmesan cheese. Bake in a medium oven (350°) for 1 hour.

## Meat Balls with Anchovies

| | |
|---|---|
| 4 fillets of anchovy | Flour |
| 1 onion | Salt and pepper |
| 2 lb. lean pork or veal | 2 buns soaked in milk |
| Butter | 1 egg |
| 2 c. bouillon stock | 2 c. sour cream |
| 1 T. Capers | Grated orange peel |

Pass the meat through a mincer with the squeezed buns and onion. Add salt and pepper and 1 egg. Mix well and form balls. Roll the balls in flour and brown in butter. Add bouillon and sour cream mixed with 1 T. of flour. Add capers and some grated orange peel. Stew on a slow flame for 30 minutes.

## Sauerkraut with Spare Ribs

| | |
|---|---|
| 3 lb. pork spare ribs | 2 onions, sliced |
| 2 lb. sauerkraut | Water |
| ¼ t. Caraway seed (opt.) | |

Cut the spare ribs into sizes for serving. Brown onions lightly. Add the spare ribs. Let them simmer together for 30 minutes. Add the sauerkraut. Cover with water and let cook slowly until the meat is tender, possibly 1 hour. The caraway seed is optional and tends to temper the flavour of the sauerkraut. It is added with the sauerkraut if used. Serve with mashed potatoes.

## Spare Ribs Stewed with Cabbage

4-5 lb. pork spare ribs | 1 carrot, chopped
1 onion, chopped | 1 T. butter
1 stalk celery, cut | Broth
Parsley, chopped | 1 T. flour
Salt and pepper | 2 small heads cabbage

Place the spare ribs in a pot with enough water to cover the meat. Simmer for 2 hours. Shred the cabbages and add to the meat, adding also onion, carrot, celery and parsley. Then stir 1 T. of butter with the flour. Dilute with broth and pour over the meat. Salt and pepper to taste. Stew for another 45 minutes. Serve with the cabbage in the middle and the meat around.

## Spare Ribs Stewed with Kohlrabi

4-5 lb. pork spare ribs | 1 T. butter
1 T. flour | Diced kholrabi
Salt and pepper | Meat stock
Sugar

Cover the meat with cold water and cook together with the diced kohlrabi. Prepare a sauce, melting the butter with the flour, salt and sugar to taste. Add meat stock slowly. Cut the meat into serving pieces and serve with the sauce.

## Pig's Feet Stuffed with Truffles

Pig's feet | Few slices bacon
1 t. basil | 4 chopped truffles
1 t. rosemary | 1 egg
½ t. thyme | Salt and pepper
1 onion | 1 piece of ham
Butter | 1 bun soaked in milk
Bread-crumbs

Scald and clean the pig's feet. Cook with herbs and onion. When tender take out the bones. Prepare the stuffing: mince the ham with 1 squeezed-out bun and a few slices of bacon. Add the chopped truffles, salt and pepper and 1 egg, and mix. Stuff the pig's feet with this filling. Then, sprinkle with melted butter and bread-crumbs. Brown in butter. Serve with sauce à la Diable (see p. 103) and potatoes or potato crôquettes.

## Pork Kidneys with Buckwheat Groats

2-3 lb. pork kidneys | 1 T. flour
1 T. butter | Salt
Broth | ¼ c. red wine
1 large chopped onion | 1 c. buckwheat groats

Soak kidneys in water. Slice in thin slices. Place in a pot and cover with water. Cook, taking off the scum from the surface. When half-done, drain, add onion and butter and stew under cover until tender. Separately cook the buckwheat groats (see p. 26) and add to the kidneys. At the end add some red wine and simmer for another 5 minutes.

## Kolduny

| | |
|---|---|
| ¼ lb. raw lamb | 1 t. dried basil |
| ¼ lb. raw veal | Bread-crumbs |
| ¼ lb. raw beef | Salt and pepper |
| 3 onions, grated | Meat stock |
| 3 T. butter | Suet |
| 1 t. marjoram | Dough |

Cut the meat evenly into small pieces. Chop the suet and cook lightly with the grated onion. Add the meat. Simmer for a few minutes with all the ingredients. Prepare on the side the dough as for ushka (see p. 27). Cut little circles with a small glass. Fill very sparingly as the meat needs room to stretch when cooking. Bring the edges closely and tightly together. Cook the kolduny in boiling meat stock for 10 to 15 minutes. Serve with broth.

## Tripe

| | |
|---|---|
| 4 lb. cooked fresh tripe | 1 onion, chopped |
| Salt and pepper | 1 soup bone |
| 1 bouillon cube | 1 T. flour |
| 3 stalks celery, cut | 2 T. butter |
| Parsley, chopped | Dash of nutmeg |
| 2 carrots, sliced | Paprika |
| ½ t. marjoram | |

Cut the cooked tripe (you can buy it cooked at your food store) in strips 2 by ½ inch. On the side cook the soup bone with all the chopped vegetables in water barely to cover. Combine the tripe with the soup and seasonings and cook for 1 hour or until tender. Remove the bone. Melt butter, blend in flour and dilute with soup broth. Then, add to tripe. Add seasonings and cook for a few more minutes. Serve.

## Tripe, French Style

| | |
|---|---|
| 4-5 lb. fresh, cooked tripe | Nutmeg |
| 2 large onions, chopped | Butter |
| 1 bouillon cube | Salt and pepper |
| 2 stalks celery, chopped | ½ t. marjoram |
| 2 T. tomato paste | 2 carrots, chopped |
| Parsley | Flour |
| 1 soup bone | 1 T. Worcestershire sauce |
| 2 c. bouillon broth | ¼ c. white wine |

Cut the tripe in strips 2 inches by ½ inch. Place the tripe with the chopped vegetables in a pot. Add butter, seasoning, broth, wine, tomato paste, Worcestershire sauce and bouillon cube. Stew for 45 minutes under cover. Before taking off the fire, sprinkle with flour and bring to a boil and serve.

### Brain Cutlets

| | |
|---|---|
| 1¼ lb. brain | Salt and pepper |
| Juice of 2 lemons | 1 large onion, chopped |
| ¼ t. thyme | Flour |
| 1 egg, beaten | Bread-crumbs |
| Butter | |

Clean the brain and cook in salted water with lemon juice, onion and thyme. Cool and chop the brain. Then, make oblong cutlets, sprinkle with flour. Roll in egg and bread-crumbs. Fry in melted butter until golden brown. Serve with a strong, sharp sauce.

### Pasztet

| | |
|---|---|
| 2 lb. calf's liver | 2 stalks celery, cut |
| ½ lb. veal | 3 onions, chopped |
| ½ lb. pork | 3 carrots, cut |
| ½ lb. duck or turkey | 3 sections garlic |
| 10 dried mushrooms | Butter |
| 5 eggs, beaten | Milk |
| ½ t. marjoram | ¼ lb. bacon |
| 1 bay leaf | Salt and pepper |
| Parsley | 3 slices dry bread |
| ¼ c. white wine | |

Soak liver in milk overnight. Simmer all the meat, except the liver, together with the herbs and seasoning in a small amount of water for about 60 minutes. Add liver and continue cooking for another 30 minutes. Drain and mince all together. Add eggs, wine and bread which has been previously soaked in milk. Salt and pepper well. Fry the bacon. Butter a mould (square if possible). Sprinkle it with bread-crumbs and arrange the bacon strips in a pattern. Pour in the mixture and bake for 45 minutes in a slow oven. Serve warm with a sauce such as tartare sauce (see p. 106) or cold as an appetizer or entrée.

### Stewed Liver Pudding

| | |
|---|---|
| 1 lb. calf's or beef liver, soaked in milk | 1 large onion, chopped |
| | 2 slices bacon |
| Salt and pepper | 6 eggs, separated |
| 2 T. butter | Bread-crumbs |
| 1 bun soaked in milk | Peel of 1 lemon |

Soak the liver in milk for 2 hours. Insert small pieces of bacon all over the liver. Salt and pepper. Sauté with chopped onion until tender. When it cools, grate and pass through a sieve, together with a squeezed-out bun. Mix 2 T. of butter with 5 egg yolks adding the strained liver. Season. Add grated lemon peel. Beat the egg whites and combine with the mixture. Place in a dish coated with butter and bread-crumbs. Cook over hot water bath for 1½ hours; serve with a strong sauce.

## Liver Stewed in Sour Cream

| | |
|---|---|
| 1½ lb. calf's or beef liver, soaked in milk | 1 T. flour |
| | 1 c. bouillon broth |
| 1 onion, chopped | Salt and pepper |
| 2 c. sour cream | 3 slices bacon |

Soak the liver for 2 hours. Then, dry with a clean cloth. Salt and pepper. Make slits in the liver. Chop the bacon and insert into the liver. Brown lightly, adding chopped onion. When the liver is browned, add some broth and stew under cover for 10 minutes. Then add the sour cream mixed with 1 T. of flour and bring to a boil. Slice the liver and garnish with potatoes. The liver should not cook more than 15 minutes because it hardens.

## Fried Liver

| | |
|---|---|
| 1½ lb. calf's liver | Butter |
| Flour | Milk |
| Salt and pepper | |

Soak the liver in milk for 2 hours. Drain and wipe with a clean cloth. Salt and pepper. Slice and sprinkle with flour. Fry in hot melted butter.

## Liver à la Nelson

| | |
|---|---|
| 1½ lb. calf's liver | 5-7 potatoes |
| Milk | ½ c. bouillon broth |
| ½ c. mushrooms, sliced | Butter |
| ½ c. sweet red wine | Salt and pepper |
| 1 onion, sliced | |

Soak the liver for 2 hours in milk. Peel and cook the potatoes. When tender, slice them. Stew the mushrooms in butter with onion. Slice the liver in strips 1 inch thick. Salt and pepper and roll in flour. Brown lightly on all sides. Then, combine with potatoes. Sprinkle with onion and mushrooms. Dilute with bouillon broth, adding wine, bring to a boil. Stew for a few minutes. Do not overcook the liver.

## Bigos

| | |
|---|---|
| Left-over meat | 1 lb. Polish sausage, diced |
| 2 lb. sauerkraut, diced | 4 dried mushrooms |
| ¼ lb. salt pork, diced | 1 T. sugar |
| Fat | 1 bouillon cube |
| Salt and pepper | 2 apples, peeled and diced |
| 2 T. mustard | 3 fresh tomatoes, diced |

Cook the sauerkraut and dried mushrooms. Add diced apples and tomatoes. Brown the salt pork with the onion. Combine with the

sauerkraut. Chop all the left-over meat. Add Polish sausage to the sauerkraut. Season well. Add sugar and mustard. Also the bouillon cube. Cook for 1 hour. Serve with potatoes. The longer it cooks the better it tastes. It is also delicious warmed-up the next day.

## Polish Sausage Stewed in Red Cabbage

| | |
|---|---|
| 1 head red cabbage | Juice of 2 lemons |
| 1 T. butter | 1 T. flour |
| ½ c. red wine | Salt and pepper |
| ½ t. Worcestershire sauce | Sugar to taste |
| ½ lb. Polish sausages, diced | |

Slice the cabbage thinly and scald with hot water, then sprinkle with a little lemon juice. Melt 1 T. of butter with the flour and dilute with wine. Combine with cabbage, salt and pepper, ½ t. of Worcestershire sauce, sugar to taste and remaining lemon juice. Cook on a slow flame. Fifteen minutes before taking off the fire, add Polish sausage and stew under cover for a few minutes. Serve with the sausage on top.

### Kishka

| | |
|---|---|
| 2 lb. pork | ¼ t. marjoram |
| Pork liver | 2 onions, chopped |
| 2 lb. buckwheat groats | 2 eggs, beaten |
| Salt and pepper | Butter |
| ¼ c. of bouillon broth | Nutmeg |

Cook the buckwheat groats. Chop the liver and the pork. Cook until tender, in water to cover, adding salt and pepper. Sauté the chopped onion in butter. Combine the onions with the meat and add the eggs, nutmeg and marjoram, and the bouillon broth. Mix with the buckwheat groats. Press into a mould and chill thoroughly. Warm before serving.

### Fried Chicken

| | |
|---|---|
| 2 broilers in pieces | 4 T. butter |
| 1 egg, beaten | 2 T. water |
| ¼ c. sweet cream | 5 T. bread-crumbs |
| ½ c. flour | Salt and pepper |

Season the cut up chicken. Roll in flour and then in egg diluted with 2 T. of water, and finally in bread-crumbs. Brown the chickens in butter. Place in the oven, add the sweet cream and bake, covered for 30 minutes, in a moderate oven.

### Chicken Polish Style

| | |
|---|---|
| 1 young chicken, quartered | Salt |
| 4 c. water | 2 carrots, sliced |
| 2 stalks celery, cut | Parsley, chopped |
| 3 dried mushrooms | 1 T. butter |
| ½ c. white wine | 2 egg yolks |

Cook the quartered chicken in salted water. Bring to a boil, adding all the vegetables and chopped mushrooms. Stew until tender for about 1 hour or less. Melt 1 T. of butter and blend in 1 T. of flour, adding to it the remaining chicken stock and cook until it thickens. Then, gradually pour in egg yolks and wine and add chicken. Simmer for a few minutes but do not boil. Serve with boiled or mashed potatoes.

### Chicken with Gooseberry Sauce

| | |
|---|---|
| 1 broiler, quartered | 1 T. sugar |
| 1 T. butter | 1 c. chicken broth |
| 1 T. flour | 1 c. not-too-ripe gooseberries |

Cook the chicken in the manner for chicken, Polish style. (See above).

Melt the butter separately and blend in flour, adding to it chicken broth and cook until it thickens. Add gooseberries and sugar. Bring to the boil. Add the chicken, and heat. Serve with sweet potatoes in butter sauce.

### Stewed Stuffed Chicken

| | |
|---|---|
| 1 young chicken | 2 t. fresh dill, chopped |
| 4 T. butter | 1 chicken liver, chopped |
| Salt and pepper | 1½ c. bread-crumbs |
| 1 onion, chopped | |

Rub the inside and outside of the chicken with salt. Prepare stuffing: Fry chopped liver in butter with chopped dill and onion. Add bread-crumbs. Stuff the chicken and cover with melted butter and bake under cover in a moderate oven until tender.

### Roast Stuffed Chicken

| | |
|---|---|
| 1 young chicken | 1 T. parsley, chopped |
| 6 T. bread-crumbs | Salt and pepper |
| ¼ c. milk | Garlic, pressed |
| 4 T. butter | 2 eggs, beaten |
| Chicken liver, chopped | |

Rub the chicken with salt and garlic inside and out. Combine chicken-liver with eggs and bread-crumbs, milk, parsley, salt and pepper. Stuff the chicken and rub it with butter. Bake in the oven (350°) for 1 hour.

### King's Chicken

| | |
|---|---|
| 1 spring chicken | ¼ c. butter |
| 2 medium onions, chopped | 2 c. sour cream |
| 1 t. paprika | Salt and pepper |
| 1 c. hot water | |

Sauté the chopped onions in butter until they are rosy. Cut up the chicken. Add to the onions and brown. Add salt and pepper. Add water and stew under cover until tender. When almost done, add sour cream and paprika. Simmer for a few minutes more. Serve with potato croquettes.

### Chicken in Dill Sauce

| | |
|---|---|
| 1 broiler, quartered, or frying chicken in pieces | 1½ c. sweet cream |
| | 1 T. butter |
| Parsley, chopped | 2 c. water |
| 1 T. flour | Salt and pepper |
| 2 t. fresh dill, chopped | 1 t. lemon juice |

Stew the chicken in butter and water until tender. Salt and pepper to taste. When ready to serve, mix together the cream, flour, lemon juice, and dill. Stir into the chicken. Simmer for a few minutes. Serve with asparagus tips, with Hollandaise sauce (see p. 100) or rice.

## Stuffed Capon

| | |
|---|---|
| 1 capon | Salt |
| ¼ lb. veal | Capon's liver |
| 3 eggs, separated | |

*Stuffing:*

| | |
|---|---|
| 4 T. butter | ½ t. grated lemon rind |
| 10 anchovies | ½ c. salt pork |
| 1¼ c. bread-crumbs | |

Sprinkle the inside and outside of the capon with salt. Prepare the stuffing in the following manner: Cook the veal in pork fat until tender, adding the liver for a few moments. Chop or grind the veal, anchovies and liver fine. Combine with lemon rind, butter, egg yolks and bread-crumbs. Fold in the beaten egg white. Stuff the capon. Bake in a moderate oven for about 30 minutes per pound and baste frequently. Serve with baked potatoes.

## Young Chicken Stuffed with Pea Purée

| | |
|---|---|
| 2-3 young chickens | ¼ lb. veal, ham or salami |
| 4 T. sweet cream | 1 can purée of peas or 1 lb. of |
| Butter | fresh peas, cooked and sieved |
| Salt and pepper | |

Heat the pureé of peas. Pass the veal through a meat grinder and mix with the purée of peas. Add salt and pepper and mix 4 T. of sweet cream. Salt the chickens inside and out and stuff them with this mixture. Then, bake them in the oven basting generously with butter. When tender, cut them in half and pour over their own sauce.

## Chicken Fricassee

| | |
|---|---|
| 2-3 young chickens, cut up | 2 onions, cut |
| Salt | 2 carrots, cut |
| Parsley | 3-4 c. water |
| 3 mushrooms | 1 T. flour |
| Chicken giblets | 2 T. butter |
| 3 egg yolks | Juice of 2 lemons |

Sprinkle the chickens with lemon to blanch. Cook in enough water to cover. Put in the vegetables and giblets. When tender remove the chicken and cut the cooked chicken livers and giblet in thin strips. Strain the chicken broth adding sauce of 1 T. of butter and 1 T. of flour. Stew the chickens in this sauce for another few minutes. Serve the chicken with rice cooked separately. Add to the sauce 3 well-beaten egg yolks mixed with 1 heaped T. of butter. If you prefer to have the chicken more colourful, brown pieces in butter first, then cook as above.

### Chicken à la Wilson

| | |
|---|---|
| 2-3 young chickens, cut up | 3 T. bread-crumbs |
| Salt | Butter |
| 1 c. sweet cream | 1 T. flour |
| 2 eggs | 2 egg yolks |
| 4 T. grated cheese, Parmesan | |

Salt the chickens and stew in butter. When they are half-cooked, sprinkle with half of the Parmesan cheese and place in a dish. Mix the sweet cream with 1 T. of flour and bring to the boil. Add a dash of salt. When it has cooled a little, beat in 2 eggs and 2 egg yolks. Mix well and pour over the chickens. Then sprinkle the chickens with 2 T. of Parmesan cheese, bread-crumbs and melted butter. Bake in a moderate oven for 20 minutes or until the browned skin becomes slightly cracked.

### Chicken Spanish Style

| | |
|---|---|
| 2-3 young chickens | 2 T. tomato paste |
| 1 lb. shallots, cut | 1 T. butter |
| Paprika | ½ c. bouillon broth |
| 1 T. flour | 1 t. soya sauce |
| ½ c. white wine | Butter |

Salt and quarter the chickens. Stew in butter under cover. Add the shallots, tomato paste, a dash of paprika and finally the wine. When the chickens are tender, prepare sauce of butter and flour, dilute with bouillon broth and some of the sauce of the chicken. Add soya sauce. Serve with potato croquettes.

### Curried Chicken

| | |
|---|---|
| 2-3 young chickens | 1 t. curry powder |
| 1 t. dry mustard | Salt |
| 2 onions, grated | 1 T. olive oil |
| 1 c. strong broth or 2 bouillon | 2 c. uncooked rice |
| cubes | 2 T. tomato paste |
| 1 T. butter | 4 T. grated cheese, Parmesan |
| Butter | |

Salt and quarter the chickens and brown them in butter. Separately, mix grated onions with dry mustard, salt, olive oil and curry. When the chickens are browned, add to them this mixture and dilute with 1 c. of bouillon. Stew under cover until tender. Separately cook the rice until almost tender. Stir in tomato paste and 1 T. of butter. Add to chicken mixture. Put in a baking dish. Shake Parmesan on the top and cook for 5 minutes in the oven.

## Chicken with Anchovies

| | |
|---|---|
| 2-3 young chickens | Salt and pepper |
| 2 cans fillets of anchovy | Juice of 1 lemon |
| 1 T. anchovy butter | 1 T. flour |
| (see page 102) | 1 c. chicken broth |
| 4 T. sour cream | |

Salt the chickens and insert anchovies in slits in the skins of the chickens, as in larding meat. Stew in anchovy butter, under cover, basting with broth, until tender. Sprinkle with flour, and sour cream and lemon juice. Stew a few minutes longer. Serve in sauce with rice.

## Hungarian Chicken

| | |
|---|---|
| 2-3 young chickens, quartered | 2 T. tomato paste |
| Paprika | Salt and pepper |
| 1 c. broth | 2 T. butter |
| 2 chopped onions | 1 T. flour |

Sprinkle the quartered chickens with paprika and place in a pan with 1 T. of butter, 2 chopped onions and tomato paste. Stew under cover, basting with broth until tender. Then prepare the sauce with 1 T. of butter and 1 T. of flour. Add some more broth and combine with the chicken sauce. The amount of butter and flour may be increased if a thicker sauce is desired. Serve with noodles or rice.

## Chicken Paprikash

| | |
|---|---|
| 2-3 young chickens | 1 onion, chopped |
| 2 T. butter | 1 T. flour |
| 1 c. sour cream | Salt and pepper |
| Paprika | 1 c. chicken broth or water |

Salt the quartered chickens and sprinkle with paprika. Brown lightly 1 chopped onion in butter and then add to it the chickens. Stew under cover until tender, basting occasionally with chicken bouillon or water. Ten minutes before serving, pour in 1 c. of sour cream mixed with 1 T. of flour and stew. Serve with fried potatoes or rice.

## Roast Chicken with Pea Soup Stuffing

| | |
|---|---|
| 1 roasting chicken | Parsley, chopped |
| Salt and pepper | ½ c. sweet or sour cream |
| 2-3 c. bread-crumbs | 1 t. poultry seasoning |
| 1 egg | 1 t. sage |
| Olive oil or salad oil | 1-2 c. pea soup |

Rinse chicken cavity with cold water and sprinkle with salt. Mix together pea soup, bread-crumbs (varying quantity with size of chicken or the state of your pantry), egg, cream, parsley, poultry seasoning, and sage. Stuff the chicken. Truss for roasting. Cover with olive oil, rubbing it on with your hands to coat every surface. Place in a large flat pan breast up, and fold metal foil over it. Roast

30 minutes per pound in a moderate (325-350°) oven. Pour on a little more oil if necessary. For the last 15 minutes, turn up oven slightly and remove foil to let the bird brown. Serve with gravy and vegetables in season. Mushrooms are particularly good when added to the chicken gravy.

### Baked Chicken with Sour Cream

| | |
|---|---|
| 1 chicken or capon, cut | 2 c. sour cream |
| 2 T. butter | Salt |
| 4 egg yolks | 1 T. flour |
| 1 c. strong bouillon broth | 1 onion |
| or 2 bouillon cubes | |

Brown the salted chicken in butter with onion. Prepare a cream out of 2 c. of sour cream combined with 4 beaten egg yolks, adding 1 T. of flour, a dash of salt, beating to a foam. Put on the fire until it thickens. Put the chicken in a baking dish. Pour the cup of bouillon over it and place in a moderate oven. When browned, begin basting with the sour cream. The pieces of chicken will absorb the cream sauce in a short time so continue basting at intervals throughout the baking time. When tender, serve with sour cream poured over the top.

### Chicken with Tomatoes

| | |
|---|---|
| 2 chickens, in pieces | ½ c. white wine |
| 2 c. chicken stock | 2 onions |
| 6 large tomatoes | ½ t. Worcestershire sauce |
| 1 T. flour | Salt |
| Olive oil | 2 carrots |

Salt the chicken parts and brown in olive oil. Add 2 c. of stock and ½ c. of white wine. Slice and add 2 onions, 2 carrots and 6 tomatoes. Stew under cover until the chicken is tender. Remove chicken. Strain broth and make a sauce by adding flour and Worcestershire sauce. Return chicken to the sauce and heat together. Serve with rice.

### Chicken with Parmesan

| | |
|---|---|
| 1 chicken in pieces | Salt and pepper |
| 2 c. sour cream | Butter |
| 1 T. flour | Broth or water |
| 2 egg yolks | 2 T. bread-crumbs |
| 4 T. Parmesan cheese | |

Brown the chicken in butter. Cover and baste with water or broth so that it does not burn. Simmer until tender. Place in a baking dish and pour over sour cream mixed with flour and egg yolk. Sprinkle with Parmesan cheese, and bread-crumbs browned in butter. Bake for 15 minutes and serve.

## Caesar's Chicken

| | |
|---|---|
| 1 chicken, in pieces | ½ t. Worcestershire sauce |
| 5 large chopped mushrooms | ¼ c. white wine |
| 2 large onions, chopped | Butter |
| 2 truffles, chopped | Salt and pepper |
| 1 T. flour | Parsley, chopped, or dill |

Brown the chicken in butter with onions. Add chopped mushrooms, truffles and wine. Stew until tender. Thicken the sauce with 1 T. of flour and ½ t. of Worcestershire sauce. Add dill, season. Serve with rice or egg noodles.

## Stewed Chicken with Ham

| | |
|---|---|
| 1 chicken, in parts | 3 mushrooms, chopped |
| 1 lb. piece of ham | Dill |
| 1 T. flour | 1 c. chicken bouillon |
| ½ t. Worcestershire sauce | Salt |
| ½ glass sherry | |

Salt the chicken parts and brown in butter, adding chopped ham, mushrooms, 1 grated onion, a handful of chopped dill. Stew under cover adding bouillon occasionally. When tender, add the sherry and make a gravy by adding a T. of flour blended with 1 T. of butter and ½ t. of Worcestershire sauce.

## Chicken Soufflé

| | |
|---|---|
| White meat of 2 chickens | 3 eggs, separated |
| (breasts) | 1 bun soaked in milk |
| 2 c. heavy cream | Salt |
| 3 mushrooms, chopped | Butter |

Pass the meat through a mincer twice, then pass through a sieve. Add 1 bun soaked in milk, not squeezed out. Place in refrigerator for 15 minutes, then beat it for 10 minutes. Add the egg yolks, the whipped cream, salt, chopped mushrooms and finally fold in stiffly beaten egg whites. Place in a buttered dish and cook over a water bath for 45 minutes.

## Chicken Risotto

| | |
|---|---|
| 1 chicken, in pieces | 1 onion |
| 2 stalks celery | 2 c. water |
| Parsley | 1 T. flour |
| 1 T. butter | 2 c. rice |
| 1 T. tomato paste | Salt and pepper |
| 4 T. grated Parmesan | 2 carrots |

Cook the chicken with vegetables under cover in salted water until tender. Then, take out the chicken, strain the broth, adding to it 1 T. of melted butter blended with 1 T. of tomato paste and add rice. There ought to be just enough broth to cover the rice. Place in a moderate oven for 25 minutes. Baste with broth when necessary.

Add grated Parmesan. Mix and place in a buttered pan, alternating rice and chicken. Pour over ½ c. of strong broth and place in the oven for 30 minutes.

### Chicken Cutlets (for each serving)

| | |
|---|---|
| 1 breast young chicken | Paprika |
| 2 T. butter | Fat |
| Salt and pepper | 1 egg |
| Bread-crumbs | |

Chill butter on ice. Add seasonings and make rolls about 2 inches long. Remove meat from bone and pound until thin. Place butter roll in the middle, and wrap securely fastening with a tooth-pick so that the butter does not leak out. Roll in breadcrumbs, dip in egg and roll in bread-crumbs again. Fry in deep fat until golden brown. Drain and place in the oven for a few minutes before serving.

### Chicken Cutlets with Truffles

| | |
|---|---|
| White meat of chicken | 2 T. Madeira wine |
| 2 truffles, chopped | Butter |
| ¼ lb. bacon | 1 T. sweet cream |
| Fat | 3 T. flour |
| 3 T. bread-crumbs | |

Prepare the chicken in the same way as the recipe for chicken cutlets. Then, insert small pieces of bacon in each piece of meat. In the middle, place a spoon of the following: chopped truffles mixed with Madeira and sweet cream. Roll and fasten securely. Cover with melted butter, and coat with flour mixed with bread-crumbs. Fry in hot fat. Place in the oven for 5 minutes. Serve with mashed potatoes.

### Ragout of Left-over Chicken

| | |
|---|---|
| Chicken left-overs | 3 T. peas, cooked |
| 3 mushrooms, chopped | 1 T. butter |
| 1 small cauliflower | 1 onion, chopped |
| 1 T. flour | 2 c. water |
| 2-3 egg yolks | |

Brown the onion lightly and simmer with the chopped left-over chicken. Separately brown the mushrooms in butter with the peas. Cook the cauliflower. Prepare the white sauce of 1 T. of butter with 1 T. of flour. Dilute with a cup of the vegetable stock. Add to it the mushrooms, meat, cauliflower in sections and all the other ingredients. Simmer another few minutes. Then add egg yolks to the sauce and serve with dumplings. (see p. 26-27).

## Vol au vent

| | |
|---|---|
| 1 chicken | ¼ c. sweet cream |
| 2 carrots | Butter |
| Parsley | 4 c. water |
| chicken giblet | Salt and pepper |
| Chicken liver | 2-3 egg yolks |
| 3 mushrooms, chopped | Juice of ¼ lemon |
| 2 T. cooked asparagus heads | 1 small can crab-meat |
| Flour | 2 stalks celery |
| 2 T. cooked peas | 1 onion, sliced |
| 24 Patty Shells | |

Cook the cleaned salted chicken in 4 c. of water, under cover, adding 1 onion, carrots, celery, a handful of chopped parsley. When the chicken is tender, take off the skin, remove the bones and chop the meat in small pieces. Cut the liver and giblet in thin strips. Cook the mushrooms and all the vegetables in broth. When everything is tender, drain. Melt 1 T. of butter and blend in 1 T. of flour. Stir in ½ c. of sweet cream, 3 egg yolks, crab meat, lemon juice. Combine with all the ingrediants, vegetables and meat. Place in a double boiler. Be careful that it does not boil. When thoroughly heated and blended, spoon into patty shells and place in a moderate oven for 15 minutes before serving.

## Chicken Salad 'Vinaigrettes'

| | |
|---|---|
| Left-overs of roast chicken, chopped | Salt and pepper |
| 4 sweet pickles, chopped | 3 marinated mushrooms |
| Parsley, chopped | Seasonings |
| | Chive, chopped |

Dice the chicken, pickles and mushrooms. Combine all the ingredients. Mix with the *Vinaigrette Sauce* which is made as follows.

| | |
|---|---|
| 4 egg yolks, hard-boiled or raw egg yolks | 4 T. olive oil |
| 1 t. salad-type mustard | 1 jigger red wine |
| 1 t. wine vinegar | Salt and pepper |
| 1 t. Worcestershire or soya sauce, optional | ¼ t. sugar |
| | Chopped chive or chopped scallions |

Pass the hard-boiled egg yolks through a sieve and mix with 4 T. of olive oil, or mix 4 egg yolks with olive oil, stirred in drop by drop. Add very gradually the mustard, wine, vinegar, salt and pepper, and sugar, stirring constantly. At the end, add a handful of chopped chive or a few chopped scallions and Worcestershire sauce.

## Chicken Livers with Rice

| | |
|---|---|
| 1 lb. chicken liver, soaked in milk | 1 chopped onion |
| 1 T. tomato paste | 2 c. stock |
| | 4 T. grated Parmesan |

Brown the liver in butter with onion. Salt. Scald the rice with hot water. Add 1 T. of butter and 1 T. of tomato paste and cook. Then, add the chicken liver, a c. of bouillon broth and place in a very hot oven for 20 minutes, under cover.      Serve with grated Parmesan cheese.

## Guinea-hen baked

| | |
|---|---|
| 2-3 guinea-hens | Bacon |
| Salt and pepper | Stuffing, similar to chicken |
| Butter | (see page 78) |
| Juice of 1 lemon | Olive oil |

Sprinkle the hens with lemon and rub with olive oil and leave standing in the refrigerator for 2 days. Salt and insert small pieces of bacon in the skin of the guinea hens. Stuff as for chicken (see p. 78). Bake in moderate oven for 1 hour.

## Baked Pigeons

For each serving

| | |
|---|---|
| 1 pigeon | Salt |
| Bacon | Butter |

Clean and soak the pigeons for about 2 hours in cold water. Salt and insert small pieces of bacon in the skin. Bake in the oven for 30 to 35 minutes basting often with a generous quantity of melted butter. Serve with blueberry compote or salad.

## Fricassee of Pigeons with Chestnuts

| | |
|---|---|
| 3-4 young pigeons | Salt |
| 1 lb. shallots | 1 jigger Madeira wine |
| Butter | 2 egg yolks |
| 1 T. flour | 3 T. bouillon broth |
| Juice of 1 lemon | ½ t. Worcestershire sauce |
| 1 lb. chestnuts, purée | 3 mushrooms, chopped |

Clean and salt the pigeons and brown in butter. Then, cut them in half. Add to the same butter, 1 T. of flour. Dilute with bouillon broth. Add the shallots and the chopped mushrooms, Worcestershire sauce, and juice of ½ lemon. Place the pigeons on top and stew under cover until they are tender. In the end add the wine. When ready to serve, beat 2 egg yolks into the sauce and pour over the pigeons. Serve with pureé of chestnuts (cooked, shelled and passed through a sieve).

## Turkey with Chestnut Stuffing I

| | |
|---|---|
| 1 turkey | Salt |
| Butter | 2 lb. fresh chestnuts |

Salt the cleaned turkey on the outside and the inside. The chestnuts should be boiled, shelled and sautéd in butter until tender. They should be stuffed whole into the turkey. Rub the whole turkey with butter or oil and bake under an oiled cloth *or* metal foil in a moderate oven (325°) until tender. Remove cloth or foil for a few minutes to brown. Serve with mashed potatoes.

## Sweet Chestnut Stuffing II

| | |
|---|---|
| 1¼ lb. chestnuts | 3 eggs, separated |
| 2 T. sweet butter | 3 T. bread-crumbs |
| 1 T. sugar | Salt |
| 4 T. heavy cream | |

Boil the chestnuts in salted water, shell and grate them. Beat the butter with egg yolks until fluffy. Add 3 T. bread-crumbs, 1 T. of sugar, chestnuts, 4 T. of heavy cream and mix well. Beat the egg whites well, and fold into mixture. Stuff the turkey and roast. It is delicious.

## Meat and Chestnut Stuffing III

| | |
|---|---|
| 1 lb. salt pork, or sausage-meat | Salt and pepper |
| 1 egg | ¼ lb. bacon |
| Nutmeg | 1 lb. cooked chestnuts |
| 2 onions, grated | 1 bun soaked in milk |

Pass the pork through a mincer with bacon, adding the squeezed out bun, nutmeg, a dash of salt and 2 grated and sautéd onions. Grate the cooked chestnuts, combine with the meat, stuff the turkey and roast as above.

## Rice Stuffing

| | |
|---|---|
| 2 c. rice | Parsley, chopped |
| 2 T. butter | 1 onion, chopped |
| 1 turkey liver | Salt and pepper |
| ¼ lb. ham | 2 eggs |
| ¼ c. sour cream | |

Boil the rice once. Then add butter and stew until tender. Slice the ham in thin strips. Chop the turkey liver. Add both to the rice when it has cooled. Combine rice and meat with eggs, sour cream, parsley, salt and pepper. Stuff turkey and roast as above.

## Left-over Turkey

| | |
|---|---|
| Turkey left-overs | 3 T. lemon juice |
| Salt | Lemon peel |
| 1 t. sugar | 1 bouillon cube |
| 3 c. cold water | |

Simmer all the ingredients, except the turkey meat, for a few minutes. Add meat. Simmer together for 5 minutes. Serve with sweet rolls or sweet breads.

### Turkey Cutlets

White meat of turkey, chopped      Salt and pepper
1 T. butter                        ¼ c. cooked or canned mushrooms
3 egg yolks

Pass the turkey through the mincer with the cooked mushrooms. Add the egg yolks, butter and salt and pepper. Form into cutlets, and roll in bread-crumbs. Fry or bake in the oven (375°) for 15 minutes.

### Goose Liver à la Strasbourg

2 large goose livers per person     1 c. sour cream
¼ lb. shallots                      Salt and pepper
1 T. flour                          1 T. capers
Butter                              3 mushrooms, chopped

Soak the livers in milk for 2 hours. Salt and sprinkle with flour and pepper. Brown in melted butter. Separately, stew in butter the chopped mushrooms and the chopped shallots. When the livers are browned, add the mushrooms and the shallots to it and stew under cover for 10 minutes. Pour in 1 c. of sour cream mixed with 1 T. of flour, and 1 T. of capers. Serve the liver with potatoes.

### Fried Goose Liver à la Naturel

2 goose livers per serving          Butter
1 onion, chopped                    Salt
Flour                               Milk

Soak the livers in milk for 2 hours. Remove from milk. Salt and dip in flour. Fry in melted butter with a chopped onion. Do not over-cook. The liver should be slightly pink inside. Serve with fried mushrooms.

### Duck Stewed in Apple Sauce

1 duck, cut up                      Salt
Butter                              6 apples or 1 can apple sauce
1 onion, chopped                    Parsley, chopped
Sugar                               1 T. flour

Cut the duck in pieces. Stew in butter with 1 chopped onion and a handful of chopped parsley until tender. Separately, cook the apples with sugar until soft, then pass through a sieve, or sweetened canned apple sauce. Stir together 1 T. of butter with 1 T. of flour, and mix with the apple sauce. Add to the duck and simmer until the flavours are mingled. Serve with mashed potatoes or rice.

## Duck Stewed in Olives

| | |
|---|---|
| 1 duck, cut in pieces | Peppercorns |
| ¼ lb. shallots | 1 T. flour |
| 2 bay leaves | ½ c. white wine |
| 1 small jar, ripe olives | A few slices of bacon |

Salt the duck and stew in bacon with shallots, a few grains of pepper and bay leaves. When brown, add wine, mixed with 1 T. of flour and olives. Simmer until tender.

## Roast Duck or Goose

| | |
|---|---|
| 1 duck or goose | Marjoram |
| Stuffing 1 | Salt and pepper |
| 5-6 oranges, peeled | Garlic, 3 sections |

Rub the duck or goose with salt, pepper and squeezed garlic inside and out. Stuff it with as many peeled oranges as will fit. Cover with sliced oranges. Roast in a moderate oven—30 minutes to a pound. Pour off fat if an excessive amount accumulates. Baste occasionally.

## Stuffing II

Use recipe No. I substituting unpeeled apples for oranges.

## Stuffing III

| | |
|---|---|
| 1 large onion, chopped | 2 lb. chestnuts |
| Goose or duck liver, chopped | 3 apples, peeled |
| Salt and pepper | ¾ c. black raisins |
| Butter | |

Fry the liver in butter with onion. Boil the chestnuts for about 45 minutes. Shell, taking off both skins, and grate. Combine all the ingredients and stuff; bake as above.

## Brown Rice Stuffing

| | |
|---|---|
| 1 c. brown rice or wild rice | 1 c. mushrooms, chopped |
| Oil or butter | 1 onion, chopped |

Brown the rice in oil or butter with onion and the chopped mushrooms. Stuff and roast the duck as above.

## Sauerkraut Stuffing

| | |
|---|---|
| 1 c. sauerkraut | 1 onion, chopped |
| Butter or margarine | |

Sauté the sauerkraut in butter with onion. Stuff the duck and roast as above.

### Duck Stewed in Red Cabbage

| | |
|---|---|
| 1 duck, cut up | Juice of 1 lemon |
| 1 red cabbage, shredded | Salt |
| ¾ c. red wine | 1 onion, chopped |
| ½ lb. bacon | |

Salt the shredded cabbage and chopped onion and leave standing for 15 minutes. Strain off the juice. Fry the bacon and add the cabbage, onion and wine. Stew under cover for 20 minutes. Cover the duck with cabbage and bake in a moderate oven until tender.

### Roast Venison with Sour Cream

| | |
|---|---|
| 5-6 lb. venison | Rosemary |
| 1 onion, chopped | Basil |
| Butter | 1 bay leaf |
| Flour | Vinegar |
| 3 slices bacon | 2 cups sour cream |

Soak the venison in vinegar, with onion and herbs for 2 days. Pound the meat well. Salt and lard with pieces of bacon. Roast in a moderate oven, 20 to 30 minutes per pound. When tender, pour over sour cream mixed with 1 T. of flour. Continue baking a few minutes more and baste several times. Serve with potatoes.

### Roast Venison

| | |
|---|---|
| 5-6 lb. venison soaked in | Butter |
|     marinade: | Salt and pepper |
| 2 c. olive oil, parsley, 2 bay | 2 c. white wine |
| leaves, 3 sections of garlic | 2 large onions, chopped |
| | Bacon |

Wash the venison. Rub with olive oil and place in the marinade for 2 days. Then salt and lard with pieces of bacon. Bake in a moderate oven for 20 to 30 minutes per pound. Baste often with butter. Serve with a strong sauce as Poivrade (see p. 103) or à la Diable (see p. 103) and a fruit compôte.

### Venison Chops with Wine

| | |
|---|---|
| 3 lb. thick venison chops | Butter |
| Salt pork or bacon, diced | Marjoram |
| 1 c. white wine | Salt and pepper |
| 1 large onion, sliced | |

Make small slits in chops. Insert pieces of salt pork or bacon in the slits. Brown the chops on both sides in butter. Place them in a large pan. Cover the meat with slices of onion and seasoning. Pour the wine on top and simmer under cover for 30 minutes. Serve with a strong sauce as "à la Diable (see p. 103) or "Poivrade" (see p. 103 in Hot Sauces).

## Rolled Venison Cutlets

| | |
|---|---|
| 2 lb. venison cutlets | 3 slices of bacon |
| ¼ lb. venison ground meat | 2 T. flour |
| 1 T. bread-crumbs | ½ c. red wine |
| 4 mushrooms, chopped | ½ c. meat stock |
| 1 onion, chopped | 1 bouillon cube, dissolved |
| 1 t. Worcestershire sauce | Salt and pepper |

Pound well venison cutlets. On the side prepare stuffing: brown the onion with chopped mushrooms, combine with chopped meat and bread-crumbs. Season. Cover each slice of venison with this stuffiing. Roll it and secure with a toothpick. Simmer in butter on a low flame. When browned, add wine and stock and continue cooking until tender.

## Venison Patties

| | |
|---|---|
| 2 lb. venison, minced | 2 egg yolks |
| 2 buns, soaked and squeezed | Bread-crumbs |
| 1 T. butter | Fat |
| Nutmeg | Salt and pepper |

Combine minced venison with squeezed buns. Beat well egg yolks with butter, pepper and nutmeg. Add this mixture to the meat. Season. Form round patties. Roll in bread-crumbs. Fry in hot fat.

## Rabbit Polish Style with Sour Cream

| | |
|---|---|
| 1 rabbit | 1 bay leaf |
| Bacon | 2 sections garlic |
| Butter | 1 onion, chopped |
| 2 c. sour cream | 1 T. flour |
| 2 c. vinegar | 3 sprigs parsley |
| 2 c. olive oil | Salt and pepper |

Clean and soak the rabbit in vinegar, with olive oil, bay leaf, garlics onion and parsley for 2 days. Salt and lard with bacon. Bake in a moderate oven, placing a few pats of butter on top. Baste frequently. When it is tender (about 1 hour) pour over the sour cream mixed with 1 T. of flour. Let the rabbit brown lightly. Pour over its own sauce and serve with a salad. A domestic rabbit does not need to be marinated as long as a wild rabbit to which the above recipe applies.

### Rabbit Hunting Style

| | |
|---|---|
| 1 rabbit, cut up | Marinade: |
| Bacon | 2 c. vinegar |
| 1 lb. shallots | 2 c. olive oil |
| Paprika | 2 cloves garlic |
| 3 T. bread-crumbs | 1 onion, chopped |
| 2 c. white wine | 2 sprigs parsley |
| Salt and pepper | |

Soak the rabbit in marinade for 2 days. Salt and pepper and place in a pan with 6 pieces of bacon and chopped shallots.

### Young Rabbit Fried

| | |
|---|---|
| 2 rabbits | 1 egg |
| Salt | Bread-crumbs |
| Butter | Flour |

Clean the rabbits. Salt inside and out. Quarter. Roll in flour, in egg and in bread-crumbs. Fry in hot melted butter. When tender, place in the oven for 15 minutes to bake. Serve with one of the strong sauces or tartare sauce (see p. 106).

### Fricassee of Rabbit

| | |
|---|---|
| 1 rabbit, cut in pieces | 1 c. white wine |
| 2 onions, chopped | 1 c. meat stock |
| ¼ lb. smoked ham or bacon, diced | Marjoram |
| | 1 lemon, juice |
| 5 mushrooms, chopped | Salt and pepper |
| 1 T. flour | Parsley |
| 1 T. butter | Butter |
| 2 egg yolks | |

Brown onions in butter. Add rabbit cut in small pieces and simmer together until the meat is brown. Add ham and mushrooms and stew under cover. Season. Add wine and stock. Continue cooking until tender. Make a roux of butter and flour, dilute it with meat gravy, add lemon juice, dash of salt and pepper, chopped parsley and finally well beaten egg yolks. Combine with meat and serve with mashed potatoes.

### Baked Wild Goose

| | |
|---|---|
| 1 wild goose | 4 slices of bacon |
| 2 onions, sliced | Salt and pepper |
| Peppercorns | Butter |
| Bay leaf | Marjoram |
| 1 c. vinegar | |

Clean the goose. Let it stand for a few days, to make the meat more tender. Marinate in hot vinegar, with onions, peppercorns and bay leaf. Let it rest in this marinade for 24 hours. Lard the goose with bacon, rub it with marjoram and salt and bake in moderate oven basting often with butter.

## Wild Duck

Prepare in the same manner as wild goose.

### Stewed Wild Duck

| | |
|---|---|
| 1 wild duck | For the marinade: |
| Handful of capers | 1 c. vinegar |
| 1 c. meat stock | 2 onions, sliced |
| 1 c. sour cream | Peppercorns |
| 1 T. flour | 2 bay leaves |
| 5 mushrooms | Salt |

Marinate the duck in hot vinegar with spices. Let it stand 36 hours. Cut it in pieces, place in a pot with meat stock, capers, mushrooms and the remaining marinade. Stew until tender. Beat sour cream with flour, fold into the meat. Warm together. Serve.

### Wild Duck or Goose with Olives

| | |
|---|---|
| Wild duck | Butter |
| Bacon | ½ T. butter |
| Thyme | ½ T. flour |
| Salt and pepper | |
| 1 onion, chopped | |
| 15 olives | For the marinade |
| Nutmeg | 1 c. vinegar |
| ½ c. red wine | 1 onion, sliced |
| ½ c. meat stock | Peppercorns |
| Bay leaf | Bay leaf |

Let the wild duck rest in the marinade for 2 days. Lard it then with bacon and brown in butter. Divide in pieces and stew with onion, meat stock, wine and all the seasoning. When tender remove the meat from the pot and prepare a roux from flour and butter, dilute with meat juice, and combine again with the meat and finally the olives. Simmer together for 15 minutes

# HOT SAUCES

Sauces are widely used in Poland. They are mostly white sauces with mushrooms or dill used rather than strong herbs. Sour cream is often liked better than milk or stock.

## White Sauce

| | |
|---|---|
| 2 T. butter or margarine | 2 T. flour |
| 2 c. stock or milk | Salt |

Melt the butter. Blend in the flour over low heat, stirring constantly. Gradually add warm stock or milk. Keep stirring. Bring to a boil and cook for 2 minutes or until the desired consistency is achieved. This is a basic sauce, served with almost everything but most commonly with fricasse of chicken, ragout of veal, and every kind of fish.

## Béchamel Sauce

This is like white sauce but is made with milk instead of meat or vegetable stock. The two names are used alternatively.

## Cheese Sauce

| | |
|---|---|
| 1 T. butter | 1 T. flour |
| 2 c. milk | 3 T. grated cheese, Parmesan |
| 4 egg yolks, beaten | |

Melt 1 T. of butter and blend in 1 T. of flour. Then add milk gradually, being careful not to make lumps. When it has cooled a little, add 3 T. of grated cheese and 3 beaten egg yolks. Serve with veal, fish, or mussels. It is good with baked dishes and can be made thick to use in casseroles.

## Paprika Sauce

| | |
|---|---|
| 1 c. of white sauce | 1 small onion |
| 1 T. butter | 2 T. sweet cream |
| ¼ t. paprika | |

Prepare the white sauce in half quantities of the recipe given (see above). Brown onion lightly in butter. Add paprika and white sauce. Cook for 5 minutes. Add sweet cream and serve with chicken, rice, or boiled meat.

## Caper Sauce

| |
|---|
| 2 T. capers to each c. of white sauce |

Add the capers to the steaming sauce. Serve with boiled meat and boiled fish.

## Dill Sauce

| |
|---|
| 2 T. dill to each c. of white sauce |

Add the dill to the hot white sauce but be careful not to boil the sauce after you have added the dill. Serve with boiled meat, potato cutlets, and puddings.

## Mushroom Sauce

½ c. mushrooms, chopped, to  1 large onion, chopped
    each c. of white sauce

Brown the onion. Then sauté the mushrooms and combine with the white sauce. Serve with veal cutlets, boiled beef, cube steak, chopped meat.

## Dried Mushroom Sauce

8 dried mushrooms  1 T. butter
1 c. sour cream  Salt and paprika
1 T. flour

Boil the dried mushrooms. When tender, take them out. Reserve the water. Chop them fine. Melt butter, add flour and dilute with the mushroom water. Add salt, paprika, sour cream and mushrooms. Serve with boiled meat, fried sausage, roast pork.

## Curry Sauce

2 T. butter or margarine  2 T. flour
2 c. stock  Curry powder
Salt

Melt butter with flour. Dilute with broth and cook for 10 minutes. Add salt and curry powder to taste. Serve with rice. For a supper dish, double this recipe and slice hard-boiled eggs into it. Serve over rice or noodles.

## Cheese with Béchamel Sauce

2 T. butter or margarine  2 T. flour
1 c. milk or sweet cream  5 T. grated cheese, Parmesan
Salt  or Romano

Melt butter with flour, adding milk or cream. Cook for 10 minutes. Add cheese and salt. Serve with noodles.

## White Lemon Sauce

1½ T. butter  1 T. flour
1½ c. bouillon broth  1 lemon
6 dry chopped mushrooms  Parsley
2 egg yolks

Mix 1 T. of butter with 1 T. of flour. Blend in some hot bouillon. Squeeze the lemon into the mixture, reserving peel to grate and sprinkle a little into the sauce for flavour. Cook. Stew mushrooms in the remainder of the broth and when tender, add the whole to the sauce and stir together. Simmer for a few minutes. Add parsley. When ready to serve add 2 egg yolks blended with ½ T. of butter. Serve with omelettes or fish.

## Chive Sauce

| | |
|---|---|
| 1 T. butter | 1 T. flour |
| 1½ c. stock | 1 c. sour cream |
| Juice of ¼ lemon | 2 T. chopped chives |
| Salt and pepper | |

Melt butter and stir in flour. Dilute with warm broth. Add sour cream and lemon juice. Season. Add finely chopped chives. Bring to a boil. Serve with boiled meats.

## Anchovy Sauce

| | |
|---|---|
| 1 T. butter | 4 fillets of anchovy or 1 T. |
| 1 c. stock | anchovy paste |
| 1 T. flour | |

Melt butter and stir in flour. Dilute it with stock. Add anchovies or anchovy paste. Bring to a boil. Serve with chopped meat or fish.

## Pickle Sauce

| | |
|---|---|
| 1 T. butter | 1 T. flour |
| 2 dill pickles | 1 c. stock |
| 1 c. sour cream | ½ c. pickle juice |
| 1 t. sugar | Salt |

Melt butter with flour. On the side peel the pickles. Cook them in the stock for a few minutes. Chop the pickles. Add 1 c. of sour cream to the butter and flour mixture. Combine with the pickles and stock. Add pickle juice, sugar and salt. Serve with fish cakes, fish ring, boiled meat—anything which does not have a strong taste of its own.

## Onion Sauce

| | |
|---|---|
| 3 T. butter | 3 onions |
| Dash of sugar and salt | 1 T. vinegar |
| 1 T. flour | 2 c. stock |

Chop and brown onion in 2 T. of butter. When tender pass them through a sieve. Melt 1 T. of butter. Add flour and brown. Dilute with warm meat or vegetable stock. Add the onions, salt, sugar, and vinegar and bring to a boil. Serve over meat or omelettes.

## Horseradish Sauce

| | |
|---|---|
| 2 T. horseradish (ready made) | 1 c. stock |
| 1 T. flour | Salt |
| 1 c. sour cream | 2 egg yolks |
| Juice of 1 lemon | 1 T. sugar |
| 1 T. butter | |

Melt butter with flour. Add the horseradish and dilute with warm stock. Add sour cream, salt, sugar, egg yolks and lemon juice. Bring to a boil. Serve with boiled meat or boiled fish.

## Sour Cream Sauce

| | |
|---|---|
| 2 egg yolks | 1 c. sour cream |
| 1 T. lemon juice | Salt and paprika |
| 1 T. parsley | |

Beat the egg yolks. Add sour cream and lemon juice. Heat in the double boiler. Season. Add parsley. Serve with vegetables.

## Tomato Sauce

| | |
|---|---|
| Olive oil | 1 onion, grated |
| 1 carrot, grated | 2 stalks celery, chopped |
| 1 green pepper, chopped | 1 can tomato purée |
| 1 c. water | Rosemary |
| 4 T. grated cheese, Parmesan or | Garlic salt |
| Romano | Basil (optional) |

Sauté the vegetables in olive oil and sieve. Replace in pot and add tomato purée, 1 c. of water and all the seasonings. Add water when needed. Cook for 2 hours on a low flame. Serve with puddings, spaghetti or omelettes.

## Tomato Sauce with Meat

Follow the recipe for tomato sauce adding $\frac{1}{2}$ lb. of chopped meat with the tomato purée.

## Tomato Sauce with Mushrooms

Follow recipe for tomato sauce adding 10 soaked, chopped, dried mushrooms.

## Quick Tomato Sauce

| | |
|---|---|
| 1 can tomato paste | Garlic salt |
| Olive oil | 1 c. sweet cream |
| Salt and pepper | 1 t. sugar |
| 4 T. grated cheese, Parmesan | Rosemary |
| or Romano | |

Cover the bottom of a pan with olive oil. Add tomato paste, cream, seasonings, and grated cheese. Cook on a low flame for 10 minutes before serving.

## Brown Butter Sauce

| | |
|---|---|
| 4 T. butter | 3 T. bread-crumbs |

Melt the butter. Add bread-crumbs. Fry until it is golden brown. Serve with vegetables.

### Genevoise Sauce

| | |
|---|---|
| 1 T. butter | 1 onion, chopped |
| 2 c. vegetable stock with | Salt and pepper |
| vegetables | 1 c. red wine |

Fry onion in butter. Sieve the vegetables. Combine them, and stock, with onion. Add red wine. Bring to a boil. Serve with boiled fish.

### Bordelaise Sauce

Follow recipe for Genevoise sauce, adding 1 heaped T. of tomato paste. Add a dash of paprika, pepper and ½ t. of Worcestershire sauce.

### Provençale Sauce

| | |
|---|---|
| 1 T. butter | 1 onion, chopped |
| 1 c. bouillon broth | 1 glass white wine |
| ½ t. bouillon extract | 3 dried and soaked mushrooms, |
| or 1 bouillon cube | chopped |
| 1 tomato | Salt |

Chop and fry an onion in butter until it is golden brown. Add some bouillon broth, 1 glass of white wine, the bouillon extract or bouillon cube, 1 fresh sliced tomato, and the mushrooms. Cook for 15 minutes. Serve over cold meat.

### Ravigotte Sauce

| | |
|---|---|
| 2 c. chicken or meat stock | Handful of chopped chive |
| Parsley, chopped | Handful of chopped dill |
| Salt and pepper | 1 T. butter |
| ½ t. Worcestershire sauce | 1 T. flour |
| 2 T. vinegar | 3 T. sweet cream |

Cook in broth the chopped chive, dill, parsley for 10 minutes. Add vinegar. On the side, melt butter in flour. Dilute with a few spoons of the stock, add salt and pepper and ½ t. of Worcestershire sauce and combine. Before taking off the fire, add about 3 T. of sweet cream. Serve with smoked meats and dark meats in general.

### Hollandaise Sauce

| | |
|---|---|
| 5 egg yolks | 2 T. butter |
| ¼ c. white wine | ¼ c. chicken stock |
| Juice of ½ lemon | Salt and pepper |
| Dash of nutmeg | 1 t. sugar (optional) |

Beat to a foam the eggs and butter. Cook the wine and chicken broth together in the top of a double boiler. Add the juice of lemon, season, and slowly pour in the eggs and butter, mixing constantly until the sauce turns light and thickens. Be careful not to let it boil. Serve with fish. Add sugar if it is to be served with vegetables.

## Mustard Sauce

| | |
|---|---|
| 3 T. butter | 2 onions |
| 1 T. flour | 1 c. chicken stock |
| ¼ c. white wine | 2 T. mustard |
| ½ t. Worcestershire sauce | ½ bouillon cube |

Chop and brown onions in butter. Add flour and dilute with stock. Stir in the ¼ c. of wine and cook together. Before removing from the flame blend in 2 T. of mustard, Worcestershire sauce, and bouillon cube. Serve with fish, sausage, liver cutlets, ham and wild game.

## Colbert Sauce

| | |
|---|---|
| 1 T. butter | 1 T. flour |
| 1 c. bouillon broth | Salt and pepper |
| Juice of ¼ lemon | ¼ t. soya sauce |
| Chopped parsley | |

Melt butter and stir in flour. Dilute with bouillon broth. Stir in other ingredients and simmer until flavours are mingled. Serve with shrimp.

## Sauce à la Russe

| | |
|---|---|
| 1 T. butter | 1 onion, grated |
| 1 T. flour | ¼ c. bouillon broth |
| 2 c. sour cream | 1 t. Worcestershire sauce |

Melt butter and fry grated onion until brown. Blend in 1 T. of flour. Dilute with bouillon broth and stir in 2 c. of sour cream and Worcestershire sauce. Serve with fried meats.

## Raisin Sauce

| | |
|---|---|
| 1 T. butter | 1 T. flour |
| 1 c. bouillon broth | 2 t. honey |
| 1 c. white wine | 2 T. vinegar |
| ¼ c. raisins | |

Melt butter and stir in flour. Add bouillon broth and bring to a boil. Add honey, wine, raisins and vinegar which have been heated. Bring to a boil again and serve with ham or corned beef.

## Milanaise Sauce

| | |
|---|---|
| 2 T. butter | 5 tomatoes, peeled and chopped |
| 1 onion, chopped | 2 carrots, chopped |
| Fresh parsley | 1 green pepper, chopped |
| 1 stalk celery | 1 c. bouillon broth |
| Bay leaf | 1 T. flour |
| Salt and pepper | Paprika |
| 1 bouillon cube | ¼ c. red wine |
| 8 green olives | ¼ lb. diced ham |

Cover and stew vegetables and bay leaf in 1 T. of butter until they are tender, adding bouillon broth when necessary to prevent sticking. Sieve all the ingredients. On the side melt 1 T. of butter and stir in 1 T. of flour. Add 4 T. of bouillon broth and the sieved vegetables. Season. Stir in the wine and bouillon cube and cook for a few minutes. Before serving add diced ham and olives. Serve with any chicken dish, steak, cutlets, or roast pork.

### Butter à la Maitre d'Hotel

| | |
|---|---|
| 4 T. sweet butter, softened | 1 t. lemon juice |
| 2 T. parsley, chopped | |

Beat the softened butter well. Add chopped parsley and lemon juice. Make butter balls with a teaspoon. Serve with a steak and any fried meats or fish.

### Garlic Butter

| | |
|---|---|
| 2 garlic sections | 3 T. butter |

Squeeze the garlic sections through a garlic squeezer and mix with the melted butter. Chill. Make balls with 2 teaspoons and serve with artichokes, lobster and any grilled meat or use to spread on bread.

### Chive Butter

| | |
|---|---|
| 3 T. butter | ¼ c. chopped chives |

Mix the melted butter with the chopped chives. This is particularly good served over new potatoes or sliced beets, also steak.

### Dill Butter

Prepare in the same manner.

### Anchovy Paste Butter

| | |
|---|---|
| 4 T. butter, softened | 2 T. anchovy paste |

Beat the butter until it is quite soft. Add anchovy paste and mix well. Make balls to serve on grilled meats or spread on crackers for hors d'oevres.

### Sauce à la Strogonov

| | |
|---|---|
| 1 T. butter | 1 onion, grated |
| 1 T. flour | ¼ c. bouillon broth |
| ¼ c. sour cream | 1 t. Worcestershire sauce |
| 2 T. tomato paste | |

Brown the onion lightly in butter. Stir in flour and dilute with the bouillon broth. Mix in sour cream, tomato paste and Worcestershire sauce. Bring to a boil and serve with meats.

## Mousseline Sauce

| | |
|---|---|
| 2 egg yolks | Salt and pepper |
| ¼ lb. butter, sweet | 2 T. water |

Mix well-beaten egg yolks with water, salt and pepper. Place in a double boiler and mix persistently until the yolks start to thicken. Then start adding butter, piece by piece (about the size of a nut). Continue mixing until all the butter is stirred in and the sauce reaches the boiling point. Serve with fish, particularly broiled fish like salmon or swordfish.

## Poivrade or Strong Sauce

| | |
|---|---|
| 2 T. butter | 1 onion, chopped |
| 2 carrots, chopped | 1 stalk celery, chopped |
| 2 c. water | 2 slices Canadian bacon, |
| 3 sardines | country-smoked bacon or ham |
| 1 c. bouillon broth | or left-over meat |
| 1 T. flour | 1 T. wine vinegar |
| 1 t. Worcestershire sauce | Salt and pepper |
| 1 t. soya sauce | 1 bouillon cube |

Stew in 1 T. of butter all the chopped vegetables. Add smoked meat and sardines and simmer, adding water occasionally to prevent burning. When everything is rosy and tender, pour over it some of the bouillon broth. Add the vinegar and continue cooking until well-blended. Then pass the meat through a mincer and all the vegetables through a sieve. On the side melt 1 T. of butter and blend in 1 T. of flour. Dilute with the rest of the bouillon and combine with the meat mixture. Add salt and an abundant amount of pepper, 1 t. of Worcestershire sauce, soya sauce, 1 bouillon cube and cook again. Serve with dark meats. It is very strong.

## Spicy Sauce à la Diable

| | |
|---|---|
| 2 T. butter | 2 onions, chopped |
| 1 carrot, grated | 1 celery stalk, chopped |
| Chopped parsley | Salt and pepper |
| 2 bay leaves | 1 T. flour |
| 1 c. bouillon broth | ½ t. paprika |
| 2 T. tarragon vinegar | ¼ c. red wine |
| Oregano | 4 chopped mushrooms |
| Sugar | Several small white cocktail onions |

Stew in 1 T. of butter the chopped onions, celery, carrots, and parsley. Add pepper, 2 bay leaves and salt. Add a little bouillon broth to prevent burning and simmer until tender. Pass the vegetables through a sieve and add them to a mixture of 1 T. of butter, 1 T. of flour and the rest of the bouillon broth which has been prepared on the side. Add paprika, tarragon vinegar, wine and a dash of oregano. Before removing from the fire add cooked chopped mushrooms, cocktail onions and salt and sugar to taste. Serve with wild game or any dark meat.

### *Polish Grey Sauce*

| | |
|---|---|
| 1 T. butter | 1 lemon, juice |
| 1 T. meat extract | 2 t. sugar |
| 1 T. flour | 1 c. stock, meat or fish |
| 2 T. raisins | (accordingly if served with |
| 2 T. almonds, blanched | fish or meat) |
| and chopped | 1 glass red wine |

Make a roux with butter and flour, dilute it with hot stock. Add meat extract, raisins and finely chopped almonds. Mix thoroughly. Add lemon juice and sugar, finally wine. Simmer for a few minutes and serve with carp or any kind of boiled meat.

### *Polish Egg Sauce*

¼ lb. butter                                      5 hard-boiled eggs

Melt the butter. Chop the eggs fine. Drop the chopped eggs into boiling butter and fry together for 2 minutes. Serve with boiled fish.

# COLD SAUCES

### Mayonnaise I

2 raw egg yolks
½ t. salt

1 c. olive oil
Juice of ½ lemon

Beat the egg yolks well. Add oil, drop by drop, mixing constantly. When the consistency is thick, add salt and lemon juice.

### Mayonnaise II

1 cooked egg yolk
1 c. olive oil
Juice of 1 lemon

1 raw egg yolk
½ t. salt

Pass the hard-boiled egg yolk through a sieve and mix with the raw egg yolk. Add oil gradually, drop by drop, mixing constantly. When the mixture is thick and smooth add salt and lemon juice.

### Mayonnaise with Wine

| | |
|---|---|
| ¼ c. white wine | 1 c. olive oil |
| 1 envelope gelatine | Juice of 2 lemons |
| Salt, pepper, sugar | 5 raw egg yolks |

Mix the white wine with the olive oil. Dissolve gelatine in lemon juice and combine. Season to taste with salt, pepper and sugar. Beat well. Then add 5 egg yolks and continue beating until the sauce thickens. Serve with fish.

### Mayonnaise without Oil

| | |
|---|---|
| 2 raw egg yolks | ½ c. sweet cream |
| 2 T. melted butter | 1 t. Worcestershire sauce |
| Juice of ½ lemon | Salt and paprika |

Beat the egg yolks with sweet cream in a double boiler. When the consistency is thick add melted butter and all the seasonings. Chill.

### Tartare Sauce

| | |
|---|---|
| 6 raw egg yolks | 6 T. olive oil |
| 1 T. dry mustard | Salt and pepper |
| ¼ t. Worcestershire sauce | Sugar |
| Chopped pickles or relish | ¼ c. cold water |

Make a mayonnaise of the egg yolks and olive oil. Add dry mustard, salt, pepper and sugar to taste, and then the Worcestershire sauce and water. Cook over a slow flame, being careful not to boil, beating constantly, until it thickens. Add pickles or relish and chill. When cold, if it is not sour enough, add lemon juice. If too thick, add water. Serve with cold ham fried fish, cold meats. In Poland this traditionally is Easter fare.

### Remoulade

| | |
|---|---|
| Mayonnaise·I (see page 105) | 2 chopped dill pickles |
| 1 T. mustard | 1 T. capers |
| 1 T. chopped parsley | 1 T. chopped chives or ¼ T. |
| 1 T. anchovy paste (opt.) | grated onion |

Mix all the ingredients with mayonnaise and serve with cold meats.

### Horseradish Sauce with Cream

| | |
|---|---|
| ½ c. grated horseradish | ½ c. sweet cream |
| 1 t. sugar | 1 T. vinegar or lemon juice |

Grate horseradish and leave standing for an hour before using or use prepared horseradish. Add cream and sugar, mixing well. Blend in vinegar or lemon juice. Serve with ham, fish or boiled beef.

### Cwikla or Beet Sauce

4 beets
Wine vinegar

1½ T. prepared horseradish
Salt

Bake or pressure-cook beets. It seems that baking or cooking quickly under pressure preserves the redness of the beets better than a long boiling process. Peel and grate the beets and mix with horseradish. Add salt. Cover with vinegar and keep cold in a jar. Serve with cold meats or boiled meats.

### Anchovy Sauce

2 T. anchovy paste or 4 chopped
　anchovy fillets
3 hard-boiled egg yolks
1 T. mustard

Juice of ½ lemon
Salt, pepper, and sugar
1 T. olive oil

Mix anchovy paste with the hard-boiled egg yolks passed through a sieve. Then mix in mustard with olive oil and juice of lemon. Salt, pepper and sugar to taste. Serve with fish. The whites of the hard-boiled eggs may be reserved to use in salads.

# SWEET SAUCES

## Hard Sauce

4 egg yolks
½ c. granulated sugar

1 c. white wine

Beat the egg yolks with sugar until the sauce becomes light. Add wine gradually, drop by drop, beating constantly. Place over a low flame and beat until thick. Chill. Serve with hot desserts.

## Cream Sauce

3 egg yolks                                 ½ c. sugar
1 t. vanilla                                 ½ t. cinnamon
1 c. hot milk

Beat eggs, adding sugar, vanilla and cinnamon. Mix in milk gradually. Cook over a low flame until thick, stirring constantly. Be sure
not to boil. Serve either hot or cold with puddings.

## Fruit Juice Sauce

1 c. water                                   1½ c. fruit juice
¼ c. sugar                                   1 T. corn starch

Mix water with the juice and bring to a boil. Add the sugar. On
the side dilute the corn starch with a little water and add to the juice
mixture. Bring to a boil again, stirring constantly. If you like the
sauce stronger add a little white wine and a dash more of cornstarch. Serve with hot desserts and puddings. For this recipe a sweet
fruit juice like raspberry, apricot or pineapple is suggested.

## Fruit Sauce

2 c. white wine                             Juice of 1 lemon
Juice of 1 orange                           Grated rind of orange and lemon
2 c. sugar                                   1 jigger liqueur, preferably apricot
5 egg yolks                                      brandy
1 c. water

Cook white wine with water, lemon juice and orange juice until it
comes to a boil. Remove from the fire and cool. Mix the sugar with
the orange and lemon rind. Beat egg yolks until light. Add sugar
and grated rind. Combine gradually with the wine mixture. Return
to the fire. Cook slowly and heat until it thickens. At the end, stir
in the liqueur and serve with either hot or cold desserts.

## Berry Sauce

2 c. strawberries, raspberries, or          Juice of ¼ lemon
    blueberries                              ½ c. sugar
1 c. sweet cream                             1 T. cornstarch
¼ c. white wine

Bring wine, lemon juice and fruit to a boil. Add sugar, stirring
constantly. Wet cornstarch with a little cream and blend into the
mixture, still stirring. Bring to a boil. Serve either hot or cold over
puddings or ice cream. Fresh fruit is preferred but either canned or
frozen fruit may be used. Canned fruit should be drained before
using.

## Apricot Sauce

| | |
|---|---|
| 1 c. apricot pulp | 1 c. heavy cream |
| Sugar | |

Pass canned or cooked apricots through a sieve. Add to cream beaten stiff. Sweeten to taste.

## Almond Sauce

| | |
|---|---|
| 1 c. almonds | 5 T. sugar |
| 6 c. milk | 1 T. cornstarch |
| 3 egg yolks | |

Blanch almonds, remove skins and pound or grind the nuts to a powder. Mix with 2 T. of sugar. Cook with all the milk, reserving 2 T. to mix with the cornstarch. Bring milk and almond powder mixture to the boiling point and strain through a sieve. Stir in the cornstarch and cold milk. Beat egg yolks with 3 T. of sugar until light. Place on a low flame and stir in the almond milk slowly. Beat and cook until it thickens. Chill and serve with fruit desserts.

## Chocolate Sauce

| | |
|---|---|
| 4 squares unsweetened chocolate | 3 T. sweet butter |
| 2 c. sweet cream | 1 T. cornstarch |
| 3 egg yolks | 3 T. sugar |

Melt chocolate in butter over hot water or very low heat. Add cream and cornstarch, which has been moistened with cream, and stir until smooth. Beat egg yolks with sugar until light and stir into chocolate, cream gradually. Continue cooking and beat until it thickens. Serve with hot puddings or ice cream.

## White Wine Sauce

| | |
|---|---|
| 5 egg yolks | 2 c. white wine |
| 5 T. sugar | |

Beat the egg yolks with sugar until light. Then place on the fire and stir the wine in gradually. Beat hard until it thickens. It is best to prepare this sauce at the last minute because it has a tendency to go flat. To serve cold—after taking off the flame place on ice and beat for a few minutes. Use for puddings, compotes, stewed fruit.

## Red Wine Sauce

| | |
|---|---|
| 2 c. red wine | 5 T. sugar |
| 1 t. cinnamon | 1 c. water |
| 3 cloves | Juice of ½ lemon |
| Grated rind of 1 lemon | 1 T. cornstarch moistened with |
| ¼ c. raisins | 2 T. water |

Cook together all the ingredients except the raisins. Bring to a boil.

Strain through a sieve and add raisins. Serve with hot puddings or with cold desserts. The sauce itself may be used either hot or cold.

### Vanilla Sauce

| | |
|---|---|
| 5 egg yolks | 5 T. sugar |
| 2 c. milk | 1 t. vanilla |

Beat the egg yolks until light. If it is possible to use vanilla beans they make a better sauce than the vanilla extract. If the beans are used cook with milk. If the extract is used, add at the end of the preparation process. Bring milk to a boil. Cool slightly and stir into the egg yolk and sugar mixture. Place on the fire and beat until it thickens. Serve with hot or cold desserts.

### Sherry Sauce

| | |
|---|---|
| 1 c. heavy cream | 2 T. sugar |
| 4 egg yolks | ½ c. sherry |
| 2 T. apricot jam | |

Beat the egg yolks with sugar until light. Beat in apricot jam. Add sherry. Place on a low fire and beat until it thickens. Do not let it boil. When cool, add the whipped cream and mix with the sauce. Serve with rice puddings, sponge cake, ice cream, or almost any kind of pudding.

### Hot Rum Sauce

| | |
|---|---|
| 2 T. butter | 1 c. powdered sugar |
| 2 eggs, separated | ½ c. cream |
| 3 T. rum | |

Cream butter and sugar together until smooth. Add beaten egg yolks and cream. Cook in a double boiler until it thickens. Pour it over stiffly beaten egg whites. Fold in rum. Serve with hot puddings.

# DAIRY DISHES

Butter, daily made, new laid eggs and cottage cheese were the products that you could most easily find in the Warsaw market or any other city market in Poland. The peasants made daily trips to town in order to deliver their goods. Poland was always an agricultural country and dairy products were its pride. The great bounty of dairy products may have accounted for the variety and originality of Polish dairy dishes.

## Eggs in Red Hats

| | |
|---|---|
| 6 hard-boiled eggs | 3 T. sour cream |
| 1 c. cottage cheese | Chive |
| Salt and pepper | Radishes |
| 6 tomatoes | |

Peel the eggs and cut off the tops and the bottoms so that they can stand. Cut the top off a fresh tomato and place on top of each egg. Mix the sour cream with cottage cheese. Season. Cut up the radishes and add them. Chop chives. Mix well. Spread on a long platter and stand the eggs with tomato-top hats in the middle.

## Eggs in White Sauce

| | |
|---|---|
| 6 hard-boiled eggs | 2 raw eggs |
| 1 T. butter | Bread-crumbs |
| 2 c. Béchamel sauce | |
| (see page 96) | |

Peel the hard-boiled eggs. Beat the raw eggs and roll the boiled ones in them; then roll them again in the bread-crumbs. Fry them lightly. Place on a platter and cover with warm Béchamel sauce. Good Lenten food.

## Stuffed Eggs I

| | |
|---|---|
| 6 hard-boiled eggs | Paprika |
| 2 T. olive oil | 1 T. sour cream |
| 5 T. tuna fish | Salt and pepper |

Peel the eggs. Cut them lengthwise and take out the yolks. Mix the tuna fish with the egg yolks. Add the sour cream and olive oil, to make it smooth. Refill the eggs and sprinkle with paprika and garnish with parsley.

## Stuffed Eggs II

| | |
|---|---|
| 6 hard-boiled eggs | 4 T. sour cream |
| 1 slice of bread, soaked in milk | 1 t. flour |
| 1 T. butter | 1 T. chive, chopped |
| 1 raw egg | Bread-crumbs |
| 6 fillets anchovy | |

Squeeze out the bread. Mix it with chopped anchovies. Cut the peeled eggs lengthwise. Take out the yolks and chop. Combine with the other mixture. Pass through the sieve. Mix and fry with butter, 1 T. of sour cream, chive and beaten egg. Refill the whites of eggs, sprinkle with bread-crumbs. Put in a baking dish and cover with sour cream beaten with one t. of flour. Bake in a moderate oven for 15 minutes.

### Eggs à la Tripe

| | |
|---|---|
| 6 eggs | 1 c. tomato sauce |
| 2 T. grated cheese | Salt and pepper |

Make several thin omelettes. Slice them lengthwise in strips ½ inch wide. Place them in a saucepan with prepared tomato sauce and simmer for 10 minutes. Place on a platter and sprinkle with grated cheese.

### Scrambled Eggs with Cottage Cheese

| | |
|---|---|
| 2 T. cottage cheese to each egg | Salt and pepper<br>Butter |

Melt the cottage cheese in butter, add the well beaten eggs. Scramble. Salt and pepper to taste. If you like a touch of colour, sprinkle with paprika or chopped chive.

### Scrambled Eggs with Chives

| | |
|---|---|
| 2 eggs per person | 1 T. sweet cream per egg |
| Chives | Salt and pepper |
| Butter | |

Beat the eggs well in a bowl, pour slowly into a frying-pan with melted butter. Add a few spoons of cream, salt and pepper and chopped chives. Stir constantly to have it thicken evenly.

### Hungarian Scrambled Eggs

| | |
|---|---|
| Smoked lard or bacon | Paprika |
| Eggs | Salt and pepper |

Cut the bacon in small pieces and fry. Take off some of the fat. Add eggs and scramble. Add paprika to taste.

### Scrambled Eggs with Ham or Polish Sausage

| | |
|---|---|
| Eggs | Polish sausage or ham, diced |
| 1 T. sweet cream for each egg | Salt and pepper |
| Chopped chive | |

Fry the sausage or ham slightly. Beat the eggs with cream, well. Add chives. Combine with the sausage and scramble, mixing constantly.

### Peacock's Eyes

| | |
|---|---|
| 5 eggs | 5 slices white bread |
| Butter | Grated cheese |
| Sweet cream | Salt and pepper |

Remove the centre of each slice of bread and discard. Then brown the remnants of the slices in butter. Sprinkle a baking dish with sweet cream. Place the toasted bread in the bottom of the dish. Drop one raw egg into middle of each crust. Sprinkle with salt and grated cheese. Add 1 T. of sweet cream on each egg. Bake in a moderate oven for 15 minutes or until firm.

### Eggs à la Carina

6 T. grated cheese
5 T. butter
2 eggs per person
1 c. sour cream

½ T. flour
½ t. Maggi's extract, or any meat extract or soya sauce

Springle a baking dish heavily with grated cheese. Add sour cream (which you have previously beaten with ½ T. of flour and Maggi's extract). Put in a hot oven for 5 minutes before serving. Break the eggs carefully into the dish. Season with salt and pepper. Cover with grated cheese and with pieces of butter. Bake in the oven long enough for the whites of egg to coagulate.

### Scrambled Eggs with Tomatoes

3 fresh tomatoes, peeled
4 eggs
Butter

Garlic powder
Salt and pepper

Sauté the tomatoes in butter. When soft and tender add a dash of garlic powder, salt and pepper and fold into beaten eggs, stirring constantly.

### Eggs in Madeira Wine

4 poached eggs
4 T. Madeira wine
Paprika
Salt and pepper

2 T. butter
2 T. flour
1 c. meat stock
Toasted bread

Melt butter and flour, mix in warm stock. Add the wine, salt, paprika and pepper. Cook for 5 minutes. On the side prepare poached eggs. (Break the egg in boiling water, when the white coagulates the poached egg is ready). Prepare toasted bread. Place the poached eggs on bread and cover with the sauce.

### French Omelette

5 eggs
2 T. sweet cream

Salt and pepper
Butter

Never make an omelette out of more than 5 eggs. To have it fluffy, add the cream to the well beaten eggs. When the butter is well melted, pour beaten eggs into the pan and do not mix. Let them get done on the bottom. With the end of a knife pick up the ends, letting the yet undone parts run underneath and get cooked, paying attention that the omelette should be slightly browned on the bottom and very fluffy on top.

## Omelette 'à la Jardinière'

| | |
|---|---|
| Cooked vegetables | Salt and pepper |
| 5 eggs | Butter |

Simmer the cooked vegetables, (carrots, green peas, string beans, onion) which have previously been very well chopped, in butter. Meanwhile prepare a fluffy omelette and fold in the vegetables.

## Omelette with Spinach

| | |
|---|---|
| ¼ lb. spinach | 2 T. grated cheese |
| 5 eggs | Fresh parsley |
| 2 T. sweet cream | Salt and pepper |
| 1 section garlic | 2 T. olive oil |

Clean the spinach. Cook in salted water. When ready chop fine and sauté in olive oil. Beat the eggs well. Add cream. Season. Add grated cheese. Add the spinach. Fry the omelette. To brown top of the omelette you can place in the oven for a short while.

## Egg Cake

| | |
|---|---|
| 4 eggs | ½ c. milk |
| 3 T. flour | ¼ lb. sliced bacon |
| 2 sections garlic | Salt and pepper |

Blend well the flour and milk taking care that there are no lumps. Sprinkle seasoning. Add eggs, well beaten. Add juice of pressed garlic. Place the bacon in the pan, cover it with the egg mixture, let it cook.

## Danish Omelette

| | |
|---|---|
| 4 eggs | |
| 4 T. butter or margarine | 2 T. butter |
| 4 T. milk | 2 onions |
| Salt | Curry powder |
| | 1 T. water |

Slice the onions. Brown them in butter. When ready, add curry and water. Separate the whites and the yolks of the eggs. Beat the whites stiff and mix with well blended egg yolks and milk. Fold in the curried onions and fry.

## Sausage Pudding

Flour
3 eggs
1 c. milk
8 sausages, diced

1 T. chives, chopped
5 T. grated cheese, Parmesan
Salt and pepper

Fry the diced sausages. Take out half of the fat. Beat the eggs, yolks and whites separately. Add flour, salt and milk to the yolks. Combine with the stiffly beaten whites. Add the chives and grated cheese. Pour the mixture over the sausages and bake in a moderately hot oven for 15 minutes. Pepper is optional.

## Egg Noodles with Ham

1 cup ham, diced
1 lb. egg noodles
2 T. fat
3 slices American cheese

Bread-crumbs
Grated cheese
Butter

Butter a baking dish and sprinkle with bread crumbs. Mix half-cooked noodles with ham, fat and diced American cheese. Place in the baking dish. Sprinkle the top with bread-crumbs and grated cheese. Bake in moderate oven for 45 minutes.

## Egg Noodles with Poppy Seed

1 lb. egg noodles
$\frac{1}{4}$ c. milk
3 T. honey
2 T. sugar

$\frac{1}{2}$ c. poppy seed
3 T. butter
$\frac{1}{4}$ c. raisins, optional

Cook the noodles. Mix the milk with poppy seed, sugar, honey and raisins if desired. Cook it over low flame for 3 minutes. Add this mixture to the noodles.

## Noodles with Cottage Cheese

1 lb. egg noodles
1 lb. cottage cheese
3 T. butter

1 egg yolk
Salt

Cook the noodles in salted water. Mix the cottage cheese with the egg yolk. Drain the noodles. Add butter and cottage cheese and serve.

## Noodles with Cheese and Milk

1 lb. egg noodles
$\frac{1}{4}$ lb. cottage cheese
$\frac{1}{2}$ c. milk

3 T. sugar
$\frac{1}{2}$ c. milk

Cook the noodles in salted water. Place in colander and strain. Warm the milk with sugar for a few minutes and pour over the noodles. Serve mixed with cottage cheese.

### Noodles Baked in the Oven

| | |
|---|---|
| 1 lb. egg noodles | 2 T. melted butter |
| 3 T. sugar | 2 T. bread-crumbs |
| 4 T. grated cheese | 2 c. sour cream |
| 2 egg yolks | |

Cook the noodles in salted water. When ready, strain under running cold water. Mix with grated cheese. Place in a buttered pan and sprinkle with bread-crumbs and sugar. Cover the noodles with melted butter and sour cream mixed with 2 beaten egg yolks. Place in a very hot oven and bake for about 30 minutes, until golden brown.

### Lazanki with Ham

| | |
|---|---|
| ½ lb. ham, chopped | 2 T. water |
| 2 c. flour | 2 T. butter |
| 3 T. sour cream | 1 T. bread-crumbs |
| 1 egg | 4 slices bacon, optional |

Make the dough with 2 c. of flour, one egg and 2 T. of water. Knead on a floured board until quite firm and then roll out flat and cut into 2 inch strips which should then be sliced lengthwise into 1 inch pieces.. Cook the "lazanki" in salted water, drain. Fry bread-crumbs in butter. Pour melted butter with bread-crumbs over the lazanki. Alternate the layers of lazanki and ham. Bake in a very hot oven for a ½ hour. You can use the prepared egg noodles instead of going into the long procedure of preparing lazanki. Bacon may be used to cover the noodles before placing them in the oven.

### Lazanki with Cottage Cheese

| | |
|---|---|
| 1 lb. noodles | 3 eggs |
| 1 c. cottage cheese | 2 c. sour cream |
| 2 T. sugar | 1 T. bread-crumbs |
| Sugar | |

Cook the prepared noodles in salted water and drain in colander. Combine the cottage cheese with the egg yolks and sugar. Add sour cream. Alternate layers of noodles with layers of cottage cheese and sprinkle with some more sugar. Bake in a very hot oven for 30 minutes, or until golden brown.

### Macaroni with Bouillon and Tomatoes

| | |
|---|---|
| 1 lb. elbow macaroni | 2 c. thick bouillon broth |
| 1 T. melted butter | 4 T. tomato paste |

Cook the macaroni in salted water. Drain in a colander. Add the tomato paste to the macaroni with 1 T. of melted butter. Place in a pan and pour over 2 c. of thick bouillon. Bake in a moderate oven until golden brown.

### Baked Macaroni with Mushrooms

| | |
|---|---|
| 1 lb. elbow macaroni | ¼ c. dried mushrooms, diced |
| 2 T. melted butter | 2 c. sour cream |

Cook the mushrooms in salted water. Drain, saving some of the mushroom broth to mix with 2 c. of sour cream. Add the mushrooms finely chopped. Separately cook the macaroni in salted water. Drain. Combine the macaroni with 2 T. of melted butter and the mixture of mushrooms and cream. Place in greased pan and bake in a moderate oven until golden brown.

### Macaroni 'au gratin'

| | |
|---|---|
| 1 lb. macaroni | 2 T. bread-crumbs |
| 3 T. butter | 4 T. grated cheese, Parmesan |

Cook the macaroni in salted water. Drain in a colander. Brown the bread-crumbs in butter lightly. Place the macaroni in a pan, sprinkle with Parmesan cheese and the browned bread-crumbs. Bake in the oven until golden brown.

### Macaroni Baked with Apples

| | |
|---|---|
| 1 lb. cooked macaroni | Cinnamon (optional) |
| 1 T. bread-crumbs | 2 T. butter |
| ¼ c. sugar | 5 apples, sliced |

Place a layer of the cooked macaroni in a buttered pan sprinkled with bread-crumbs. Slice the apples finely and sprinkle with sugar and cinnamon. Alternate layers of macaroni and apples so that the macaroni layer is on the top. Top with bread-crumbs and butter. Bake in a moderate oven for 1 hour.

### Bread Cakes

| | |
|---|---|
| 1 c. milk | powdered sugar |
| 4 eggs | Cinnamon |
| Vienna bread, thinly cut | Butter |

Beat the eggs well. Dip the slices of bread in milk on both sides, and then into the eggs. Fry in butter and dust with powdered sugar and cinnamon if desired. This is known elsewhere as French toast.

### Pierogi Lenive or Lazy Pierogi

| | |
|---|---|
| 4 eggs, separated | ¼ c. flour |
| 6 T. butter | Bread-crumbs |
| 1 lb. cottage cheese | Dash of sugar |
| Salt | |

Beat together 1 T. of butter with 4 egg yolks. On the side prepare the cottage cheese. Drain off all the water, sieve and then mix it with the egg yolks. Beat the egg whites stiff and add to the whole mixture.

Fold in the flour. On a floured board, cut out pieces of dough. Make long rolls out of them, not thicker than 2 fingers, 2 inches long. Cook in boiling water for 10 or 15 minutes. Serve with buttered, browned bread-crumbs.

### Fluffy Pancakes

| | |
|---|---|
| 6 egg yolks | 6 egg whites, stiffly beaten |
| $\frac{1}{4}$ c. sugar | Powdered sugar |
| $1\frac{1}{2}$ c. flour | 1 c. sweet cream |
| Fat | Fat |

Beat the egg yolks with sugar until light. Add flour and cream. Fold the egg-whites in very softly and mix carefully. Drop from the spoon. Cook in an iron frying pan, well greased. Fry the pancakes on both sides. Serve with powdered sugar, strawberry jam or cinnamon and sugar.

### Polish Blintzes or Nalesniki

| | |
|---|---|
| 3 eggs | Salt |
| Powdered sugar | 2 T. flour |
| $\frac{1}{2}$ c. milk | Fat |
| 1 egg yolk | Jam or cottage cheese |
| 2 T. sugar | |

Beat the eggs well. Add flour gradually. When it is dissolved, add milk. Use a pastry brush for spreading the fat on the frying pan. When the pan is very hot, pour 1 T. of batter for each nalesniki. When light brown, take it off the fire and place it on a wooden board. Spread it with jam, or cottage cheese that you have previously softened with one egg yolk and 2 T. of sugar. Roll the pancakes and sprinkle with powdered sugar. Serve warm or cold. You may prepare them ahead of time, and if you want them warm, just put them in the oven for a few minutes.

### Sour Cream Blintzes

| | |
|---|---|
| 2 c. sour cream | Salt |
| 2 c. flour | Parsley, chopped |
| 4 eggs, separated | 5 T. Swiss cheese, grated |
| Butter or margarine | (or Parmesan) |

Mix sour cream with flour in a bowl, adding chopped parsley and egg yolks. When it is well mixed, add beaten egg whites and mix gently. Pour into hot fat and fry like pancakes on both sides. When ready, sprinkle with grated cheese, and serve.

### Bliny

| | |
|---|---|
| 2 c. buckwheat flour | Salt |
| 2 c. white flour | 2 c. sour cream |
| 2 yeast cakes | $\frac{1}{4}$ lb. margarine |
| 2 eggs | 3 c. milk |

Put the buckwheat flour into a bowl. Scald with boiling milk. Mix well. When cooled off, add crushed yeast. Mix with a spoon and let it stand for 30 minutes. Then add salt and the eggs and finally the flour. Stir all the ingredients thoroughly, adding milk. Pour the batter into individual buttered muffin tins and let it rise again. Bake in a hot oven (375°) until brown. Serve with butter and sour cream. Bliny is also good with chopped chives.

### Yeast Blintzes or Nalesniki

| | |
|---|---|
| 2 c. flour | 1½ c. milk |
| 2 eggs | 1 T. sugar |
| 2 egg yolks | 2 yeast cakes |
| Butter, margarine or lard | Dash of salt |

Mix the yeast with the lukewarm milk, let it stand for ½ hour. Combine with well-beaten eggs, fold in all the remaining ingredients slowly. Cover and let it stand in a warm place, possibly without a draught. After 2 hours, take the dough up with a spoon and fry on both sides in a very hot iron frying pan. Serve with any fruit preserve; wild rose preserve is really delicious with the yeast nalesniki.

### Nalesniki with Jam

| | |
|---|---|
| 4 egg yolks | 4 egg whites |
| 1 c. milk | Salt |
| 2 c. flour | 1 T. butter, melted |
| 1 c. water | Any preserved fruit |

Beat 4 egg yolks, adding 2 c. of flour and a dash of salt; mix constantly, adding water and milk gradually and 1 T. of melted and cooled butter. The batter should be prepared for pouring. When ready to fry the "nalesniki," add 4 stiffly beaten egg whites to the batter. Fry on a greased pan. When each is done do not turn over on the other side but take out and place on a board. Spread some fruit jam on each one and roll into a trumpet shape. Serve, sprinkled with powdered sugar.

### Nalesniki with Cheese

| | |
|---|---|
| 4 eggs, separated | Salt |
| 1 c. milk | Cinnamon, if desired |
| 1 c. water | Powdered sugar |
| 2 c. flour | 1 T. butter, melted |

*Cheese filling:*

| | |
|---|---|
| ½ lb. cottage cheese | Sugar |
| 2 egg yolks | Vanilla |
| 2 egg whites | 2 T. sour cream |
| ¼ c. raisins | |

Prepared in the same way as the nalesniki with jam, but instead of jam use cottage cheese mixed with 2 egg yolks, 2 T. of sour cream, raisins, sugar and the stifflly beaten egg whites. A drop of vanilla may be added. Spread on the nalesniki.

## Nalesniki with Cream

Batter for nalesniki, and prepare as above.

*Cream filling for 12 nalesniki:*

| | |
|---|---|
| 4 egg yolks | 3 T. sugar |
| 1 T. flour | 2 c. sweet cream |
| Vanilla | Grated lemon peel |

Mix egg yolks with sugar until they are light, then add flour. Dilute with sweet cream, beating constantly and place in a double boiler; cook and beat until it thickens. Take off the flame. Add a drop of vanilla, and some grated lemon peel. When cool spread on the nalesniki. Roll them as above.

## Polish Blinki with Potatoes

| | |
|---|---|
| 3 buns without crust | Salt |
| soaked in milk | 2 T. sour cream |
| 3 egg yolks | Butter or any fat |
| 3 egg whites | Milk, if necessary |
| 2 c. potatoes, grated | Sour cream |

Pass the squeezed buns through a sieve, and mix with 3 egg yolks, 2 T. of sour cream; add to this the grated potatoes, salt and the beaten whites of the eggs. Mix thoroughly. If it is too thick, add a little milk. Leave standing for about 3 hours. Then fry in very hot fat, pouring 1 T. for each blinka and browning it on both sides. Serve on a hot platter, with sour cream, if desired.

## Plum Knedle

| | |
|---|---|
| 4 c. raw potatoes, grated | Butter |
| 2½ c. flour | Bread-crumbs |
| 3 eggs | Sour cream |
| Plums (not too ripe) | 1 T. sugar to each plum |
| Salt | |

Drain the water of the grated potatoes. Add flour, a dash of salt and the eggs. Mix the ingredients well on a floured board, roll out the dough and cut circles about 2 inches in diameter. To prepare the plums, remove stones and put a spoonful of sugar in place of each stone. Place the plum in the centre of the circle of dough and fold over, so that it is completely folded in. Cook in a large amount of salted water for 10 minutes or until they float to the surface. Serve with melted butter with bread-crumbs sprinkled with powdered sugar. Sour cream may be served on the side.

## Plum Knedle II

| | |
|---|---|
| 4 c. flour | Warm milk |
| 2 egg yolks | ¼ c. of sugar |
| Plums | 3 T. butter |

Mix the flour with the beaten egg yolks, blend in as much luke-warm milk as the dough soaks up. Knead until firm and then cover with a plate for half an hour. Roll out flat and thin circles, cut with a glass. Wrap each plum, stone free, with this dough. Before serving, throw into boiling salted water and cook until they float. Drain and cover the knedle with melted butter and sugar.

## Knedle with Prunes

Prepared in the same way as plum knedle, but using prunes instead of plums.

## Knedle with Cheese Batter

| | |
|---|---|
| 2 c. of flour | Plums or apricots |
| 3 egg yolks | Powdered sugar |
| ¼ lb. cottage cheese | Sour cream |
| Salt | 3 T. butter |

Pass the cheese through the sieve. Add the flour, salt and egg yolks. Work into a dough. If it seems too thick add a drop of milk. Cut out the pieces, make round knedle, filled with plums or apricots (stone free). Cook in boiling water for 5 minutes or until they float. Take out. Pour melted butter on top of them. Sprinkle with powdered sugar and serve with sour cream.

## Knedle with Cherries

| | |
|---|---|
| 1 lb. cherries | 4 T. butter |
| 1 lb. flour | ¼ c. milk |
| 3 egg yolks | Powdered sugar |
| ¼ lb. bread-crumbs | |

Mix butter with egg yolks. Add bread-crumbs and milk, salt and flour. Make a soft dough. Take by spoonfuls on to a floured board and put a cherry inside. Fold the dough around to make a ball, and roll in flour. Cook in boiling water until they float. Serve with melted butter, sprinkled with sugar.

## Knedle made with Cream of Wheat

| | |
|---|---|
| ½ lb. cream of wheat | 4 eggs, separated |
| ½ c. milk | Salt |
| 1 lb. cottage cheese | 4 T. butter |
| 3 T. bread-crumbs | |

Mix the cream of wheat with milk, let it stand for an hour. Pass the cheese through the sieve, add the egg yolks and a dash of salt. Mix well together. Add the stiffly-beaten egg white and the cream of wheat, work into a smooth paste and cut out the round knedle. Cook in boiling water, until they float. Serve with butter melted with bread-crumbs.

### Knedle made with Cream of Wheat II

| | |
|---|---|
| 3 T. soft butter | 4 T. butter, melted |
| 4 eggs | 2 T. bread-crumbs |
| ½ lb. cottage cheese | ½ c. cream of wheat |

Beat the butter well, adding the egg yolk gradually. Combine with the cheese which has been previously passed through the sieve. When the paste is smooth enough, add the egg whites stiffly beaten, and also the cream of wheat. Mix. Make into an oblong form. Place in cheese cloth and cook in boiling water for 30 minutes. Remove the cheese cloth, pour on butter melted with bread-crumbs. Serve with prune preserve.

### Mamalyga or Corn Meal

| | |
|---|---|
| 1 lb. corn meal | 8 c. water, or more |
| Salt | Slices of bacon |
| 3 T. bacon fat | |

Bring the water to a boil, adding salt. Pour the corn meal in gradually, stirring constantly. Cook for 10 minutes. Add bacon fat. Put in an oven-proof dish. Cover with slices of bacon and bake in a hot oven for 15 minutes. Serve with cottage cheese or buttermilk.

### Prazuha

| | |
|---|---|
| 1 lb. wheat or whole wheat flour | Salt |
| 5 c. boiling water | 4 T. bacon fat |

Put the flour in a large frying pan and let it get brown. Stir continuously. Add slowly to boiling salted water. When the whole paste is smooth, put the pan into the oven for 15 minutes. Make round patties with a large spoon, which should be dipped each time in fat, and arrange on a platter. Serve with meat or with sugar and cinnamon, as a dessert.

### Buckwheat Groats or Kasza

| | |
|---|---|
| ½ c. dried mushrooms, diced | 2 bouillon cubes |
| 2 c. buckwheat groats | Salt |
| 2 T. butter | 5 c. water |

Cook the diced mushrooms in water. Remove. Cook the buckwheat groats in the boiling mushroom broth, for 10 minutes with the butter and bouillon cubes. Then bake the groats mixed with mushrooms in a moderate oven for 25 minutes.

### Buckwheat Pudding

| | |
|---|---|
| 1 lb. buckwheat flour | 1 T. salt |
| 2 T. bacon fat | ¼ lb. white flour |
| 2 c. water | Sour cream |
| 2 yeast cakes | |

Place the buckwheat flour in a bowl. Pour in hot fat. Mix well. Add the flour, yeast and salt. Add warm water and mix once more. Put in a warm place and let it rise. Cut down and place in a buttered pan. Let it rise again. Put in a hot oven and bake for 1 hour. Serve with sour cream.

### Buckwheat Dumplings with Cheese

| | |
|---|---|
| 3 c. buckwheat flour | 1 T. salt |
| 3 T. flour | ½ lb. cottage cheese |
| 1½ c. hot water | Butter |

Put the buckwheat flour in a frying pan, dry it well on a low flame. Take care not to brown it too much. Place in a bowl and add salt and hot water. Mix into a dough. Add white flour and mix some more. Add a drop of cold water. Bring a pan of salted water to the boil. Make dumplings with 2 spoons, forming balls, and cook for about 15 minutes in the water. Drain. Combine with cottage cheese. Pour on some melted butter and serve.

### Rice

| | |
|---|---|
| 1 c. rice | Salt |
| Butter | |

Place rice in a strainer and pour boiling water into it. Place in a baking dish. Add the butter and warm water to cover. Cover the dish tightly and bake in a moderate oven for about 25 minutes. Watch; adding some water every once in a while if needed, so that it does not dry up. When it is done each grain is separate and fluffy.

### Rice with Tomatoes

| | |
|---|---|
| 3-4 tomatoes | 1 c. stock (preferably meat) |
| 3 c. rice | Salt |
| 3 T. butter | 3 T. grated cheese, Parmesan |

Stew the tomatoes in butter and, when tender, strain through the sieve. Cook the rice until it is half done and mix with the tomatoes and salt. Sprinkle with Parmesan, cover and cook until tender on a low flame.

## Rice Cakes

| | |
|---|---|
| 2 c. rice | 3 T. butter |
| 2 eggs | 2 T. mushrooms, diced |
| Salt | Parsley, chopped |
| Bread-crumbs | Milk |
| 1 T. flour | 3 T. sour cream |

Cook the rice in milk until tender. Milk should cover the rice. Mix 1 T. of butter with 2 eggs. Add chopped mushrooms, salt, chopped parsley, and combine with the strained rice. Make patties and roll them in bread-crumbs. Fry in melted butter. On the side, prepare a mushroom sauce with the left-over mushroom broth; melt 1 T. of butter with flour and dilute with the mushroom broth. Add sour cream. Serve together.

## Risi-bisi (Rice with Peas)

| | |
|---|---|
| ½ lb. of young peas or frozen peas | 4 c. stock |
| | 3 T. grated cheese, Parmesan |
| Butter | 2 c. rice |

Stew the peas in butter. Cook the rice separately in stock (chicken or bouillon), until tender. Butter a baking dish or mould. Put the rice on the bottom and on the sides, and the peas in the middle. Bake in a moderate oven for about 15 minutes and sprinkle with Parmesan cheese and cover with lumps of butter.

## Rice with Honey and Poppy Seed

| | |
|---|---|
| 1¼ c. rice | ½ c. poppy seed |
| 2 T. sugar | ½ c. blanched almonds |
| ¼ c. raisins | 4 T. honey |

Cook the rice in water or milk. When it has cooled off, mix with poppy seed and honey. Add sugar, raisins and chopped almonds. When serving, sprinkle with raisins and almonds.

## Rice with Saffron

| | |
|---|---|
| 1½ c. rice | 4 c. milk |
| 3 T. butter | 1 jigger rum |
| 3 T. sugar | Dash of saffron |
| 2 squares baking chocolate | |

Cook the rice with milk. When ready divide in two parts. Mix 1 part with grated chocolate, the other with rum which has been mixed with saffron. Butter a baking dish generously and put in the rice in layers, first the black, then the yellow. Sprinkle with butter. Serve with raspberry preserve. Orange marmalade may be used instead. You may garnish the rice with whipped cream, or sour cream whipped with 2 T. of powdered sugar.

### Rice Crôquettes

| | |
|---|---|
| 3 c. rice | Milk or stock |
| 4 egg yolks | 3 T. butter |
| Bread-crumbs | 3 T. grated cheese, Parmesan |
| Salt | 1 section of garlic, squeezed |

Cook the rice in milk or in stock. Cool. Mix 1 T. of butter with 3 egg yolks, garlic and the grated Parmesan cheese and combine with the rice. Make oblong croquettes and roll them in bread-crumbs. Fry in melted butter until golden brown. Chopped browned mushrooms or other vegetables may be added to this recipe either to improve the flavour or to use left-overs in an appetizing manner.

### Pierogi with Yeast Dough

| | |
|---|---|
| 3 c. flour | 3 eggs, separated |
| ¼ c. warm water | Meat filling |
| ½ c. milk | 2 yeast cakes |
| 4 T. butter | Dash of salt |
| 2 T. sugar | |

Dissolve the yeast in the warm water. Add it to 2 c. of flour and milk. Cover with a towel and set aside to rise for about 1 hour. Beat the egg whites stiff. Mix the egg yolks with sugar and beat them well. Add melted butter. Salt. Fold in the egg whites. Mix with flour and yeast dough. Add 1 c. of flour and possibly more. Knead on floured board. Fill buttered muffin tins with balls of dough and set aside to rise for 1 hour. When double in bulk, insert the filling. Meat filling is the best (see p. 28). Bake in moderate oven for 30 minutes or until lightly browned.

### Paszteciki

| | |
|---|---|
| 1½ c. flour | ¼ lb. margarine or butter |
| 3 T. sour cream or buttermilk | Meat filling (see page 28) |

Mix the softened margarine with flour and buttermilk. Work the dough on a floured board. Roll out several times and fold in again. Place in a cold spot (in the refrigerator) until ready to use. Put meat filling on rolled out round patties, seal the ends, bake in a moderate oven for 30 minutes or until golden brown. Serve very hot. It is a delicious appetizer for an elegant dinner. You can substitute for this filling a piece of the Italian melting cheese, Mozzarella.

### Pierogi with Cheese and Potatoes

| | |
|---|---|
| 3½ c. flour | Margarine |
| 1 egg | Salt |
| 1 lb. cooked potatoes | Melted butter |
| ½ lb. cottage cheese | ¼ c. warm water |
| 1 small onion, chopped | Sour cream |

Make a dough with flour, warm water, egg and a dash of salt. Form a hole in the middle; add the other ingredients. If the dough is sticky add more flour. Roll out on a floured board until it is very thin and cut out round forms with a glass or biscuit cutter. Make the filling out of well-cooked, mashed potatoes, mixed with cottage cheese, salt, pepper and lightly browned onion. Place a T. of filling in each piece of dough and close the pierogi well, so that they do not open when boiling. Cook in boiling salted water for 5 minutes or until they float. Serve with melted butter and sour cream. The potato and cheese pierogi left-overs are delicious when fried after previously being boiled. Also serve with sour cream.

### Pierogi with Cheese and Sour Cream

Dough as for above recipe

Filling:
| | |
|---|---|
| 1 egg | ¾ lb. cottage cheese |
| 3 T. butter | 1 c. sour cream |
| Salt | |

Make a dough precisely as the one for the pierogi with potatoes and cheese. Pass the cottage cheese through the sieve, mix it with the eggs and salt. Fill the pierogi with cheese filling, taking care that only a small amount of cheese is put in each, as in cooking they rise. Cook for 5 minutes in boiling water. Serve with melted butter and sour cream.

### Pierogi with Cabbage

| | |
|---|---|
| Dough as for above recipe | 2 small heads of cabbage |
| Butter or margarine | Melted butter |
| 1 onion, chopped | Salt and pepper |
| 1 T. mushrooms, chopped | |

Shred the 2 heads of cabbage and boil in salted water, until they are partially cooked. Drain. Chop fine and steam in butter or margarine, in which you have browned an onion. Add mushrooms and some pepper. Fill the pierogi in the same manner as potato pierogi. Cook for 5 minutes in boiling, salted water and serve with melted butter and browned bread-crumbs.

### Pierogi with Blueberries

| | |
|---|---|
| Dough as above | 1 qt. blueberries |
| Sugar | Sour cream |
| Powdered sugar | |

Mix the blueberries with granulated sugar to taste and fill the pierogi. Cook for 5 minutes or until they float. Serve with powdered sugar and sour cream, beaten with sugar.

## Buckwheat Pierogi

| | |
|---|---|
| 1 c. buckwheat flour | Salt |
| 2 T. flour | 1 c. sour cream |
| 4 T. cottage cheese | 1 c. boiling water |
| 1 egg yolk | 4 T. butter |

Place the buckwheat flour in a bowl. Add salt and boiling water, mixing until a thick paste is formed. Add flour, a drop of cold water and work into a dough. Place on a floured board. Roll it out until it is moderately thin. Cut out round forms with a glass or biscuit cutter. Fill with the cheese, after mixing the cheese with a dash of salt and an egg yolk. Close up the ends, drop in boiling water and boil for 5 minutes or until they float. Serve with melted butter and sour cream.

## Pierogi with Buckwheat Groats

| | |
|---|---|
| 2 c. buckwheat flour | 2 c. water |
| 1 c. white flour | 1 egg |
| Salt | 2 c. cottage cheese |
| | Butter |
| | Sour cream |
| | Salted water |

Mix the buckwheat flour and the white flour in a pot. Place it on a slow fire and stir constantly, for about 3 minutes. Take off the flame. Season. Add 2 c. of boiling water—enough to make a dough which is not too thick. Roll out on a floured board, not too thin, cut out small pieces, fill with cheese, prepared with an egg. Seal the pierogi and cook in boiling water. When they are ready they will come to the surface. Drain. Pour on melted butter and serve with sour cream on the side.

## Ormian Pierogi

| | |
|---|---|
| 3 egg yolks | 2 c. flour |
| 4 T. butter, melted | ½ c. sour cream |
| 2 yeast cakes | 2 T. sugar |
| *Filling:* | |
| 1 egg | ¼ lb. cooked lamb |
| 3 T. bread-crumbs | ¼ lb. cooked ham |
| Butter | 1 onion |

Mix the butter with egg yolks, add salt, sour cream, sugar, beat well together. Beat the egg whites and add them to the mixture. Squash the yeast, dilute it with a drop of water. Combine with the eggs, finally add the flour. Work all the ingredients well together. Cover the dough and let it rise. Cut out small pieces, roll them out and fill with the meat filling. Turn into small rolls. Cut out of brown paper 3-4 inch squares of paper. Butter them, place each roll on a paper. Let them rise again. Place in a moderate oven and bake for 20 minutes. The meat filling you prepare in the following manner: mince the lamb and the ham. Brown the chopped onion in butter. Add the meat and sauté. Add bread-crumbs and sour cream, and fill the pierogi. A good variation might be to use, instead of ham, chopped mushrooms. The dry mushrooms are much tastier, but they must be soaked and pre-cooked before browning.

# MUSHROOMS

Mushroom picking or rather mushroom expeditions were a popular and frequent occupation of youth in Poland. It was like a social event: a group of young people would meet to go mushroom hunting, instead of going to a ball game. There is a great variety of mushrooms in the woods of Poland. The elders would teach the young to recognize which ones are edible and which ones to discard. At the end of an adventurous day in the woods many baskets full of mushrooms were brought home for fresh cooking or for drying for winter. The fame of the mushroom hunts is well depicted in Polish literature, for instance in "Pan Tadeusz" by Mickiewicz.

### Mushrooms with Butter

| 1 lb. mushrooms | Salt and pepper |
| Butter | 1 onion, minced |

Clean fresh mushrooms and separate the heads from the stems.
Slice fine and place in a pot with salt and pepper. Add 1 minced
onion and stew under cover, stirring occasionally, so they do not get
burned. When they give off their own juice, add a heaped T. of butter
and cook for another 5 minutes.

### Mushrooms Stewed in Sour Cream

Follow the recipe for the mushrooms with butter and 5 minutes before serving add 2 c. of sour cream mixed with 1 T. of flour.

### Mushrooms au Gratin

| 1½ lb. mushrooms | 4 T. grated cheese, Parmesan |
| 1 onion, chopped | 1 T. flour |
| Butter | 2 T. bread-crumbs |
| 2 c. sour cream | |

Peel very young and fresh mushrooms and separate the heads from
the stems. Stew whole in butter with chopped onion. Then, place
in a baking dish. Cover with 2 cups of sour cream mixed with 1 T.
of flour, 4 T. of grated Parmesan cheese. On top sprinkle about 2
T. of bread-crumbs. Place a few drops of butter on the surface. Then,
bake in a very hot oven for 30 minutes.

### Mushroom Pudding

| 1 lb. mushrooms | 1 onion |
| 2 c. milk | 4 eggs, separated |
| 3 T. butter, melted | 2 T. bread-crumbs |
| 2 T. grated cheese, Parmesan | Salt and pepper |
| ¼ bouillon cube | |

Clean, separate heads from stems and slice the mushrooms. Add
salt and pepper. Stew with chopped onion in butter. On the side, mix
2 c. of milk with 2 heaped T. of flour and pour in a pot with 1 T. of
melted butter. Stir until the sauce thickens and then take off the
flame. Add to it 4 well-beaten egg yolks, 2 T. of Parmesan and combine with the mushrooms. When the mixture has cooled off, add 4

beaten whites of eggs, $\frac{1}{2}$ t. of bouillon extract or 1 T. of dissolved bouillon cube. Place in a well greased baking tin, sprinkle with bread-crumbs. Bake in a moderate oven between 30 and 45 minutes. Test with a straw to see if it is done. Serve with melted butter.

## Mushroom Cutlets

| | |
|---|---|
| 1 lb. fresh mushrooms or | Salt and pepper |
| 2 cans mushrooms | 2 buns, soaked in milk |
| 1 onion | 2 eggs |
| 1 T. parsley, chopped | Bread-crumbs |
| Butter | Water |

Clean mushrooms and cook in water until they are tender. Drain. Reserving the water. Then pass them through a mincer with 2 buns soaked in milk and squeezed out. Grate I onion and sauté in butter. Combine with the mushrooms. Add salt and pepper and fry on a low flame. Take off the fire and add 2 well-beaten eggs and chopped parsley. Form oblong cutlets, roll in bread-crumbs. Fry in butter. Serve with mushroom sauce or potatoes cooked in the left-over mushroom stock.

## Stuffed Mushrooms

| | |
|---|---|
| 1 lb. large fresh mushrooms | 2 T. chopped dill or parsley |
| $\frac{1}{4}$ lb. small mushrooms | 1 piece baked ham |
| Butter | Water |
| 2 T. bread-crumbs | Salt and pepper |
| 1 onion, chopped | |

*Filling:*

| | |
|---|---|
| 1 egg | 2 T. butter |
| 2 T. bread-crumbs | |

Separate the heads from the stems of the mushrooms. Chop the stems with the small mushrooms. Add 1 chopped and sautéd onion. Add some chopped dill or parsley, 2 T. of bread-crumbs, and a piece of baked ham which has been minced, salt and pepper. Cook the large mushrooms for a few minutes in salted water. Drain off the water and fill. The filling consists of 1 egg 2 T. of bread-crumbs and 2 T. of melted butter. Mix these ingredients well. Combine with chopped mushroom mixture. Fill the mushroom heads and bake in the oven until golden brown. Serve with meats as a vegetable or separately with a dill sauce (see p. 96). Boiled potatoes are delicious with the stuffed mushrooms.

### Mushrooms with Sour Cream and Eggs

| | |
|---|---|
| 1 lb. mushrooms | Chopped dill |
| Butter | Salt and pepper |
| 1 c. sour cream | 1 bouillon cube |
| 1 onion, chopped | 2 eggs, separated |

Sauté a well chopped onion. Add finely chopped mushrooms, and simmer until tender. Season to taste. Add sour cream and 2 beaten egg yolks. When ready to serve, fold in egg whites stiffly beaten and sprinkle with dill. Serve with boiled potatoes.

### Mushroom Patties

| | |
|---|---|
| 1 lb. mushrooms | Parsley, chopped |
| 2 onions, chopped | Bread-crumbs |
| 2 T. butter | Flour |
| 2 T. flour | 2 eggs, beaten |
| ½ c. cream | Fat |
| 2 egg yolks | |

Clean and wash the mushrooms. Sauté the onions with chopped mushrooms and parsley. Season. Make a thick white sauce with butter, flour and cream and combine with mushrooms. Simmer together for a few minutes. Cool. Add egg yolks one by one. With large spoon scoop out mushroom mixture and roll in flour, then in egg and bread-crumbs and fry in hot fat.

### Dried Mushroom Cutlets

| | |
|---|---|
| ¼ lb. dried mushrooms | 2 eggs |
| 2 buns, soaked, squeezed | 2 T. parsley, chopped |
| 1 onion, grated | Bread-crumbs |
| Salt and pepper | Butter |

Cook dried mushrooms until tender. Pass through mincer together with squeezed buns. Stew grated onion in butter, add to the mushroom mixture. Season. Simmer together for 5 minutes on a low flame. Cool. When completely cooled off add eggs and parsley. Form cutlets, roll in bread-crumbs and fry in butter. Serve with any strong flavoured sauce.

### Purée of Mushrooms

| | |
|---|---|
| 1 lb. mushrooms | ½ c. sweet cream |
| 1 onion, grated | 3 egg yolks |
| 1 lemon, juice | Butter |
| ¼ T. flour | Salt and pepper |

Wash and clean the mushrooms. Take off the skin. Slice. Sprinkle with lemon juice. Stew in butter with onion. Season. When tender pass through a strainer. Mix flour with cream and combine with mushrooms purée. Simmer together. Cool and fold in egg yolks.

### Marinated Mushrooms

| | |
|---|---|
| 2 lb. mushroom heads | Peppercorns |
| 5 onions, sliced | 3 bay leaves |
| 1 c. water | Salt |
| 2 c. vinegar | |

Simmer mushroom heads with onion in water. When tender add vinegar and all the spices and boil together for a few minutes. Cool off. Conserve in glass jars.

# VEGETABLES

Cabbage in all its forms is one of the oldest traditional foods in Poland. Bigos, the Polish cabbage and sausage stew, was always eaten after hunting and during cold winter evenings. Potatoes, especially boiled and garnished with fresh dill are also traditional in their daily use. During winter with hot barshch, during summer with a bowl of buttermilk.

## Eggplant Stewed in Butter

| | |
|---|---|
| 1 large eggplant | Paprika |
| Butter | Salt and pepper |

Slice eggplant in small pieces and stew in butter until soft. Season with salt, pepper and paprika.

## Eggplant 'à la Provençale'

| | |
|---|---|
| 6 small eggplants | Water |
| 1 onion, chopped | 2 egg yolks |
| Olive oil | 1 T. dill |
| 1 T. parsley, chopped | 4 T. bread-crumbs |

Cut off the tops of the eggplants. Scoop out the meat from the inside and cook it in salted water. Chop the onion together with the strained eggplant meat and sauté in olive oil. Add 2 T. of bread-crumbs, the chopped parsley, dill, salt and pepper. Mix well. Take off the flame and add 2 well-beaten egg yolks. Stuff the eggplant skins with the mixture, cover with the cut-off tops and place in the oven, in a greased baking dish. Sprinkle with the remaining bread-crumbs and olive oil. Bake in a moderate oven for 45 minutes.

## Stuffed Eggplant

| | |
|---|---|
| 6 small eggplants | 1 onion, chopped |
| Olive oil | 4 T. bread-crumbs |
| 2 c. Béchamel sauce | 2 egg yolks |
| (see page 96) | Grated cheese, optional |
| 4 pieces bacon, chopped and broiled | 1 t. chopped parsley |

Cut the eggplants in half. Scoop out all the meat from the inside and chop fine. Brown the chopped onion. Sauté the eggplant meat with the onion. Add parsley. Season to taste. Combine with béchamel sauce and bacon. Add well-beaten egg yolks. Mix well. Stuff the eggplant skins again. Place in a greased baking dish. Sprinkle with bread-crumbs and olive oil. Bake in a moderate oven for 45 minutes. You may add grated cheese before baking if you like the taste of cheese.

## Scooped out Turnips or Turnip Balls

| | |
|---|---|
| Turnips | 4 T. stock |
| Butter | 1 T. flour |
| Salted water | |

Peel the turnips and with a butter-ball spoon scoop out little round balls of turnip. Cook in salted water until tender. Then sauté in melted butter. Cover them with flour and sauté lightly again. Then add a few spoons of broth and serve.

### Stewed Shallots

| | |
|---|---|
| 1 lb. shallots | Salt and pepper |
| 2 c. stock | ¼ c. white wine (optional) |
| Butter | 1 bouillon cube |
| Flour | |

Peel the shallots. Cook in stock. Drain and reserve the broth. Brown in butter. Sprinkle with flour. Sauté lightly. Then, pour over the broth in which they were cooked. Add white wine, if desired, and a bouillon cube.

### Beets with Sour Cream

| | |
|---|---|
| 6 large beets cooked or 1 large | Dash of salt |
| can of beets | 1 T. flour |
| 1 T. sugar | 3 T. butter |
| 1 t. caraway seed | 1 T. vinegar |
| ¼ c. sour cream | |

Grate the beets. Melt butter. Add flour slowly. Let it boil for 1 minute. Add vinegar, salt and sugar, and finally caraway seeds. Add the beets and let them cook together for 5 minutes. Add sour cream and serve.

### Purée of Beets and Apples

| | |
|---|---|
| 5-6 large beets | Sugar |
| 4 sour apples | Salt and pepper |
| Juice of ¼ lemon | 1 T. flour |
| 2 T. sour cream | |

Peel the beets and the apples and grate on a large grater. Then place them in a pot with their own juice and salt and pepper. Add lemon juice and sugar to taste. Simmer for 20 minutes. Then add sour cream mixed with flour. Serve to garnish meats.

### Beets with Lemon Juice

| | |
|---|---|
| 1 can beets | 1 T. flour |
| 2 T. butter | Salt |
| Juice of 1 lemon | |

Grate the beets. Melt the butter with flour. Brown it slightly. Add the grated beets. Add the lemon juice. Warm thoroughly. Season to taste and serve.

### Beet Salad with Tomatoes

| | |
|---|---|
| 1 can beets | Olive oil |
| 4 fresh tomatoes | Salt and pepper |
| 4 scallions | Tarragon vinegar |
| Garlic salt | |

Slice the beets and tomatoes. Add finely chopped scallions. Mix in with all the seasonings, vinegar and olive oil according to taste.

### String Beans with Sour Cream

| | |
|---|---|
| 1 lb. cooked string beans | Juice of 1 lemon or 2 T. vinegar |
| 1 T. butter | Salt and pepper |
| 1 c. sour cream | 1 T. flour |

Cut the cooked string beans. Season. Add butter. Pour over the sour cream which has previously been beaten with flour, and finally add lemon juice or vinegar. Warm together and serve.

### Cauliflower with Bread-crumbs

| | |
|---|---|
| 1 cauliflower | 3 T. butter |
| Bread-crumbs | |

Cook the cauliflower. Place on a platter. Melt the butter with bread-crumbs, brown them lightly, and pour over the cauliflower.

### Cauliflower with Cheese

| | |
|---|---|
| 1 cauliflower | 1 c. Béchamel sauce |
| 4 T. crated cheese | (see page 96) |
| Salt | 4 T. butter |

Cook the cauliflower. Place in a greased baking dish. Cover with béchamel sauce and grated cheese. Place in a moderate oven and bake for 30 minutes.

### Cauliflower with Anchovies

| | |
|---|---|
| 1 cauliflower | 1 T. chopped parsley |
| 1 c. Béchamel sauce | Salt and pepper |
| (see page 96) | 6 filllets anchovy, chopped |
| 4 T. grated cheese | 2 T. butter |
| 2 slices of American type cheese | |

Cook the cauliflower. Put in a casserole. Mix the béchamel sauce with grated cheese, salt and pepper. Cut anchovies, and pour the mixture over the cauliflower. Cover with diced American cheese and melted butter and bake in a moderate oven for 30 minutes.

### Cauliflower 'au gratin'

| | |
|---|---|
| 1 large cauliflower | Grated cheese, Parmesan |
| Béchamel sauce | Bread-crumbs |
| (see page 96) | Butter |
| Salt | |

Cook cauliflower in salted water until tender. Place face up on a greased baking dish. Pour over it béchamel sauce, approximately 1 c., a good quantity of grated parmesan cheese (about 4 T.) and sprinkle with bread-crumbs. Place a few pats of butter on top. Bake for 20 minutes in a very hot oven.

## Pumpkin

1 lb. pumpkin
2 T. sugar
2⅔ c. milk

Salt
1 T. cinnamon
2 T. butter

Peel and cut the pumkin into small pieces. Cook in milk with all the other ingredients. Mash and serve.

## Stewed Pumpkin

1-2 lb. pumpkin
Butter
Salt

Parsley, chopped
Sugar

Slice the pumpkin in thin slices, cook twice, changing water. Then, place in pan and stew under a cover in butter, with a dash of sugar, salt and chopped parsley.

## Cabbage, Polish Style

1 head cabbage
3 T. cider vinegar
Pork fat
1 T. flour

Sugar (optional)
Water
1 onion, chopped
1 T. butter

Shred the cabbage, salt and leave standing for an hour, so that it gives off water. Squeeze the cabbage well. Place in a pot and cover with cold water. Add vinegar and cook until tender. Fry a piece of pork fat. Chop and add to cabbage. Simmer together for a few minutes. On the side sauté the chopped onion with flour and butter and dilute with the juice of the cabbage. Serve this sauce over the cabbage.

### Cabbage with Apples

Follow recipe of Cabbage Polish Style and add 4 peeled and diced sour apples. Simmer together.

### Cabbage with Tomatoes

Follow the recipe for cabbage with apples and add 4 sautéd tomatoes. Cook until the flavours are well-blended.

### Sauerkraut with Sour Cream

1 lb. sauerkraut
1 onion
Butter

2 c. sour cream
1 T. flour

Brown 1 chopped onion. Add to the sauerkraut and let it simmer 10-15 minutes adding butter and the sour cream, mixed with the flour.

## Sweet Cabbage

| | |
|---|---|
| 2 heads cabbage | ½ T. soya sauce |
| ¼ c. stock or more | ¼ lb. pork fat |
| ½ T. flour | Salt and pepper |

Cut cabbage in quarters. Soak them in salted water for 10 minutes. Drain well. Place in a pot with a small piece of pork fat. Add ½ c. of stock and stew under cover, for 2 hours, adding stock if necessary. Before serving prepare a sauce of soya sauce and browned flour. Pour over the cabbage and serve.

## Sweet Cabbage with Caraway Seeds

| | |
|---|---|
| 2 heads cabbages | 1 T. melted butter |
| 1 onion, chopped | 3 T. stock |
| 2 t. caraway seeds | Salt and pepper |
| 1 T. flour | 1 t. soya sauce |

Cut the cabbage in chunks and cook in salted water for 10 minutes. Drain and sauté in pork fat with finely chopped onion. Add the stock, salt and pepper. Stew under cover until tender. Before serving, add sauce made from 1 T. of butter, 1 T. of flour and soya sauce. The caraway seeds may be added together with the soya sauce or, if a stronger flavour is preferred, just in the midst of sautéing.

## 'Golabki' from Sweet Cabbage

| | |
|---|---|
| 2 heads cabbage | ½ T. flour |
| 2 c. rice | 1 onion |
| 1 c. or more ready-made barshch | 4 T. butter |
| 2 c. sour cream | Mushroom sauce |
| 3 cans mushrooms or 1 lb. dried mushrooms | optional (see page 97) |

Cut the cabbages in half and cook in salted water. Drain and separate the leaves. Cook the rice. Brown onion and mushrooms in butter. Add salt and pepper and combine with rice. Wrap the rice mixture in the individual cabbage leaves. Place the rolled stuffed cabbage leaves one next to the other on a baking dish. Pour over them barshch and 2 T. of butter. Cover and bake in the oven under cover until they are tender. This may be simmered slowly on top of the stove also. Prepare a sauce from flour and 1 T. of butter. Dilute with more warm barshch and add sour cream. Pour over and warm before serving. Mushroom sauce may be used instead of butter and flour roux.

## 'Golabki' with Meat

Follow recipe I. Golabki can be made with a meat stuffing. Minced pork may be used instead of mushrooms in the above recipe.

## Potato Pancakes

| | |
|---|---|
| 8 large potatoes | 1 large grated onion |
| 2 eggs | Salt and pepper |
| 2 T. flour | Fat |
| Sour cream | |

Grate the peeled potatoes. Add onion, seasoning, flour and the eggs. Mix all the ingredients well. Drop with a wooden spoon into hot fat, counting 2 T. for each pancake. Fry on both sides, taking care that they are crisp. Serve immediately with sour cream.

## Potato Crôquettes

| | |
|---|---|
| 2 c. mashed potatoes | Chopped dill and parsley |
| 4 eggs | Bread-crumbs |
| Salt and pepper | Flour |

Add chopped dill, parsley, salt and pepper, 3 beaten eggs to the potato purée. Mix well. Shape into oblong forms. Dip in flour and in 1 beaten egg. Sprinkle with bread-crumbs. Fry in fat until golden brown.

## Potato Croquettes with Mushrooms

Follow the recipe for potato croquettes, adding 2 T. of chopped and cooked mushrooms. Chopped onion is optional. Fry in fat until golden brown.

## Potato Biscuits

| | |
|---|---|
| 10 potatoes, cooked | Salt and pepper |
| 2 T. butter | Flour |
| 3 T. grated cheese | Parsley or dill, chopped |
| 3 eggs, separated | 2 T. sour cream |

Pass the cooked potatoes through a vegetable strainer. Beat 1 T. of butter with the 3 egg yolks. Add this mixture to the potatoes. Sprinkle with grated cheese and parsley. Mix in the sour cream, salt and pepper, and finally the egg whites stiffly beaten. Butter muffin tins or any biscuit tins. Fill with the potato mixture and bake for 15 minutes in a hot oven. Serve with mushroom sauce (see p. 97).

### Potatoes Stuffed with Meat

| | |
|---|---|
| 4 potatoes | 1 onion, chopped |
| 2 hard-boiled eggs | Salt and pepper |
| ¼ lb. minced meat (raw) | Butter |
| 2 T. sour cream | |

Peel the potatoes. Cut off the top. Scoop out the insides with a spoon. Fry the meat with chopped onion. Add the chopped hard-boiled eggs and sour cream, season and stuff the potatoes. Salt the potatoes on the outside. Cover with the tops that had been cut off. Place side by side in a greased pan and bake in a very hot oven, basting often with butter. Bake until golden brown. Serve with mushroom sauce (see p. 97), a tomato sauce (see p. 99) or as desired.

### Potatoes Stuffed with Mushrooms

| | |
|---|---|
| 4 potatoes | Salt and pepper |
| 2 hard-boiled eggs | 1 onion, chopped |
| 2 T. mushrooms, chopped | Butter |
| 1 T. parsley, chopped | Breadcrumbs |

Bake the potatoes. When tender, cut them in half length-wise. Scoop out the inside. Mash it together with sautéd mushrooms and onion, chopped eggs and parsley. Season. Refill the potato shells. Sprinkle them with bread-crumbs. Cover with melted butter and bake for 15 minutes in a hot oven.

### Potatoes Stuffed with Parmesan Cheese

| | |
|---|---|
| 4 potatoes | Butter |
| 4 T. sour cream | Salt and pepper |
| 2 egg yolks | Paprika |
| 3 T. grated cheese, Parmesan | |

You can use the recipe for potatoes stuffed with mushrooms, but instead of mushrooms, combine the potatoes with grated cheese, sour cream and egg yolks. When ready to serve, sprinkle with paprika.

### Potatoes Stewed with Sour Cream

| | |
|---|---|
| 2 lb. potatoes | 4 T. sour cream |
| 2 onions | Salt and pepper |
| 1 T. chopped parsley | |

Peel and slice the potatoes. Scald them with boiling water. Place them with chopped onions and butter in a baking dish. Add parsley and the sour cream. Season and cook under cover in a hot oven until they are soft.

### Baked Potatoes with Hard-boiled Eggs and Sour Cream

| | |
|---|---|
| 8 potatoes | 4 hard-boiled eggs |
| Butter | Flour |
| 4 T. sour cream | Seasoning |

Cook the peeled potatoes. When they are cold, slice. Also slice the hard-boiled eggs. Grease a pan with butter, sprinkle with flour and place the slices of potatoes and eggs in the pan. Pour over 1 T. of butter and 4 T. of sour cream. Cover and bake in a very hot oven for about 30 minutes.

### Potatoes in the American Style with Anchovies

| | |
|---|---|
| 6 potatoes | 6 fillets of anchovy |
| 1 T. butter | 2 hard-boiled egg (optional) |
| Juice of 1 lemon | 2 c. sour cream |
| $\frac{1}{2}$ T. flour | Capers (optional) |

Melt butter and blend in flour. Dilute with 2 c. of sour cream. Add lemon juice to taste and finely chopped anchovies. Slice and place peeled, half-cooked potatoes in a buttered baking dish. The addition of chopped hard-boiled eggs with some capers is optional. Pour the hot sauce over the potatoes. Place in a very hot oven for 15 minutes. It makes a very fine Lenten dish.

### Potato Patties

| | |
|---|---|
| 2 lb. potatoes | Flour |
| 3 eggs | Fat |
| Salt and pepper | |

Pass cooked potatoes through a vegetable strainer. Add 2 beaten eggs, salt and pepper. Shape them into round patties. Roll them in the remaining egg and flour, then fry. Serve with mushroom, (see p. 97), tomato (see p. 99), or caper sauce (see p. 96).

### Brigand Noodles from Raw Potatoes

| | |
|---|---|
| 6 large potatoes | Milk |
| 2 slices white bread | 1 T. butter |
| 2 egg yolks | Salt and pepper |

Peel and grate the raw potatoes. Drain them in a piece of cheese cloth or paper towels. Squeeze all the water out. Remove and place in a bowl. Soak bread slices in milk and stir into potato mixture. Add salt and pepper. Beat egg yolks with butter and add to the potatoes. Make dumplings with a spoon and drop into boiling salted water. Let them cook for 10 minutes. Drain them and serve with a roast.

### Potato Noodles

| | |
|---|---|
| 10 medium potatoes | Salt and pepper |
| 1 T. butter | Buttered bread-crumbs |
| 2 eggs, beaten | ½ lb. cottage cheese |
| Flour | 2 T. milk |

Mash the cooked potatoes with butter and eggs. Add cheese, salt and pepper. Dilute with milk. Mix well. Place the dough on a floured board. Roll it out, making small squares or circles. Cook in boiling salted water for a few minutes. Drain and serve with buttered bread-crumbs.

### Potato Cakes

| | |
|---|---|
| 10 potatoes | Fat |
| 1 T. butter | 3 T. sugar |
| 3 egg yolks | 3 stiffly beaten egg whites |
| 2 T. sour cream | Powdered sugar |

Mash the cooked potatoes. When they cool off, add the butter, sour cream, egg yolks, sugar and finally fold in beaten egg whites. Mix lightly. Make round patties. Fry. Serve covered with powdered sugar.

### Spinach with Sour Cream

| | |
|---|---|
| 2 lb. spinach | 2 eggs, beaten |
| 1 c. sour cream | 1 small onion |
| 3-4 T. grated cheese | Salt and pepper |

Clean and cook the spinach briefly. Drain. Chop it fine. Brown the onion lightly. Add the spinach and simmer for 2 minutes. Add the sour cream, salt and pepper and let it cook on a low flame for 5 minutes. Add the grated cheese and the well-beaten eggs and serve.

### Spinach Patties

| | |
|---|---|
| 2 lb. spinach | ½ c. bread-crumbs |
| 2 eggs, beaten | Salt and pepper |
| 1 T. butter | Fat |

Cook the spinach. Drain and chop it fine. Add bread-crumbs, eggs and butter. Season. Mix well. Make round patties, roll in bread-crumbs and fry.

## Spinach with Parmesan

| | |
|---|---|
| 2 lb. spinach | 1 egg white, optional |
| 5 T. grated cheese, Parmesan | Olive oil |
| 2 sections garlic | Salt and pepper |
| Bread-crumbs | |

Clean and cook the spinach in salted water. Strain. Chop and place in a pan with olive oil and garlic. Let simmer under cover for 5 minutes. Add grated cheese. Season to taste and serve. This may also be finished in the oven by placing in a baking dish and topping with cheese, bread-crumbs and beaten egg white.

## Spinach Soufflé

| | |
|---|---|
| 2 lb. spinach | 4 T. grated cheese, Parmesan |
| 2 c. Béchamal sauce | Salt and pepper |
| (see page 96) | Bread-crumbs |
| 2 eggs, separated | 1 onion, chopped |
| Butter | |

Clean and cook the spinach. Chop it well after straining. Brown the onion with butter. Add the spinach and sauté them on a low flame for 5 minutes. Mix with 2 c. of warm béchamel sauce. Add egg yolks and grated cheese. Finally fold in the remaining egg whites, stiffly beaten. Place in a greased baking dish or pudding tin. (Smear the tin with butter and sprinkle it with bread-crumbs). Cover the spinach with bread-crumbs and cook in moderate oven for 30 minutes, or in a double boiler for 1 hour. When ready, take out of the tin and serve immediately with ragout or a thick mushroom sauce (see p. 97).

## Green Peas à la Marseillese

| | |
|---|---|
| 2 cans peas or 2 lb. frozen, | 2 T. chopped parsley |
| cooked peas | 4 T. olive oil |
| 3 garlic sections | 2 bouillon cubes |
| Salt and pepper | |

Drain peas and mix the ingredients. Cook on low flame for 10 minutes. Serve.

## Green Peas with Mushrooms

| | |
|---|---|
| 2 cans peas or 2 lb. frozen | Salt and pepper |
| peas, cooked | 1 chopped onion, optional |
| 3 T. butter | 1 c. mushrooms |

Sauté the mushrooms in butter. If you like a stronger flavour add 1 chopped, slightly browned onion. Add peas and seasoning. Let simmer under cover for 10 minutes. Serve.

### Carrots in Batter

Carrots                                      Batter (see Haddock in Batter,
                                                  page 41)

Slice the carrots thin, cook them in salted water until tender and
dip them in batter and fry.

### Purée of Carrots

10 large carrots                             1 T. sugar
2 T. butter                                  Salt
4 T. sweet cream

Cook the carrots in a little salted water. When very soft, mash them,
adding the butter, sweet cream and sugar.

### Soufflé of Carrots

10 large carrots                             5 eggs, separated
2 T. butter                                  4 T. sweet cream
1 T. sugar                                   Salt

Prepare purée of carrots as in the previous recipe. Add 5 egg yolks
and mix well. Fold in 5 egg whites stiffly beaten. Mix carefully. Place
in a greased baking dish and bake in moderate oven for 25 minutes.

### Sautéed Carrots with Peas

3 c. raw carrots, diced                      ½ c. water
2 c. raw or frozen peas                      Sugar
3 T. butter                                  Salt and pepper
1 T. flour

Sauté cut carrots with peas in butter, adding peas only when the
carrots are tender. Combine with salt and sugar and ½ c. of water.
Cook under cover until tender. Stir in 1 T. of flour. Simmer for a
few minutes and serve.

### Brussels Sprouts

1 lb. Brussels sprouts                       Salt and pepper
2 T. butter                                  2 T. bread-crumbs

Soak the brussels sprouts in salted water for 30 minutes. Drain well
and wash again. Place in boiling water and cook until tender. Drain
the water off and season. Brown the bread-crumbs in butter and pour
them over the brussels sprouts.

### Stuffed Cucumbers

5 cucumbers                                  ½ c. mushrooms
1 onion, chopped                             1 egg
¼ lb. chopped meat                           Butter
Bread-crumbs                                 Salt and pepper

Cut the cucumbers lengthwise. Scoop out the seedy sections. Sauté
the onion with mushrooms, adding the meat and 1 egg. Mix well.

Fill the cucumbers and place them in a greased baking dish. Cover them with bread-crumbs and bake in a 350° oven for 30 minutes.

### Stuffed Squash

You can use the preceding recipe for zucchini and yellow summer squash.

### Chick Peas

| | |
|---|---|
| 1 can chick peas | Olive oil |
| Salt and pepper | |

Drain and season the chick peas well with salt and pepper. Add olive oil and mix. Serve cold.

### White Beans or Fasola

| | |
|---|---|
| 2 c. white dried beans | 5 T. bean water |
| 1 onion | 1 t. baking soda |
| 1 T. butter | 3 T. vinegar |
| 1 T. flour | |

Soak the beans overnight. Cook them well in water to cover, adding salt and 1 t. of baking soda. Sauté chopped onion in butter and brown slightly. Dilute with warm bean water. Add the cooked and strained beans. Add vinegar and simmer together for 10 minutes.

### Red Cabbage with Caraway Seeds

| | |
|---|---|
| 1 head red cabbage | Salt and pepper |
| 1 t. caraway seed | Lemon juice or vinegar |
| 4 T. butter | |

Grate the cabbage. Scald it with boiling water and drain. Let it stand covered liberally with salt for 1 hour. Simmer it under cover in butter and caraway seed. When tender, add lemon juice or vinegar to taste and serve.

### Asparagus

| | |
|---|---|
| 1 lb. asparagus | Salt |
| 3 T. butter | 2 T. bread-crumbs |

Break off the tough end of the asparagus. Clean top. Cook in boiling salted water until tender but do not over-cook. Carefully drain and place in serving dish. Brown the bread-crumbs in butter and pour over the asparagus.

### Asparagus with Grated Cheese

| | |
|---|---|
| 1 lb. asparagus. | 3 T. grated cheese |
| 3 T. butter | Salt |

Prepare as the previous recipe with the only difference in the use of grated cheese instead of bread-crumbs.

## Asparagus with Sour Cream

| | |
|---|---|
| 1 c. sour cream | 1 lb. cooked asparagus |
| Butter | Salt |
| Bread-crumbs | |

Arrange the cooked asparagus in a baking dish. Pour over them the sour cream and sprinkle with bread-crumbs. Add chunks of butter on top and bake for 20 minutes in a moderate oven.

## Artichokes Boiled

| | |
|---|---|
| Artichokes | Vinegar, optional |
| Salt | Butter, melted |
| Garlic, pressed | |

Boil the artichokes in salted water, drain and serve on plates with individual bowls of melted butter, which you may mix with pressed garlic. If you like a stronger taste, add a drop of vinegar to the butter. Dip each leaf separately in the butter.

## Stewed Artichokes

| | |
|---|---|
| 6 artichokes | 1 onion, chopped |
| 3 garlic sections | Salt and pepper |
| Olive oil | 1 t. rosemary |

Quarter the artichokes. Cut off the tops and clean the insides. Boil the quarters in salted water until half-done. In the meanwhile sauté the onion with garlic in olive oil. Add the rosemary (fresh, if possible, but dried will do.) Place the half-cooked artichokes in a pan with the rest of the ingredients and stew under cover for 30 minutes.

## Artichokes with Wine

| | |
|---|---|
| 6 artichokes | Salt and pepper |
| 2 T. butter | ½ c. white wine |

Half-boil the quartered and cleaned artichokes. Place them in a pot with butter, wine and seasoning. Stew under cover until tender. Serve in the liquid.

## Stuffed Artichokes

| | |
|---|---|
| 6 artichokes | 2 T. Bread-crumbs |
| 4 T. tuna fish | 3 T. grated cheese, Parmesan |
| Salt and pepper | 2 eggs |
| 2 T. butter | |

Cut off the tops of the artichokes and the outer leaves. Half-boil them in salted water. Carefully open the leaves to reach the bottom. Scoop out the hairy part of the vegetable and fill with the tuna fish which has been prepared in the following way: Pass the tuna fish through the sieve, mix with the bread-crumbs and the eggs. Add the seasoning and the grated cheese. Place the filled artichokes on a buttered baking dish and bake them for 30 minutes in a moderate oven.

### Stuffed Peppers

| | |
|---|---|
| 6-8 green peppers | Butter |
| ½ lb. chopped meat | 1 T. tomato paste |
| 1 c. cooked rice | Salt and pepper |
| 1 chopped onion | 1 t. basil (optional) |

Clean the peppers, cutting off the top and taking out the inside. Half-boil them and drain. Make the filling by combining the rice with the meat, sauté with onion and butter, and tomato paste. Season it well. Fill the peppers. Place in a greased baking dish and bake for 20 minutes in a moderate oven.

### Stuffed Tomatoes

| | |
|---|---|
| 7 tomatoes | 3 slices white bread soaked in |
| Garlic | vinegar |
| Parsley, chopped | 2 T. grated cheese |
| Basil | Salt and pepper |
| Olive oil | |

Cut the tomatoes in half. Take out all the seed, and reserve. Chop the bread with garlic and parsley until very fine. Season it with salt and pepper and basil. Add grated cheese. Pass the seeds and juice through a sieve. Fill the tomatoes with the bread and garlic mixture, cover with strained tomato juice. Put in a buttered baking dish. Cover them with bread-crumbs and sprinkle with olive oil. Bake in a moderate oven for 30 minutes.

### Tomatoes in Batter

| | |
|---|---|
| 8 medium tomatoes | Salt and pepper |
| 1 T. dill | Fat |
| 1 T. parsley, chopped | Batter (see page 41) |

Slice the tomatoes, draining all the seeds and water out of them. Season the slices with salt and pepper. Cover with chopped dill and parsley and dip in thick batter. Fry in hot fat and serve as soon as ready.

### Tomatoes with Meat Filling

| | |
|---|---|
| 8 tomatoes | 3 T. bread-crumbs |
| ½ lb. chopped meat | 1 T. chive |
| 1 small onion | 1 egg |
| 1 T. dill or parsley | Salt and pepper |

Scoop inside out of tomatoes. Prepare the filling in the following manner: Brown the chopped onion with the meat. Season. Sprinkle with parsley, dill and chives. Add bread-crumbs and egg. Fill the tomatoes. Place in a moderate oven for 30 minutes.

### Stuffed Tomatoes with Sour Cream

8 tomatoes
½ lb. chopped meat
1 onion, chopped
1 T. dill or parsley
3 T. grated cheese, Parmesan

1 t. chive
2 c. sour cream
1 T. soya bean sauce
3 T. cooked rice

Prepare as previous recipe with the following change: instead of bread-crumbs use 3 T. of cooked rice and add 3 T. of Parmesan. Before placing in the oven, beat well 2 c. of sour cream and the soya sauce and pour over the tomatoes. Bake in a moderate oven for about 30 minutes.

### Celery in Batter

Cooked celery
Fat

Batter (see page 41)

Cut cooked celery in slices. Dip the pieces in batter and fry in very hot fat.

### Celery Stewed in Wine

Celery
2 T. butter
¼ c. white wine
Salt and pepper

1 c. stock
Paprika
¼ T. flour

Cut round balls out of the celery with a butter scoop, (or use chunks of celery). Scald them with boiling water. Place in a pot. Season. Add stock and white wine and simmer under cover until tender. On the side, mix butter with flour and add to the celery. Before serving, sprinkle with paprika for colour effect.

# SALADS

Not a long time ago, but certainly before the value of proper food balance and the importance of vitamins were as widely discussed as today, a young Polish nobleman went to France for a supposedly lengthy sojourn. He returned to Poland much before the fixed date. Upon questioning, he admitted that the Frenchmen were feeding him "grass," much to his dislike and he was obliged to come back sooner, to more hearty food. However, the "grass" is quite popular now in Poland and Poles acquired, maybe later than the Frenchmen, the habit of eating salads with their meals.

### Polish Style Salad with Sour Cream

| | |
|---|---|
| 2 heads lettuce | 2 to 3 hard-boiled eggs |
| 1 t. sugar | Juice of 1 lemon |
| 1 c. sour cream | Salt |

Seperate the leaves of lettuce and wash well. Grate 1 or 2 egg yolks and mix 1 t. of sugar. Add lemon juice and sour cream. Salt the lettuce and pour the dressing over it. Cut the remaining eggs in chunks and use to garnish the salad.

### Salad with Olive Oil

| | |
|---|---|
| 1 head lettuce | Juice of 1 lemon |
| Salt | 4 T. olive oil |
| 2 hard-boiled eggs | |

Wash and separate the lettuce. Sprinkle with lemon, salt, and pour over olive oil. Garnish with chunks of eggs.

### Scalded Salad with Bacon

| | |
|---|---|
| 1 head lettuce | 6 pieces of bacon |
| Juice of ½ lemon | Salt |
| 3 T. water | |

Wash and separate the lettuce. Cut the bacon in small pieces and fry with lemon juice and 3 T. of water. Pour over the lettuce and serve immediately.

### Sauerkraut Salad

| | |
|---|---|
| 1 lb. sauerkraut | 2 T. sugar |
| 2 T. olive oil | 1 apple |
| Pepper | |

Sprinkle the sauerkraut with sugar. Pour over olive oil and add apple sliced thin. Shake pepper over it. Toss and serve.

### Red Cabbage Salad

| | |
|---|---|
| 1 head red cabbage | Salt and pepper |
| Juice of 1 lemon | 2 T. sugar |
| 4 T. olive oil | |

Place grated cabbage in a collander and scald with boiling water. Sprinkle with other ingredients after the water has been drained from it. Toss and serve.

### Cabbage and Onion Salad

| | |
|---|---|
| 1 head cabbage | 2 large sweet onions |
| ½ c. parsley, chopped | 4 T. olive oil |
| 2 T. sugar | 2 T. wine vinegar |
| 1 t. salt | |

Grate cabbage coarsely. Slice onions in rings. Add parsley and toss together. Make a dressing of the remaining ingredients and pour over the cabbage mixture before serving. Left-overs may be kept chilled in a closed jar and used as a relish.

### Cucumber Salad

| | |
|---|---|
| 3 to 4 cucumbers | Salt and pepper |
| 3 T. olive oil | 2 T. vinegar |

Peel the cucumbers and slice very thin. Salt and leave standing for 30 minutes so that the water is drawn from the cucumbers. Place in a napkin and squeeze out the liquid. Pepper and mix with oil and vinegar.

### Cucumber Salad with Sour Cream

| | |
|---|---|
| 3 to 4 cucumbers | Salt and white pepper |
| 1 c. sour cream | |

Prepare the cucumbers as above. Pepper and pour over sour cream. Yoghurt may be substituted for sour cream.

### Potato Salad with Celery

| | |
|---|---|
| 1 to 2 lb. potatoes | 1 bunch celery |
| Salt and pepper | 1 onion, chopped, or chopped |
| Dill | chive |
| 3 T. olive oil | 2 T. vinegar |

Peel the potatoes and cook until tender in salted water. Separately cook the celery. Dice the potatoes and celery, mix them together. Season well. Add chopped chive and dill. Mix olive oil with vinegar and pour over the potato and celery salad. You can prepare the same salad using raw celery instead of cooked.

### Potato Salad in Egg Sauce

| | |
|---|---|
| 1 to 2 lb potatoes | 3 hard-boiled egg yolks |
| 4 T. olive oil | Juice of 1 lemon |
| Salt and pepper | 1 jigger white wine |
| Chive, chopped | Parsley, chopped |

Cook the potatoes unpeeled. When tender cool, peel and slice. Grate the egg yolks and mix with oil, lemon juice and white wine. Pour over the dressing and sprinkle with chopped chive and parsley.

### Potato Salad with Apples and Capers

| | |
|---|---|
| 1 to 2 lb. potatoes | 2 apples |
| 2 T. capers | 1 jigger white wine |
| Juice of ½ lemon | Salt and pepper |
| 3 T. olive oil | |

Cook the potatoes unpeeled. When tender cool and peel. Slice and combine with sliced, peeled apples. Sprinkle with lemon juice. Add capers, oil, salt, pepper and white wine. Mix and chill.

### Potato Salad with Anchovies

| | |
|---|---|
| 1 to 2 lb. potatoes | 3 T. oil |
| ¼ onion, chopped | 6 fillets of anchovy |
| Salt and pepper | 2 T. vinegar |
| | Parsley and chives, chopped |

Cook the unpeeled potatoes. When tender cool, peel and slice. Cut the anchovies in pieces. Add with onion. Season and pour over oil and vinegar. Garnish with parsley and chives.

### Herring Salad

| | |
|---|---|
| 3 potatoes, cooked | 5 marinated mushrooms or |
| 2 apples | pickles |
| ¼ onion, chopped | Salt and pepper |
| 3 T. olive oil | 2 T. vinegar |
| 3 fresh salted herring | |

Soak the herring several hours, changing the water several times. Cook the potatoes. Peel and slice. Chop the herring fine, with the peeled apples, mushrooms or pickles. Salt and pepper and add oil and vinegar. Mix well.

### Mixed Cooked Salad

Vegetables such as potatoes, green beans, red cabbage, lima beans may be used. Arrange on bed of lettuce, mix with Russian or French dressing.

### Asparagus Tips

Cooked or canned asparagus on thin tomato slices with Hollandaise sauce (see p. 100).

### Cauliflower

Raw or cooked cauliflower sliced very thin or separated in small flowerets. Serve with mayonnaise or oil and vinegar. Cauliflower may be mixed with grated raw carrots.

### Turkish Salad

| | |
|---|---|
| 5-6 potatoes | Parsley, chopped |
| 1 c. walnuts, chopped | Dill, chopped |
| 3-4 apples | 2 hard-boiled eggs |
| 1 c. prepared mayonnaise | ¼ c. Marsala wine |

Cook the potatoes, unpeeled, until tender. Peel and slice together with the whites of eggs. Peel and cut the apples. Add to potatoes. Mix 1 c. of mayonnaise with wine, chopped parsley, dill and walnuts with the rest of the salad. Season. Place in a salad bowl. Pass the egg yolks through a sieve over the salad bowl to garnish.

## Potato Salad with Mushrooms

| | |
|---|---|
| 5-6 potatoes | 2 T. butter |
| ¼ lb. mushrooms | White pepper |
| 1 onion, chopped | Mayonnaise |
| 1 hard-boiled egg | Salt |
| 2 celery stalks | |

Sauté the chopped mushrooms in butter with salt. When they are browned combine with cooked potatoes sliced in strips, cooked sliced celery and chopped onion. Prepare the mayonnaise and mix a part of it with the vegetables. Then, pour rest of the mayonnaise on top of the salad. Sprinkle with white pepper. Garnish with hard-boiled egg quartered.

## Jellied Crab Meat

| | |
|---|---|
| 2 c. crab meat | 8 stuffed olives |
| ¼ green pepper, diced | 1 potato, diced |
| Salt and pepper | 2 T. gelatine |
| ¼ c. cold water | 1 c. boiling water |
| 1 c. mayonnaise | 1 c. cream, whipped |

Mix mayonnaise with crab meat, olives, whipped cream, green pepper, salt and pepper, and tomato. Dissolve gelatine in cold water. Add boiling water and allow to cool slightly. Combine with mayonnaise crabmeat mixture. Place in mould and chill. Then set it. Turn out on a platter with lettuce. Garnish with tomatoes and cucumbers.

## Royal Salad

| | |
|---|---|
| 3 c. cooked potatoes, diced | 2 c. beets, diced |
| 3 c. apples, diced | cooked or canned |
| 1 c. mayonnaise | 1 can herring fillets |
| ¼ c. sour cream | 2 hard-boiled eggs, quartered |
| 1 T. mustard | 3 T. scallions, chopped |
| 2 dill pickles, diced | Lettuce |

Combine all the vegetables with the apples, eggs and herring. Combine mayonnaise with ½ c. of sour cream and T. of mustard Mix well. Combine with all the ingredients. Serve on lettuce.

## Warsaw Salad

| | |
|---|---|
| 2 c. beets, cooked or canned | 1 can crab meat |
| 3 pickles, diced | 2 c. peas, cooked or canned |
| 2 c. kidney beans, cooked or | 3 scallions, chopped |
| canned | 1 hard-boiled egg |
| 1 c. prepared mayonnaise | ½ c. sour cream |
| 1 T. mustard | Carrots and radishes to garnish |

Mix the diced cooked or canned vegetables with diced pickles, can of crab meat and scallions. Prepare mayonnaise and combine with sour cream and mustard. Pour over the salad. Garnish with a quartered egg, strips of carrots and rose radishes.

### Jellied Vegetable Salad

| | |
|---|---|
| 1 c. peas, cooked or canned | 1 c. kidney beans, cooked or |
| 1 carrot | canned |
| 1 celery stalk | 5 sardines |
| 1 apple | Salt and pepper |
| 1 cauliflower, cooked | 2 c. cold water |
| 4 envelopes gelatine | 2 c. boiling water |
| 2 T. salt | ¼ c. lemon juice |
| Red cabbage, shredded | 2 hard-boiled eggs |
| 1 cucumber | |

Slice or grate vegetables. Separate the cauliflower flowerettes. Mix sardines and all vegetables except red cabbage. Make a mayonnaise dressing. Dissolve the gelatine and add 4 c. of water, 2 T. of salt and ¼ c. of lemon juice. Allow to set partially. Then mix with salad and place in salad bowl. Chill until set. Take out of the bowl and place on a plate. Garnish with shredded, scalded red cabbage and hard-boiled eggs quartered.

### Veal Salad

| | |
|---|---|
| ½ lb. roast veal | 4 cooked potatoes, diced |
| 1 herring fillet | ¼ lb. smoked tongue or canned |
| 2 tomatoes | ham |
| 1 onion | 2 cucumbers or large dill pickles |

Slice the ingredients into thin strips and mix with chopped onion. Combine with mustard sauce (see p. 101).

### String Bean Salad

| | |
|---|---|
| String beans | 3 T. olive oil |
| 1 onion | Juice of 1 lemon |
| Salt and pepper | Dash of basil |

Cut the string beans in thick strips. Cook in salted water until tender and drain. (Or use left-over beans). Mix with chopped onion, basil, oil and lemon dressing.

### Tomato Salad

| | |
|---|---|
| 2 heads lettuce | 1 onion, grated |
| 1 section garlic | 2 tomatoes |
| Salt and pepper | 2 T. sugar |
| 2 hard-boiled eggs | ¼ c. oil |
| Juice of 1 lemon | |

Wash and separate the lettuce. Rub the salad bowl with garlic. Slice the tomatoes. Place lettuce and tomatoes in salad bowl. Combine oil with lemon juice, grated onion, salt and pepper, sugar, and pour over salad. Garnish with hard-boiled eggs, quartered.

## Rose Salad

| | |
|---|---|
| 10 small potatoes, cooked | 4 celery stalks, sliced lengthwise |
| 2 c. shell beans, cooked | 4 beets, cooked or canned |
|    or canned | 4 T. olive oil |
| 2 heads shredded red cabbage | Salt and pepper |
| Juice of 1 lemon | 1 T. sugar |
| ¼ lb. sauerkraut | 3 T. tarragon vinegar |
| 1 T. water | |

Mix the lemon juice with oil and sugar diluted in water. Add salt and pepper. Pour over all the vegetables with the exception of the sauerkraut and the cabbage. Scald the red cabbage and sprinkle with vinegar to regain colour. Arrange the vegetables on a large platter with the slices of beets forming a large rose in the middle of the red cabbage. Around these place the other vegetables in sections like the petals of a rose. Finally garnish with lettuce leaves.

## Potato Salad with Wine

| | |
|---|---|
| 5-6 potatoes | 1 c. white wine |
| 4 T. olive oil | Juice of 1 lemon |
| 1 celery stalk, cooked | Chive, chopped |
| Parsley, chopped | Dill, chopped |

Cook the potatoes in salted water. Slice thin. Pour over the wine. Let stand for ½ hour. Cook the celery and then pass through a sieve. Mix chive, dill and parsley with oil and lemon. Add salt and pepper. Pour dressing over the salad. Toss and serve.

## Herring Salad

| | |
|---|---|
| 5-6 potatoes, cooked, diced | 3 herrings, soaked overnight |
| 1 large pickle, diced |    in water |
| Juice of 1 lemon | 2 apples, diced |
| Salt | 2 T. olive oil |

Combine all the cooked and diced vegetables with the chopped herring. Mix lemon and oil. Salt and pour over salad.

## Fruit Salad

| | |
|---|---|
| 3 oranges | Juice of ½ lemon |
| 3 apples | 3 pears |
| ¼ cup sugar | ½ lb. seeded grapes |
| 1 c. white wine | ¼ c. mustard |

Peel all the fruit. Remove the skin from the oranges. Slice the oranges, apples and pears. Mix the mustard with the sugar and dilute with wine. Add lemon juice. Pour over the fruit. Place in the refrigerator for 2 to 3 hours. Serve very cold.

### Party Salad in Shells

| | |
|---|---|
| 2 potatoes cooked | 2 T. olive oil |
| 1 piece of baked veal | 1 pickle |
| 1 egg yolk | Chicken left-overs or |
| 4 chopped marinated mushrooms | 1 can chicken |
| Salt and pepper | 1 hard-boiled egg |
| 2 T. capers | ½ can fillets of anchovy |
| Chive chopped | Olives |

Dice potatoes, veal, pickle and mushrooms. Beat the egg yolk and add oil drop by drop, stirring constantly. Then, add lemon juice, salt and pepper and pour over salad. Mix and serve in large oyster shells or shell dishes. Garnish with anchovies, olives, capers and chopped chive. Makes a very elegant salad.

### Spring Salad

| | |
|---|---|
| 1 c. cooked peas | 1 head lettuce |
| 1 cucumber, sliced | ½ can asparagus tips |
| 2 carrots, sliced | 8 radishes, sliced |
| 3 scallions, diced | 1 T. chopped parsley |
| 1 T. chive, chopped | Hollandaise sauce (see page 100) |

Combine all the sliced and diced vegetables with Hollandaise sauce.

### Imperial Salad

| | |
|---|---|
| Asparagus tips, cooked or canned | 2 T. tarragon vinegar |
| Salt and white pepper | 1 can anchovies |
| 3 T. oil | String beans, cooked or canned |

Place the vegetables on a platter and place the anchovies on top crossing the vegetables. Then pour over the dressing of oil, vinegar and seasonings.

### Diplomatic Salad

| | |
|---|---|
| 4 tomatoes, peeled and diced | 1 t. Worcestershire sauce |
| 3 bananas, sliced | ½ c. pineapple wedges |
| 2 truffles, sliced in strips | 5-6 cooked potatoes, sliced |
| ¼ c. Rhine wine or any white wine | 4 sliced black olives |
| | 1 c. prepared mayonnaise |

Mix 1 t. of Worcestershire sauce with the prepared mayonnaise and add wine. Combine all the other ingredients and pour over them the dressing. Place in the refrigerator to chill thoroughly, preferably overnight.

## Spanish Onion Salad

| | |
|---|---|
| 4 large red onions, sliced thin | 3 T. olive oil |
| Tarragon | 3 T. garlic vinegar |
| Salt and pepper | |

Scald the onions with hot garlic vinegar and let them stand in it for about 3 minutes. Drain. Sprinkle with tarragon, salt and pepper and mix with oil and vinegar. Serve with roasts.

## Russian Salad

| | |
|---|---|
| 3 truffles, sliced in strips | 10 stuffed olives |
| 1 can salmon | Caviar |
| 8 sliced black olives | Prepared mayonnaise |
| 1 can chicken | Salt and pepper |
| 6 anchovies, chopped | 2 T. olive oil |
| 3 T. capers | 2 T. vinegar |

Combine all the ingredients except the caviar with salt, oil and vinegar. Place a glass in the middle of the salad platter and arrange the salad around it. Then, remove the glass and place the caviar in the middle. Serve the mayonnaise separately.

## Japanese Salad

| | |
|---|---|
| 4 potatoes, diced | 2 T. capers |
| 1 t. tarragon | 1 T. chopped dill |
| 1 jigger white wine | 1 T. Worcestershire sauce |
| 3 truffles, sliced | 1 T. tarragon vinegar |
| 6 mussels or clams | 2 T. oil |
| Juice of 1 lemon | 2 hard-boiled eggs |

Steam the mussels until they open, then take out of shell and dice. Cook the potatoes and dice. Sprinkle the mussels with juice of $\frac{1}{2}$ lemon and combine with potatoes. Mix remaining lemon juice with oil, tarragon and white wine and pour over salad. Garnish the salad with truffles and sliced, hard-boiled eggs.

## Island Salad

| | |
|---|---|
| 3 potatoes | 3 T. olive oil |
| 1 stalk celery, cooked and diced | 2 T. capers |
| 2 pickles, diced | 1 T. chopped dill |
| 1 small can lobster meat | 1 t. Worcestershire sauce |
| 1 T. mustard | 1 T. tarragon vinegar |

Combine all the salad ingredients. Mix mustard with chopped dill, capers, Worcestershire sauce, oil and vinegar and pour over salad.

### Sardine Salad

| | |
|---|---|
| 1 can sardines | 1 T. tarragon |
| 1 T. chopped dill | 1 T. chopped parsley |
| 1 T. chive | 1 T. capers |
| 2 T. mustard | 2 T. olive oil |

Drain the oil from the sardines and reserve oil.Remove bones and slice. Dilute the mustard with sardine oil. Add olive oil. Pour over the sardines and sprinkle with rest of the ingredients. Serve garnished with lettuce.

### Cooked Vegetable Salad

| | |
|---|---|
| 1 c. peas, diced | 3 hard-boiled eggs |
| 1 c. carrots, diced | 1 c. apples, diced |
| 1 c. chick peas | 3 scallions, chopped |
| 1 c. potatoes, diced | 1 c. mayonnaise |
| 1 c. fresh tomatoes, diced | ½ c. sour cream |
| 1 c. beets, diced | 2 T. mustard |

Mix all the vegetables, prepare the dressing out of mustard with mayonnaise and sour cream, add to the vegetables and garnish with slices of hard-boiled eggs. If you like a varied colour scheme you can add for decoration a sliced tomato, some parsley and thin slices of green pepper.

### Vegetable Salad with Tomatoes

| | |
|---|---|
| 8 large tomatoes | Mayonnaise |
| ½ c. cooked peas | 3 T. sour cream |
| ½ c. cooked carrots, diced | 1 T. mustard |
| ½ c. cooked potatoes, diced | Salt and pepper |
| ½ c. beets, diced | |

Cut the tomatoes in half. Season. Scoop out the seeds and drain. Fill with the mixture of peas, potatoes, beets and carrots in mayonnaise. Mix the mayonnaise with mustard and sour cream. The ready-made mayonnaise may be used. Serve during hot summer days.

# DESSERTS

It is often said that you can judge really good cooks by the way they prepare desserts.

It was certainly true in the olden times, when the cook had to blend the qualities of an artist with those of a politician, all the time offering pleasant thrills for the guests' mouths. . . . With the dessert the table was changed sometimes into a garden with exotic flowers, and the oldest bottles would be dusted off for a worthy finale.

There was room for imagination, effect, sometimes for wit. Desserts varied with the occasion: at times honouring a particular day, at times a special guest. Thus Poland was famous for its sophisticated home baked cakes and its fancy pâtisserie.

## Milk Pudding

| | |
|---|---|
| 4 eggs, separated | 2 T. sugar |
| 1 T. melted butter | 2 c. of warm milk |
| ¼ t. pure vanilla extract | Bread-crumbs |
| 1 T. flour | |

Beat the egg yolks with 2 T. of sugar, 1 T. of melted butter, 2 c. of milk, vanilla and flour. Combine with beaten whites. Place in a baking dish which is also a serving dish and which has been sprinkled with bread-crumbs and cook on top of the stove over a double boiler or in a moderate oven.

## Vanilla Pudding

| | |
|---|---|
| 1 c. flour | 8 eggs, separated |
| 1 T. butter | 2 c. milk |
| ½ t. vanilla | Bread-crumbs |
| ½ c. sugar | |

Mix the flour with the milk, carefully avoiding any lumps. Add 1 T. of butter and sugar and cook until the mixture begins to thicken. Take off the flame. Add vanilla. When it is cool place in a bowl, add the egg yolks one by one, beating constantly. Combine with the beaten whites of the 8 eggs. Place in buttered pudding mould which has been sprinkled with bread-crumbs and steam for 1 hour, either on top of the stove over a double boiler or in a moderate oven.

## Almond Pudding

| | |
|---|---|
| 6 eggs, separated | ½ c. sugar |
| ¼ lb. chopped almonds | Bread-crumbs |

Beat the egg yolks with the sugar until they are light. Scald the almonds, peel and chop, adding to the beaten whites of eggs. Combine with the egg yolks. Fold into buttered pudding dish sprinkled with bread-crumbs. Steam for 1 hour.

## Nut Pudding

Prepared in the same way as the almond pudding, adding another variety of nuts instead of almonds.

## Cheese Pudding

| | |
|---|---|
| 6 eggs, separated | ½ c. almonds |
| ¼ lb. sweet butter | 3 T. bread-crumbs |
| ¼ lb. cottage cheese | Butter |
| ½ c. sugar | |

Beat the egg yolks with softened butter and cottage cheese, adding sugar and peeled and grated almonds. Finally beat the egg whites.

Fold them into the mixture and mix gently. Add bread-crumbs. Place in a dish, greased and sprinkled with bread-crumbs, and bake in moderate oven for 30 minutes.

## Dried Fruit Pudding

| | |
|---|---|
| 1 c. figs, chopped | 4 T. granulated sugar |
| 1 c. almonds, chopped | 6 egg whites |
| 1 c. dates, chopped | 2 T. sugar |
| ¼ c. raisins | 1 c. wine |
| 1 c. red wine | |

Cut all the dried fruit in small pieces, add wine, sugar, chopped almonds and bring to a boil together. Place in a bowl. When completely cool fold in 6 egg whites beaten stiff with 2 T. of confectioners sugar. Place in a well-buttered baking dish and bake in moderate oven for 20 minutes.

## Raisin Pudding

| | |
|---|---|
| 6 eggs, separated | 2 buns |
| 3 T. sugar | Milk |
| 1 c. almonds, chopped | Butter |
| 1 c. raisins | |

Beat the egg yolks with sugar until they become light. Add almonds and raisins. Soak the buns in milk. Drain the milk out, sieve and add. Place on low flame and stir constantly with a spoon until it thickens. Remove from fire and fold in stiffly beaten egg white. Place in a round buttered pudding bowl and steam in double boiler for 1 hour.

## Fancy Pudding

| | |
|---|---|
| 5 eggs, separated | 1 T. cornstarch |
| 1 c. sugar | 2 T. butter |
| ¾ c. corn starch | 1 c. fruit syrup |
| Flour | ¼ c. rum |
| Strawberry or apricot jam | 1 T. apricot jam |

Beat the egg yolks with sugar until they are light. Beat the egg whites stiff, fold them into the yolks. Then add the cornstarch gradually. Place in a buttered dish and bake in a hot oven for 30 minutes. When the cake is cool, slice and arrange on a large platter. Cover each slice with jam, and pour over the following sauce. Cook 2 T. of butter with 1 T. of cornstarch. Dilute it with a c. of fruit syrup and rum. Add 1 T. of jam and mix well together. Have the sauce warm when you pour it over the cake.

## Wine Pudding

| | |
|---|---|
| 1 c. bread-crumbs | 1 T. butter |
| ½ c. white wine | 1 jigger cherry brandy |
| ½ c. water | ¼ lb. butter |
| ½ c. sugar | 8 eggs, separated |
| Lemon peel, grated | Fruit syrup |

Lightly brown bread-crumbs with butter. Add cherry brandy, wine and water. Bring to a boil, then place in a bowl and work into a thick paste. Separately mix butter with sugar and egg yolks. Add lemon peel. Mix both pastes together. Beat the egg whites and fold them in. Butter a baking dish. Sprinkle with bread-crumbs. Pour the paste in and bake in a moderate oven for 30 minutes. Serve with fruit syrup.

## Tip-top Pudding

| | |
|---|---|
| 1 c. milk | 6 eggs, separated |
| 1 T. butter | Lemon peel, grated |
| ¾ c. cornstarch | Dash of nutmeg |
| Butter | Bread-crumbs |
| Fruit syrup | |

Place in a pot 1 T. of butter and c. of milk. Add ½ c. of sugar. When it reaches the boiling point pour ¾ c. of corn starch, stirring constantly so that there are no lumps. Leave it on the flame until it forms a ball in the middle of the pot. When it is cool, add the egg yolks one by one. Add 2 more T. of sugar a dash of nutmeg grated lemon peel. Fold in stiffly beaten egg whites. Mix lightly. Place in a pudding bowl which has been buttered and sprinkled with bread-crumbs. Place in a larger container with boiling water and cook it for 1 hour. Serve with fruit syrup.

## Chocolate Pudding

| | |
|---|---|
| 1 c. bread-crumbs | 1 c. milk |
| ¼ c. sugar | ¾ bar semi-sweet chocolate, melted |
| 8 eggs, separated | ½ t. vanilla |
| Butter | |

Melt the chocolate over hot water. Separately scald the bread-crumbs with milk, stirring away all the lumps. Stir in the sugar, vanilla and chocolate. Beat until the mixture thickens. Take off the flame and cool. Beat in the egg yolks one by one. Then fold in the beaten whites. Place in a pudding bowl, which has been buttered and sprinkled with bread-crumbs. Steam for 1 hour over hot water.

## Fruit in Rum Pudding

| | |
|---|---|
| 6 eggs, separated | 2 lemons |
| 2 oranges, peeled | Juice of 1 lemon |
| Juice of two oranges | 2 jiggers rum |
| ¼ lb. almonds, blanched | 3 T. bread-crumbs |
| 1 c. sugar | |

Dice the fruit and roll in sugar. Beat the egg yolks with sugar until they are light. Mortar the fruit into a paste. Combine the egg yolks with the fruit adding: the juice of 2 oranges, 1 lemon, grated almonds, bread-crumbs, rum and stiffly beaten egg whites. Mix well and place in a pudding bowl. Steam over hot water. When ready to serve pour over some rum and light. Separately serve a fruit sauce.

## Bread Pudding

| | |
|---|---|
| 1 c. pumpernickel | ½ t. ground cloves |
| breadcrumbs | 1 T. melted butter |
| 6 eggs, separated | Bread-crumbs |
| 6 T. sugar | ½ t. cinnamon |
| Sour cream | Powdered sugar |

Grate dry pumpernickel bread to make 1 c. of bread-crumbs. Beat the egg yolks with sugar until they are light. Add bread-crumbs, cinnamon and cloves. Melt butter and pour it in. Fold in stiffly beaten egg whites. Place in a buttered pan and bake in moderate oven for 30 minutes. Serve cool with sour cream beaten with powdered sugar on the side.

## Chestnut Pudding with Fruit

| | |
|---|---|
| 1 lb. chestnuts | 6 egg whites |
| 2 c. milk | 3 T. powdered sugar |
| 3 T. granulated sugar | Vanilla |
| Dried fruit: pears, apricots | Prunes |

Cook the chestnuts for 20 minutes. Peel them and place them in a pot with milk. Cook until soft adding 3 T. of granulated sugar and a few drops of vanilla extract. Pass through a sieve into a large oven-proof platter, shaping into a pyramid. Cook the dried fruit in a little water with sugar, and place around the chestnuts. Cover all with beaten egg whites, sweetened with powdered sugar while beating. Bake in a moderate oven for 20 minutes. When the meringue becomes slightly brown, the chestnut pudding is ready. You may serve it warm or cold.

## Potato Pudding

| | |
|---|---|
| 1 c. mashed potato | 3 T. sugar |
| 2 T. margarine | 1 t. grated lemon rind |
| 3 eggs, separated | Juice of 1 lemon |
| 4 T. almonds, peeled and chopped | |

Mix the mashed potatoes with melted margarine. Add almonds, sugar, lemon juice, grated lemon rind, egg yolks, and finally fold in stiffly beaten egg whites. Place in a buttered pudding form and cook in double boiler for 45 minutes. Serve with fruit syrup.

## Rum Pudding

| | |
|---|---|
| 4 egg yolks | Raspberry jam to garnish |
| 1 T. rum | 1½ pkts. gelatine dissolved in |
| 1 c. sugar | 1 T. water |
| 1¼ c. heavy cream | |

Mix the egg yolks with sugar in a pan. Add rum and place over low flame stirring constantly until the mixture takes a heavier consistency. When it is cooled, add whipped cream and at the end the dissolved gelatine. Chill. Serve with raspberry jam.

## Caramel Pudding

| | |
|---|---|
| 5 eggs | *For Caramel:* |
| 4 T. sugar | ½ c. sugar |
| ½ t. vanilla | 1 c. water |
| 2 c. sweet cream | |

Beat the whole eggs. Bring the cream to the boil mixed with the sugar and vanilla and mix it slowly with the eggs. Prepare a caramel, by browning sugar and diluting with water. Place caramel in bottom of oven-proof cups or 1 large bowl. Cover it with custard and bake for 20 minutes. Chill.

## Cranberry Pudding

| | |
|---|---|
| 1 lb. cranberries | 1 t. cinnamon |
| 2 c. sugar | ½ c. cornstarch |
| 2 whole cloves | 2 T. water |
| 4 c. water | |

Cook the cranberries in 1 c. of water until tender. Pass through a sieve. Take 1 c. of cranberry liquid and combine with 4 c. of water. Add cinnamon, cloves and sugar and cook to the boiling point. Dilute the corn starch with 2 T. of cold water. Add to the cranberry sauce and cook until it thickens. Take out the cloves and pour into a pudding dish. Serve chilled with whipped cream if desired.

## Rice Pudding

| | |
|---|---|
| 1 c. well-cooked rice | 3 T. sugar |
| 2 T. flour | 3 T. margarine |
| 1 egg | ¼ t. pure vanilla extract |
| Raisins | 3 T. apricot brandy |

Mix the cooked rice with flour, egg and sugar, vanilla and melted margarine. Add raisins and liqueur, and fry in margarine on both sides until browned.

## Cabinet Pudding

| | |
|---|---|
| 2 c. milk | 20 small macaroons or |
| 8 eggs | left-over cakes |
| 4 T. sugar | 2 T. marashino cherries |
| Sherry or rum | 1 t. vanilla extract |
| ½ c. strawberry jam | |

Sprinkle the cake or macaroons with sherry or rum and line the bottom of a buttered mould with part of it. Make a custard by cooking milk, vanilla, beaten eggs and sugar. When it coats the spoon, remove from fire and strain. Spread the cake or macaroons with jam and cherries. Pour on some custard. Take another layer of cake, then jam then custard, continuing until ingredients are used up, managing to finish with a custard layer. Cover the mould and cook in double boiler in moderate oven for nearly an hour. Serve in slices with whipped cream. Other jams or fruit may be used.

## Frozen Pudding with Apricots

| | |
|---|---|
| ½ c. cherries, sliced | ¼ c. pecans, halved |
| ¼ c. shredded pineapple, drained | ½ c. pineapple juice |
| Apricot syrup | 1 c. sugar |
| 4 egg whites, beaten | 2 T. rum |
| 1 pt. heavy cream | 1 c. whole apricots |

Cook pineapple juice with sugar, boiling for 5 minutes. Beat egg whites until fluffy. Add cherries, nuts, and pineapple, rum and whipped cream. Chill in the refrigerator for several hours. Heat the apricots in apricot syrup and arrange around pudding. Serve.

## Apple Compôte in Wine

| | |
|---|---|
| Apples | ½ c. white wine |
| 1 c. sugar | |

Peel and slice the apples. Make the syrup with enough water to cover the apples and 1 c. of sugar. Add white wine. Bring to the boil and cook the apples until tender. Serve garnished with jam.

## Compôte of Stuffed Apples

8-10 apples                          1 c. sugar
2¼ c. hot water                      Jam, apricot or raspberry
Candied orange peel                  1 jigger apricot brandy

Peel the apples and carefully scoop out the cores. Place them in cold water. Prepare a light syrup of water and sugar. Add brandy. Place the apples in a saucepan and pour over the syrup so that all the apples are covered. Cook the apples until tender. Add more sugar if the syrup is too thin. Garnish the apples with fruit gelatine or jam. On the top place a few pieces of candied orange peel. Surround with other fruit to give a festive look.

## Apricot or Peach Compôte

1 lb. apricots or peaches            1 c. water
¼ c. sugar

Take out the stones and drop the peaches or apricots into boiling syrup of 1 c. of water and sugar. When the fruit is tender place in a low bowl and pour on the syrup. Chill.

## Apple Sauce from Baked Apples

4-5 apples                           Sugar to taste

Bake the apples, then peel and pass through a sieve, adding sugar to taste. Simmer on a low flame.

## Melon Compôte

1 honeydew melon                     1 c. boiling water
¼ c. sugar                           1 jigger rum

Peel the melon. Slice into small pieces discarding seeds. Place in a low bowl. Pour over it rum and let it stand for an hour. At the end of that time pour over it thick syrup from 1 c. of water boiled with ½ c. of sugar. Let it stand for a few hours. Serve chilled.

## Orange and Apple Compôte

3-4 apples                           3-4 oranges
¼ c. of good white wine              Powdered sugar

Peel the oranges and apples, taking the white skin as well as the outer from the oranges, and slice in thin pieces. Place carefully on a dessert platter sprinkling each layer generously with sugar. Let it stand for an hour and then add wine. Place on ice for 2 hours.

## Rhubarb Compôte

| | |
|---|---|
| 1 lb. rhubarb | Lemon peel |
| 1 c. sugar | Water |

Peel the tough skin from the rhubarb. Cut into pieces 2 inches long. Scald with boiling water. Drain. Then place in thick syrup, using sugar with water. The rhubarb ought to be just covered with water. Cook until tender. Add a few pieces of lemon peel for flavour.

## Strawberry Compôte with Wine

| | |
|---|---|
| 2 c. strawberries | Sugar |
| $\frac{1}{2}$ c. red wine | |

Remove the stems of the strawberries. Cut. Sprinkle with a generous quantity of sugar and leave standing for 1 hour. Boil for a few minutes. Then, pour over red wine and place on ice for a few hours.

## Cherry Compôte

| | |
|---|---|
| 1 lb. cherries | 1 c. water |
| $\frac{1}{2}$ c. sugar | Juice of 1 lemon |
| $\frac{1}{4}$ c. grape or cherry jelly | 5 whole cloves |

Remove stones from cherries. Simmer cherries in water slowly, with cloves and sugar for 10—15 minutes. Strain but retain 2 c. of the liquid. Combine the cherry liquid with the remaining ingredients and cook until it thickens. Cool and pour over cherries. Chill for a few hours in the refrigerator. Serve with whipped cream if desired.

## Whole Pear Compôte

| | |
|---|---|
| 8 pears | $\frac{1}{2}$ t. pure vanilla extract |
| 2 c. red wine | 1 c. sugar |

Bring the wine to the boil with vanilla and sugar. Peel whole pears leaving the stems attached. Simmer the pears in the liquid until transparent. Then, place pears in the serving dish and cook syrup until it thickens. Pour over pears and serve chilled with cottage cheese.

## Blueberry Compôte

| | |
|---|---|
| 1 qt. blueberries | 1$\frac{1}{4}$ c. sugar |
| 1 c. water | |

Sprinkle the berries with $\frac{1}{2}$ c. of sugar and let stand for 1 hour. Cook water and 1 c. sugar until it thickens into a syrup. Pour over fruit and let stand another hour before serving.

## Gooseberry Compôte

| | |
|---|---|
| 1 lb. gooseberries | 1 c. sugar |
| 1 c. water | 1 cinnamon stick |

Wash the berries. Scald with boiling water and drain. Boil the water sugar and cinnamon and add gooseberries when it thickens. Bring to a boil and pour into a serving dish. Serve chilled. Remove cinnamon stick before serving.

## Cherry Compôte, Marinated

| | |
|---|---|
| Sweet cherries | Wine vinegar |
| 12 cloves | 1 c. sugar to 1 c. of cherries |

Stone the cherries and soak in vinegar with cloves overnight. Strain off the vinegar. Measure off 1 c. of cherries to 1 c. of sugar. Mix well. Cover and store in the refrigerator for several days before serving, stirring occasionally to dissolve sugar better. This compôte keeps almost indefinitely.

## Pears in Rum

| | |
|---|---|
| 8 pears | ½ c. loganberry jam |
| 2 c. water | 1 t. cornstarch |
| 1 c. sugar | 1 T. cold water |
| Rum | |

Cook the water and sugar until it is a thin syrup. Peel the pears leaving the stems attached. Put in syrup and simmer until soft. Then place in a bowl. Reduce the syrup by boiling to about half the amount. Add jam, thicken with cornstarch diluted with 1 T. of water. Pour over pears keeping them hot. Before serving, warm rum and add to pears and serve flaming.

## Brown Pears

| | |
|---|---|
| 6 pears | ½ c. of sugar |
| 1 c. water or more | 1 c. heavy cream |

Peel the pears and brown them in the caramel syrup of brown sugar diluted with water. When the pears are soft they should be taken off and cooled and covered with the whipped cream which has been mixed with the caramel.

## Pears in Wine Sauce

| | |
|---|---|
| 10 small pears | 1 egg |
| 3 T. butter | 3 T. flour |
| 5 T. sugar, powdered | ¼ c. sweet wine |
| 2 T. raisins | |

Quarter the peeled pears. Grease baking dish and place the pieces of pears in the bottom. Sprinkle them with 3 T. of water. Add the raisins. Place on the board the flour, 2 T. of sugar, 3 T. of butter, 1 egg, 1 T. of water. Work all the ingredients into a dough. Let it rest for 10 minutes. Roll it out to the size of the baking dish, so that you can cover it. Bake in a moderate oven for about 30 minutes or until the paste is nicely browned.

### Black Cherries Flambé

| | |
|---|---|
| 1 can black cherries | ¾ c. rum |

Strain off the cherry juice and pour rum over cherries. Leave standing for a few hours; then drain off the rum and warm it using a chafing dish. Place the cherries in the warm rum and light. Spoon the lighted sauce over the cherries in a stirring motion until rum is almost burned out. Serve over ice cream or cake.

### Brandied Peaches Flambé

| | |
|---|---|
| 6-8 peaches | Sugar |
| ¼ c. brandy | ¼ c. chopped nuts |

Place peaches cut in half in a baking dish. Sprinkle with sugar and nuts. Bake in a low oven for 15 minutes. Just before serving pour over heated brandy and light.

### Stuffed Peaches

| | |
|---|---|
| Large peaches | 6 egg whites |
| 1 T. sugar to each peach | 6 T. sugar |
| Strawberries | ¼ lb. almonds, peeled and chopped |
| Rum | Raspberries |

Peel the peaches and take out the seed carefully from one side. Sprinkle the centre of each peach with 1 T. of sugar. Add some varied fresh fruits as strawberries, raspberries, etc. Put the peaches in a baking dish, pour over some rum and cover each peach with beaten egg white, mixed with sugar and almonds. Bake 15 to 20 minutes in a moderate oven.

### Stuffed Melon

| | |
|---|---|
| 1 melon | 2 c. blueberries |
| ½ c. pineapple, chopped | 2 c. strawberries |
| ½ c. sugar | 1 jigger cherry brandy |

Cut off the top of the melon. Scoop out the inside without damaging the skin and dice the melon meat. Slice the strawberries. Add blueberries, and diced pineapple and replace everything in the melon, sprinkling with a generous amount of sugar. Let it stand for 1 hour and then cover with cherry brandy. Place on ice for a few hours.

### Stuffed Pineapple

Prepared in the same way as stuffed melon can be stuffed with strawberries, raspberries and the pineapple scooped out from the inside and diced, white wine should be used instead of liqueur.

### Quick Dessert

| | |
|---|---|
| 4 egg whites | 2 T. plum jam |
| Juice of 1 lemon | ½ c. sugar |

Beat all the ingredients together until thick. Serve with lady fingers.

### Sour Cream with Strawberries

| | |
|---|---|
| 2 c. strawberries | 1 c. sour cream |
| ½ c. sugar | Drop of vanilla extract |
| 1 jigger sweet liqueur | |

Cut the strawberries in small pieces. Mix them with half of the sugar. Add liqueur. Beat sour cream with the remaining sugar. Add vanilla and mix with the strawberries, just before serving. In place of strawberries you may use blueberries or wild strawberries.

### Strawberry Cream

| | |
|---|---|
| 2 c. strawberries | ½ c. cold water |
| 1½ T. gelatine | 1 c. heavy cream |
| Juice of 1 lemon | 1 c. sugar |

Wash the strawberries and press through sieve. Add lemon juice and sugar, stirring until dissolved. Dilute the gelatine in cold water and mix with strawberries. Beat heavy cream until stiff and fold into the strawberry mixture when it begins to thicken. Chill in the refrigerator until solid.

### Strawberries with Bananas in Sour Cream

| | |
|---|---|
| 2 c. strawberries | 2-3 bananas, thinly sliced |
| Granulated sugar | 1 c. sour cream |
| Powdered sugar | |

Sprinkle sliced strawberries and bananas with sugar. Let stand for 30 minutes. Then pour over sour cream. Serve sprinkled with powdered sugar as desired.

### Quick Fresh Fruit Salad

| | |
|---|---|
| 1 c. seeded grapes | Juice of 1 lemon |
| 1 c. cherries | Powdered sugar |
| 1 c. orange sections | 3 T. brandy |
| Peach halves, 1 per person | 1 c. pineapple wedges |

Place the fruits on a large platter and mix. Sprinkle with powdered sugar and brandy.

## Orange—Banana Cup

| | |
|---|---|
| 2 oranges in sections | 2 bananas, thinly sliced |
| ¼ c. chopped walnuts | Sugar |

Cut the orange sections in half and combine with sliced bananas. Sprinkle with sugar and chill. Serve topped with walnuts.

## Strawberries in Red Wine

| | |
|---|---|
| Strawberries | Sugar |
| 1 glass red wine | |

Wash the strawberries and place in a serving bowl. Sprinkle with sugar and wine. Leave standing covered in the refrigerator for 1 hour.

## Sour Cream Whip

| | |
|---|---|
| 2 c. sour cream | 2 c. heavy cream |
| 2 c. sugar | 1 c. jam |
| 2 envelopes gelatine | 2 T. water |

Beat the sour cream and the heavy cream separately on ice each with 1 c. of sugar. Then add the jam and combine all the ingredients. Add the dissolved gelatine and mix. Chill in the refrigerator until solidified.

## Coffee Cream

| | |
|---|---|
| 1 c. strong coffee | 2 c. heavy cream |
| 2 c. sugar | 2 c. sweet cream |
| ¼ t. vanilla extract | 2 envelopes gelatine |
| 8 egg yolks | 2 T. water |

Beat the egg yolks with 1 c. sugar until they are light and fold into a pot with sweet cream. Cook for a few minutes, until it thickens. Separately beat the heavy cream with 1 c. of sugar. Prepare 1 c. of very strong coffee and combine with whipped cream. Add dissolved gelatine. Combine the 2 mixtures. Beat for another 5 minutes, then pour into a form sprinkled with sugar and water and freeze.

## Cream with Orange Peel

| | |
|---|---|
| 2 c. sweet cream | 1 c. sugar |
| ¼ lb. candied orange peel | 1 envelope of gelatine dissolved in milk |

Beat the sweet cream on ice gradually adding sugar and very finely chopped candied orange peel. Add gelatine dissolved in milk. Pour into a mould and freeze.

## Pineapple Cream

| | |
|---|---|
| 1 small can pineapple or | 2 egg whites |
|   fresh pineapple | 2 c. sweet cream |
| 1 c. powdered sugar | ½ c. granulated sugar |
| 1 envelope gelatine | |

Grate the pineapple, then pass through a sieve and mix with powdered sugar. Add 2 egg whites and beat well on ice. Separately, beat the sweet cream with granulated sugar. When the pineapple mixture gets fluffy, combine with the cream, adding gelatine dissolved in pineapple juice. Continue beating for another 5 minutes or more. Place in a mould and freeze.

## Lemon Fromage

| | |
|---|---|
| 3 eggs, separated | 2 T. sherry |
| ¾ c. sugar | 2 envelopes gelatine |
| Juice of 1 lemon | 2 T. water |
| 1 c. heavy cream | |

Beat the egg yolks with sugar until light. Dissolve gelatine in water. Mix lemon juice with sherry and add to the egg yolks. Prepare very stiff beaten egg whites. Separately beat the cream and fold both gradually into the other mixture. Chill and serve very cold.

## Mousse au Chocolat

| | |
|---|---|
| 4 egg yolks | 1½ c. heavy cream |
| ⅛ lb. semi-sweet chocolate | |

Beat the egg yolks until they are light. Melt the chocolate over double boiler. When it is completely melted mix it with the egg yolks. Beat the cream and fold into the chocolate. Keep in the refrigerator until ready to serve.

## Coffee Fromage

| | |
|---|---|
| 1 c. strong coffee | 1 c. sugar |
| 2 c. heavy cream | 4 T. water |
| 2 envelopes gelatine | |

Beat the cream until it is thick. Mix it with coffee and sugar, and the gelatine dissolved in water. Mix thoroughly. Chill and serve very cold.

## Pineapple Fromage

| | |
|---|---|
| 2 eggs | 2 envelopes gelatine |
| ¼ c. sugar | 1½ c. heavy cream |
| Juice of 1 lemon | 1 c. pineapple, sliced |
| ¼ c. pineapple juice | |

Mix the egg yolks with sugar. Dissolve the gelatine and mix it with pineapple and lemon juice. Add to the egg yolks. Add the slices of pineapple and finally the stiffly beaten egg whites. Fold in whipped cream. Chill in the refrigerator.

## Raspberry Soufflé

| | |
|---|---|
| 6 eggs, separated | Bread-crumbs |
| 6 T. sugar | Butter |
| 2 c. raspberries | |

Pass the raspberries through a sieve. Separately, mix egg yolks with sugar. Add the strained raspberries, the stiffly beaten egg whites, and finally 2 T. of bread-crumbs. Put in a pudding form, buttered and sprinkled with bread-crumbs and cook in a double boiler for 1 hour.

### Cherry Soufflé

| | |
|---|---|
| 2 buns, soaked in milk | ¾ c. sugar |
| 1½ lb. cherries | ½ c. almonds, chopped |
| ¼ t. cinnamon | 2 T. butter |
| 3 eggs, separated | |

Add cinnamon, sugar, egg yolks, melted butter to the sieved softened buns. Combine with stoned cherries. Fold in egg whites beaten stiff. Pour mixture into a buttered mould which has been sprinkled with sugar. Bake in a moderate oven for 15 to 20 minutes and serve immediately.

### Fruit Soufflé

| | |
|---|---|
| 3 T. strawberry or apricot jam | 6 T. sugar |
| 6 egg whites | |

Mix the jam with the stiffly beaten egg whites and gradually add the sugar, stirring until all the ingredients are well mixed. Fold mixture into a greased oven-proof dish. Make the soufflé at the last moment before serving as there is always the danger that it might fall. Bake in a moderate oven for 20 to 25 minutes.

### Apple Soufflé

| | |
|---|---|
| 6-8 large apples | Almonds |
| 8 egg whites | ½ c. sugar |

Bake 8 apples in the oven. When soft, pass them through a sieve and allow to cool. Beat with egg-beater for a few minutes. Separately beat the egg whites stiff. When ready, fold in the apple sauce and gradually add the sugar. Place on a buttered baking dish. Cover with peeled, sliced almonds and bake for 25 minutes in a moderate oven. Sweetened apple sauce may be used for this recipe.

### Chestnut Soufflé

| | |
|---|---|
| 1 lb. chestnuts | 1 c. sweet cream |
| 2 c. milk | ½ c. sugar |
| 1 T. butter | A few drops vanilla extract |
| 1 T. flour | 6 eggs, separated |

Half cook the chestnuts. Peel them. Place them in the pot with 2

c. of milk and cook until tender. Pass them through a sieve. Mix 1 T. of butter with flour, on a low flame. Dilute with 1 c. of sweet cream. When it boils and becomes thick, put it on ice in order to cool off entirely. To this mixture add the chestnuts, sugar, vanilla and one by one the egg yolks, beating constantly. Finally fold in the stiffly beaten egg whites. Place in a buttered baking dish and bake in a moderate oven for 20 minutes.

## Royal Soufflé

| | |
|---|---|
| 3 soft buns | 2 T. raisins |
| 1 T. butter | 2 T. jam |
| 3 T. sugar | 1 T. peeled almonds |
| Milk to cover the buns | 4 eggs, separated |
| 3 T. apricot brandy | |

Slice the buns. Add the butter and sugar and cover with boiling milk. When they swell and soften, sieve. Add the raisins to the sieved buns and 2 T. of jam. Pound chopped almonds to a powder. Add them to the mixture. Add egg yolks, one by one, beating constantly. Finally fold in stiffly beaten egg whites. In a buttered baking dish, place a layer of each freely sprinkled with liqueur. Add pudding. Bake in moderate oven for 25 minutes. Serve with sherry sauce (see p. 112).

## Cream Mushroom

| | |
|---|---|
| 6 eggs, separated | 1 T. grated lemon peel |
| 1 T. butter | 1½ c. sour cream |
| ¼ c. powdered sugar | Butter |
| 2 c. flour | Jam |

Mix the egg yolks with 1 T. of butter and powdered sugar. When thoroughly mixed add flour and lemon peel. Add sour cream. Fold in well beaten egg whites. Mix softly and divide in 2 sections. Fry in butter in two similar frying pans browning both sides. Cover each layer with jam put the one on top of the other and sprinkle with powdered sugar.

## Sour Cream Soufflé

| | |
|---|---|
| 2 egg yolks | 1 c. sour cream |
| ½ c. sugar | ½ t. cinnamon |
| ½ t. cloves | |

*The Meringue:*

| | |
|---|---|
| 4 T. sugar | ½ t. vanilla extract |
| 2 egg whites | ⅛ t. salt |

Mix egg yolks with sugar. Add cinnamon and cloves. Cook all the ingredients in a double boiler stirring until it thickens. Cool a little

then place in a buttered baking dish. Cover with meringue made as follows: Beat the egg whites until frothy, add a dash of salt, then whip until stiff but not dry. Beat in gradually 4 T. of sugar and vanilla. Bake in the oven for 15 minutes.

## Lemon Soufflé

| | |
|---|---|
| 3 grated lemons with rind | 5 eggs, separated |
| ¼ c. sugar | 1 T. flour |

Grate three whole lemons, throwing away the seed. Mix with 5 egg yolks. Add 1 T. of flour and blend in sugar gradually. Beat well. Fold in the beaten whites of 5 eggs. Put in a buttered pan and bake for 20 minutes in a moderate oven.

## Orange Soufflé

Prepared in the same way as the lemon soufflé using oranges instead of lemons.

## Coffee Soufflé

| | |
|---|---|
| 3 T. ground coffee | 1 c. sugar |
| 6 eggs, separated | 1 T. cornstarch |
| Butter | 2 c. sweet cream |

Put the ground coffee in sweet cream and bring to the boil once. Cover, cool. Strain through a cheese cloth. Add to it the sugar beaten with 6 egg yolks. Pour it into the top of a double boiler and continue beating until it thickens. Take off the flame, and cool. Stir in 1 T. of cornstarch. Fold in stiffly beaten egg whites. Place in a greased baking dish in a moderate oven for 15 to 20 minutes.

## Tea Soufflé

Prepared as above, adding instead of coffee 1 T. of tea. Place the tea in the boiling cream. Cover and do not cook. Then follow recipe above.

## Sweet Mushrooms

| | |
|---|---|
| 1 T. melted butter | 5 eggs, separated |
| 2 T. sugar | 2 c. flour |
| Salt | Butter |
| ¼ c. raisins | Vanilla |
| 2 c. milk | |

Mix 1 T. of melted butter, with milk, 2 T. of sugar, a dash of salt, 5 egg yolks, flour and raisins. Combine with stiffly beaten egg whites of 5 eggs. Place in a low greased baking dish and bake for 20 minutes in a very hot oven or until it is lightly browned. Cut the cake into small pieces. Put on a platter and sprinkle with sugar. Serve.

## Kutia

| | |
|---|---|
| 2 c. wheat grains | 1 c. honey |
| 1 c. poppy seeds | 1 c. ground, blanched almonds |

Soak the wheat grains. Place them in a muslin bag and try to remove the husks by beating with a wooden spoon. Wash the husks away in hot water. When clean add water to cover and simmer for 3 hours or until the grains are soft and tender. When cooled off mix with poppy seed paste and honey. (see p.199). Add ground almonds. Place in refrigerator and serve cold.

## Baked Apples in Sweet Wine

5 large apples
Strawberry or raspberry jam

1 c. sweet wine
½ c. sugar

Remove the cores being careful not to bore through the apples. Fill the centres with jam. Then, sprinkle with sugar and wine and place in a baking dish. Bake under cover at 350° for about 1 hour, serve hot or cold, with or without whipped cream.

## Jellied Apples

5 red apples
1 jigger sweet red wine
3 T. sugar
Peel of ½ lemon

10-12 almonds, chopped
2 T. cold water
1 t. gelatine
1 c. water

Simmer peeled whole apples in water with 2 T. of sugar, wine and lemon peel until transparent. Then, place in a bowl, keeping them whole. Add 1 T. of sugar to the apple broth, bring to a boil. Add gelatine dissolved in cold water. Stir until completely blended. Cool the liquid and pour over the apples. Serve with whipped cream.

## Swedish Apples

4 apples
1 c. flour
¼ lb. grated potatoes
¼ lb. margarine

3 T. sugar
2 T. of almonds
Powdered sugar
1 t. baking powder

Prepare a dough out of grated potatoes, melted margarine and flour. Add the baking soda. Divide the dough in four pieces. Peel the whole apples and scoop out the core. Peel the almonds, chop them and mix with powdered sugar. Fill the inside of the apples with this mixture. Cover the apple in the individual dough. Place on buttered baking dish. Cover with the egg white and sprinkle with powdered sugar and bake in a moderate oven about 30 to 45 minutes or until they are evenly browned. May be served with sour cream beaten with powdered sugar.

## Rice with Apples

4 apples
3 large macaroons, opt.
1 c. rice
Cream:
2 egg yolks
1 T. cornstarch
3 T. sugar

2 T. of loganberry jam
1 pt. sweet cream

1 t. vanilla extract
1 c. of cream

Cook the rice. Prepare a cream sauce in the following manner: mix the egg yolks with cream, sugar and vanilla extract. Add the cornstarch. Place on low flame, stirring constantly until the sauce thickens.

Peel the whole apples. Scoop the core and fill with the jam. Place the apples on the cooked rice and in a baking dish. Cover with cream sauce and crushed macaroons. Place in a moderate oven and bake until the apples are soft.

### Apple Cake

| | |
|---|---|
| 6-8 apples | 3 T. flour |
| Cinnamon and sugar | 1 c. cream |
| 5 T. sherry | ½ c. whipped cream to garnish |
| ¼ lb. sweet almonds | 8 egg yolks |

Peel the apples. Slice them and mix with sugar, cinnamon and sherry. Prepare a batter with egg yolks beaten with sugar until light, adding flour, cream and peeled chopped almonds. Butter a baking dish and place the sliced apples on the bottom. Cover with the batter and bake in a moderate oven for 1 hour. Serve in the baking dish with whipped cream on top.

### Apple Sauce with Bread-crumbs

| | |
|---|---|
| 4 c. ready-made apple sauce | 4 T. sugar |
| Butter | 5 T. bread-crumbs |

Mix the bread-crumbs with the sugar and brown the mixture in butter. Grease a baking dish. Place a layer of apple sauce and a layer of bread-crumbs finishing with the layer of bread-crumbs. Cover with lumps of butter and place in a moderate oven for 15 minutes.

### Soufflé of Apples

| | |
|---|---|
| 5 large apples | Bread crumbs |
| ½ c. granulated sugar | Butter |
| 6 egg whites | |

Make a purée out of the apples, stirring or baking until they are very soft and then sieving them. Add the sugar and mix well. Beat the egg whites stiff and fold them into the apples. Place the mixture in a buttered baking dish, cover with bread-crumbs and put in a moderate oven for 15 minutes.

### Apples in Blankets

| | |
|---|---|
| 5 sour apples | Fat |
| 3 eggs, separated | Powdered sugar |
| 1 c. warm milk | Vanilla |
| ½ c. granulated sugar | Cinnamon |
| Flour | |

Peel the apples; scoop the core and slice in rings. Prepare the batter in the following manner; mix 3 egg yolks well, 1 c. of warm milk and sugar and beat with enough flour to make a thick batter. Fold in egg whites. Dip the apple rings in the batter and fry in very hot fat. When brown and crisp, sprinkle with vanilla, cinnamon and powdered sugar as desired. Serve hot.

## Apples in Crispy Dough

| | |
|---|---|
| 5 sour apples | ½ c. sugar |
| 2 T. raspberry jam | Flour |
| ¼ c. sour cream | 1 T. butter |

Peel the apples; scoop out the core and fill with jam. Prepare the dough in the following manner: mix the sour cream with melted butter, sugar and flour (enough to make a thick dough). Roll out thinly and cut squares twice the size of the apples. Put the apples in the middle of the dough; bring the corners together and bake in a moderate oven for 30-45 minutes.

## Apple in Crust

| | |
|---|---|
| 1 c. sour cream | 1 T. butter |
| ½ c. sugar | Flour |
| 5 peeled apples | Any kind of jam |

Peel and cut the apples in slices. Roll in sugar and cover with fruit jam. Prepare the dough with ½ c. of sour cream, 1 T. of butter, ½ c. of sugar and enough flour to make the dough workable. Knead and roll out flat. Cut the dough in 4 inch squares. Place apples in the centre of each piece of the dough and secure with a cross of dough. Put in a very hot oven for about 30 minutes or until the crust is crisp.

## Apple 'Grisette'

| | |
|---|---|
| ¼ lb. butter | 4 eggs, separated |
| 2 c. apple butter or jam | ½ c. sugar |
| 1 c. bread-crumbs | Lemon peel |
| ¼ lb. raisins | Olive oil |

Mix the butter with 4 egg yolks. Add 2 c. of thick apple jam or butter, sugar, bread-crumbs, some lemon peel, raisins, and fold in the beaten egg whites. Place in a greased baking dish and bake for 30 minutes in a moderate oven. Serve with any sweet sauces (see p. 109-112).

## Apple Fritters

| | |
|---|---|
| 1 egg | 3 T. butter or margarine |
| 2 T. sugar | 5-6 apples |
| 1 c. flour | 1 t. baking soda |
| ¼ c. buttermilk | Fat |

Slice the apples. Beat the flour with milk, sugar and egg. Add melted margarine or butter. Dissolve the soda with a few drops of water and add to the mixture. Dip the apple-slices in the batter and fry in hot fat.

## Orange Fritters

| | |
|---|---|
| 6 oranges | Lemon juice |
| 1 egg beaten | Powdered sugar |
| ½ c. flour | ¼ t. salt |
| 1 T. melted butter | 1 egg white, beaten stiff |

Sift flour with salt. Cream butter and add flour and egg. Let it stand for 1½ hours so that the batter becomes foamy. Then fold in beaten egg white. In the meantime peel both skins from the oranges and cut in slices. Sprinkle with powdered sugar and lemon juice and let stand for 45 minutes. Dip in batter and fry in deep fat. Serve with powdered sugar.

## Carrots and Apples

| | |
|---|---|
| 6 grated carrots | 4 apples, grated |
| Juice of 1 lemon | 1 T. sugar |

Mix juice with sugar and pour over the carrots and apples. May be served as a salad or a dessert.

## Banana Fritters

| | |
|---|---|
| Bananas | Fat |
| Powdered sugar | Batter (see Orange Fritters) |
| ½ lemon, juice | |

Peel the bananas. Cut in half. Sprinkle with sugar and lemon juice and let stand for 20 minutes. Dip in batter and fry in deep fat. Remove from the fat and sprinkle with powdered sugar. Serve with whipped cream.

## Apricot or Peach Cobbler

| | |
|---|---|
| 2½ c. sliced peaches or apricots | ¾ c. powdered sugar |
| | Apricot or peach stones |
| 2 eggs, separated | 2 T. sugar |

Take out the stones. Break them and take out the seeds, and blanch these. Pound them to a fine powder, adding sugar. Beat the yolks with powdered sugar until they lighten. Add the powdered seeds, combine with egg whites, beaten stiff. Spread half the batter on a buttered dish. Put in the fruits and cover with the rest of the batter. Bake for 30 minutes in a moderate oven. Serve hot with whipped cream.

## Fried Pear with Cottage Cheese and Chocolate Sauce

| | |
|---|---|
| 5 pears | 1 c. sugar |
| 1½ squares chocolate | 1 c. cottage cheese |
| ½ c. water | 3 T. sherry |
| ¼ t. pure vanilla extract | Butter |

Cook the sugar and water for 5 minutes. Melt the chocolate in a double boiler. Add the sugar and water gradually to the chocolate.

Then add sherry. Cut peeled pears in quarters and sauté in butter until lightly brown. Serve with cottage cheese and chocolate sauce.

## Decked Plums

| | |
|---|---|
| 2¼ lb. fresh plums | 1 c. wine, red and sweet |
| 1 t. vanilla extract | 1½ c. sugar |
| 2 T. sugar | 4 egg whites |

Cook wine with sugar till it boils. Remove stones from plums and simmer in syrup until soft. Press plum mixture into buttered mould. Flavour stiffly beaten egg whites with sugar and vanilla. Pour on top of plums. Bake in a hot oven until brown. Serve hot.

## Rice with Chocolate

| | |
|---|---|
| 2 c. rice | 4 T. sugar |
| 4 eggs, separated | 7 squares chocolate |
| Butter | Bread-crumbs |
| Milk | |

Cook the rice in milk and strain. Beat the egg yolks with sugar. Melt the chocolate in a little bit of butter and add to the yolks. Beat the whites and combine with rice and the chocolate mixture. Place in a greased dish which has been sprinkled with bread-crumbs and bake in a moderate oven for 30 minutes.

## Rice with Marmalade

| | |
|---|---|
| 2 c. rice | Cherry preserve |
| 2 c. milk | 1 c. sour cream |
| Lemon peel | Sugar |
| 1 egg | |

Cook the rice in sugared milk, with a few pieces of lemon peel. When tender, add the egg. Mix well. Place in a moistened cup and make shapes turning them over on an oven-proof platter. Cover each mould with cherry preserve and add sour cream previously beaten with sugar as desired. Put in a moderate oven for 10 minutes.

## Sweet Omelette on Fire

| | |
|---|---|
| 5 eggs, separated | Powdered sugar |
| 5 T. sugar, granulated | 1 jigger curacao or cherry |
| 1 T. flour | brandy |
| 5 T. raspberry jam | 2 T. alcohol |

Beat the egg yolks with the sugar until they are light. Add the flour and fold in the stiffly beaten egg whites. Put in a low baking dish which has been buttered and sprinkled with flour. Bake in a moderate oven for 25-30 minutes. When ready, cover with jam and fold. Sprinkle with the liqueur. Light up the alcohol and bring to the table while it is flaming.

## Cream of Wheat with Grenadine

| | |
|---|---|
| 2 c. milk | Heavy cream, optional |
| ¼ c. cream of wheat | 4 T. grenadine |
| Lemon or orange peel | 2 T. raisins |
| Sugar | |

Cook the cream of wheat in milk, adding sugar and lemon peel as desired, and raisins. When ready, put the whole in a moistened pudding dish. When completely cooled off, remove from the dish and pour the grenadine over it. Any fruit syrup may be used. Cover with whipped cream.

## Poppy Seed Dessert

| | |
|---|---|
| ¼ lb. poppy seeds | 6 eggs, separated |
| 1 c. almonds, chopped | 4 T. bread-crumbs |
| ¼ c. sugar | |

Scald the poppy seeds with boiling water, strain and pass through a mincer or powder with a spoon. Beat the egg yolks until they are light, adding sugar, scalded almonds chopped fine, and 4 T. of bread-crumbs. Combine with stiffly beaten egg whites. Put in a round baking dish, buttered and sprinkled with bread-crumbs. Bake in a moderate oven. Serve with jam or cream.

## White or Lemon Icing

| | |
|---|---|
| 5 egg whites | Juice of 1 lemon |
| 1 lb. powdered sugar | |

Beat the egg whites until they are stiff. Add the sugar little by little, and continue beating 5 minutes. Add juice of a lemon gradually until well blended. Cover the cake with this frosting and put it in a slow oven for 5 minutes.

## Transparent Icing

| | |
|---|---|
| 1 lb. powdered sugar | 3 T. rum |
| ¼ c. water or enough to | |
| liquify the sugar | |

Mix the powdered sugar with enough water to form a soft paste. Add the water drop by drop. When it is all transparent, add the rum and cover the cake. Place it in a lukewarm oven for 5 minutes.

## Coffee Icing

| | |
|---|---|
| 2 c. sugar | ½ pint coffee |
| ¼ c. cream | |

Pour the coffee over the sugar in a saucepan, let it dissolve and boil slowly for 15 minutes. Do not let it overboil, because this icing runs over easily. When sufficiently boiled, beat and then dilute slightly with cream.

## Chocolate Icing

| | |
|---|---|
| 1 c. sugar | 8 oz. chocolate |
| 3 T. butter | ½ c. milk |

Boil the sugar with milk, add the melted or grated chocolate, and mix well over a very low flame without letting it boil. Cream the butter in a bowl, add the chocolate dissolved in milk or water, mix fast and when the icing thickens, pour it on the cake, and let it run over, then smooth the sides with a knife.

## Paste-like Icing

| | |
|---|---|
| 1 c. sugar | Rum, brandy, or black coffee or |
| ½ c. water | strong tea |
| 1 lemon | |

Cook water and sugar until a thick syrup forms and until it spins a thread when lifted on a spoon. Pour into a bowl and stir in one direction until it makes a paste. For flavouring use lemon juice or extract, rum, brandy, coffee, tea, etc. After spreading on cake, chill.

## 2 Coloured Layer Cake

| | |
|---|---|
| ½ lb. almonds, blanched and peeled | ½ lb. almonds with peel |
| 5 egg whites | 6 eggs, separated |
| 3 c. sugar | ½ t. vanilla extract |
| 1 lemon | Strawberry jam |

Pass the peeled almonds through nut grinder. Mix them with 5 stiffly beaten egg whites and 1 c. of sugar, adding the juice of 1 lemon. Bake in a moderate oven in a round buttered cake pan which has been sprinkled with bread-crumbs, taking care that it only dries a little but does not brown. Prepare a similar layer with the unpeeled almonds, ground and mixed to a paste with 6 egg yolks, which have been beaten with the remaining c. of sugar. Fold in stiffly beaten egg whites and vanilla extract and place in a cake pan the same size as the previous one buttered and sprinkled with bread-crumbs. Bake this layer in a hot oven, and let it brown. Put jam, or, and fruit preserve in between the layers and cover with frosting.

## Walnut Cake

| | |
|---|---|
| 12 eggs, separated | *Filling:* |
| 1 c. sugar | ¼ lb. walnuts |
| ½ lb. walnuts, ground finely | 1 c. sugar |
| 1 c. flour | 4 T. sweet cream |
| Halves of walnuts dipped in heavy syrup | |

Beat the egg yolks until thick. Add sugar slowly, beating constantly. Mix ground walnuts and flour. When smooth, add the beaten egg whites. Divide the mixture in half and bake in two cake pans of the same size, which have been buttered and sprinkled with bread-crumbs. Prepare the filling in the following manner. Grind the walnuts and mix them with the sugar, moisten with sweet cream. Spread the fiilling and place the cake in a low oven for 10 minutes. After it has completely cooled off garnish it with walnut halves, dipped in syrup and cover with paste-like icing. (see above).

## Nut Layer Cake

| | |
|---|---|
| 6 egg yolks | 1 c. sugar |
| ½ c. walnuts, finely chopped | ½ c. almonds, finely chopped |
| 2 T. bread-crumbs | 1 t. vanilla extract |

Beat the egg yolks. Add sugar beating constantly. Add the finely chopped almonds and walnuts, bread-crumbs and vanilla and beat until all the ingredients are thoroughly blended or from 5-7 minutes. Finally fold in stiffly beaten egg whites. Divide in 2 equal parts. Place in prepared pans and bake in moderate oven. When cooled off spread the filling between the two layers and cover with the desired frosting.

*Almond filling:*

| | |
|---|---|
| ½ lb. powdered sugar | ½ lb. blanched almonds |
| Juice of 1 lemon or | |
|    2-3 T. sweet cream | |

Blanch and peel the almonds. Grind them. Mix with the sugar and dilute with either lemon juice or sweet cream.

*Coffee filling:*

| | |
|---|---|
| ½ lb. sweet butter | 5 eggs, separated |
| 1 c. confectioners' sugar | ⅓ c. strong coffee |

Cream the butter with sugar, adding egg yolks gradually. Add the coffee drop by drop, stirring constantly. When it is thick and smooth spread on the cake and cover with coffee frosting. (see p. 188).

*Chocolate filling:*

| | |
|---|---|
| 4 squares chocolate | ½ lb. sweet butter |
| 4 egg yolks | 4 T. sugar |

Place the chocolate in a double boiler. When it is completely soft, mix with the butter in a bowl. After blending, add egg yolks one by one and beat constantly. Fill the cake and cover with transparent frosting (see p. 188).

## Chocolate Cake

| | |
|---|---|
| 1 lb. almonds blanched and | 2 whole eggs |
|    ground | Chocolate icing (see page 189) |
| 1 t. vanilla extract | 4 squares chocolate, grated |
| 10 egg yolks, hard-boiled | 2 c. sugar |

*Filling:*

| | |
|---|---|
| ½ lb. almonds | 1 c. sugar |
| Juice of 1 lemon | 4 T. sweet cream |

Mix the chopped almonds, vanilla and grated chocolate. Add 10 hard-boiled egg yolks which have been passed through the sieve. Add the sugar and 2 eggs and mix all the ingredients well. Divide in 2 equal parts and place in 2 round buttered baking dishes. Bake in a moderate oven. When the cake is cooked, make the filling out of the ground almonds, sugar, lemon juice and cream. Cover with chocolate icing (see p. 189).

## Unbaked Chocolate Cake

| | |
|---|---|
| ¼ lb. sweet butter | Almonds for garnishing |
| 1 c. sugar | 5 T. sweet cream |
| 4 squares grated chocolate | ¼ lb. walnuts, ground |
| | Chocolate icing (see page 189) |

Cream the butter with sugar and the chocolate. When the paste is smooth, place it in a buttered layer cake pan and put in the refrigerator. On the side grind the walnuts. Mix with sugar. Add the sweet cream. Mix well again and spread the mixture on the chocolate one. Cover with chocolate icing and make flowers out of almonds, using, as centres, dots of orange peel.

## Coffee Cake

| | |
|---|---|
| ¾ lb. sweet butter | 3 c. flour |
| 2 eggs | 1½ c. sugar |
| ¼ lb. almonds, ground | |

*Filling:*

| | |
|---|---|
| 4 egg yolks | ½ c. sweet cream |
| 4 T. sugar | 1 t. vanilla extract |
| 1 T. flour | ¼ c. strong coffee |

Beat the butter well. Add the eggs and sugar. Mix well. Add the ground almonds. Mix again and add the flour. Divide in 3 portions and bake in identical buttered pans in a moderate oven. When they are cool, spread them with the filling. Beat the egg yolks with sugar. When they become light add the flour gradually. Bring the cream to a boil with the vanilla. Pour the eggs over the cream and mix until smooth on a very low flame. When it cools off add the coffee. Spread the filling on the layers. Let them stand over-night. Cover with coffee icing (see p. 188).

## Napoleon Cake

| | |
|---|---|
| ¼ lb. sweet butter | Lemon peel, grated |
| 1 c. sugar | 2 squares chocolate, grated |
| 4 eggs, separated | ¼ c. flour |
| ¼ lb. almonds, unpeeled, chopped | Chocolate filling (see page 191) |

Cream the butter with sugar and egg yolks. Add ground almonds, grated chocolate, grated lemon peel and flour. Mix all the ingredients well. Then fold in stiffly beaten egg whites. Divide in 2 equal portions and bake in moderate oven in 2 buttered baking pans. When the layers cool off, place a chocolate filling in between them and cover with the desired icing.

## Chestnut Cake

½ lb. blanched almonds
1 c. sugar
12 egg whites

Lemon icing (see page 188)
Bread-crumbs

*Filling:*

4 c. milk
2 lbs. chestnuts

½ lb. sweet butter
Sugar and vanilla to taste

Pass the blanched almonds through a nut grinder. Mix with sugar and stiffly beaten egg whites. Divide in half and bake in 2 buttered baking pans sprinkled with bread-crumbs. When they are cool, spread with chestnut filling prepared in the following manner: Half-cook the chestnuts. Peel them. Then cook them in milk, stirring often so that they do not burn. When completely soft, add the sugar and vanilla to taste and sieve. On the side, melt the butter. Place it in a bowl. Let it cool, then beat hard. Mix with chestnut mixture and spread on the layers. Cover with lemon icing.

## Marzipan Cake

1 lb. almonds, unpeeled
½ lb. sweet butter
2 c. sugar
8 egg yolks, hard-boiled

2 T. flour
3 eggs
1 t. vanilla
White icing (see page 188)

Pass the unpeeled almonds through a nut grinder. Cream the butter with the sugar, beating continuously. Add hard-boiled egg yolks, after having sieved them. Add the whole eggs, almonds, vanilla and the flour. Mix all the ingredients well. Set aside a small part of the mixture, for garnishing the cake. Place in a buttered baking dish, sprinkled with bread-crumbs, and bake in a moderate oven, after having garnished the top with the remaining paste. When ready, cover with white icing.

## Sandy Cake

¾ lb. butter
3¼ c. flour
½ c. sugar
Apricot jam

Powdered sugar
1 t. vanilla
Bread-crumbs

Beat the butter well. Add the flour and mix. Add the sugar and the vanilla. Beat all the ingredients. Divide the mixture in 3 parts and bake in buttered pans sprinkled with bread-crumbs in a moderate oven. Be careful that it does not become too brown. When cool, spread each layer with apricot jam and cover with powdered sugar.

## Dobosz Cake

*Filling:*

| | |
|---|---|
| 1¼ c. sugar | 6 egg yolks |
| 3 T. cornstarch | ½ lb. sweet butter |
| Powdered sugar | 3 squares chocolate |
| 8 eggs, separated | 1 c. sugar |

Mix the sugar with egg yolks until they become thick and light. Add stiffly beaten egg whites and cornstarch. Mix lightly and divide into 3 portions, bake them separately on buttered baking dishes, in a moderate oven. When they cool, spread with the following filling: Beat together 6 egg yolks with a c. of sugar and vanilla. Then place in a double-boiler, and stir constantly until the mixture is thick. Cool off. On the side beat the butter. Add to it cooled eggs and grated chocolate. When the paste is smooth, spread the layers with it and cover with powdered sugar.

## Almond Mazurek

| | |
|---|---|
| 1 lb. almonds, blanched | Lemon icing (see page 188) |
| 2 c. sugar | 2 eggs |
| Juice of 1 lemon | Bread-crumbs |

Pass the blanched almonds through the grinder. Mix them with sugar, eggs and add lemon juice. Place in a buttered pan, sprinkled with bread-crumbs. Bake in a moderate oven. When cool, cover with lemon icing.

## Sultan's Mazurek

| | |
|---|---|
| 12 egg yolks | 1 c. raisins |
| 2 c. sugar | 1 c. almonds, blanched |
| 4 c. flour | 1 c. dried figs, chopped |

Beat the egg yolks with sugar until light. Then gradually add the flour beating constantly. Chop the dried fruit finely, and mix with the paste. Spread the mixture on a low buttered baking dish, sprinkled with flour, and bake in a low oven for about 35 minutes.

## Apple Mazurek

| | |
|---|---|
| 1 lb. sweet butter | 8 eggs |
| 1 lb. blanched almonds | 4 c. flour |
| 2 c. sugar | |

*Filling:*

| | |
|---|---|
| 1 c. water | Lemon rind, grated |
| 2 c. sugar | 5 apples |

Beat softened butter with ground almonds and sugar. Add the eggs and flour, beating constantly. Work it into a good dough. Roll out to make a thin layer. Grease a baking sheet. Sprinkle with flour, and place the layer of dough on it. Bake in a moderate oven. On the side prepare a thick syrup out of the water and sugar. Peel and slice the apples. Stew them in the syrup until they are cooked to jam. Add grated lemon rind and stir occasionally with a spoon, so that apples will not stick to the bottom of the pot. Cover the warm pastry with this.

## Date Mazurek

| | |
|---|---|
| 6 egg whites | ¼ lb. almonds, blanched and |
| ¼ lb. dates, sliced | chopped |
| 8 squares chocolate, grated | Paste-like icing (see page 189) |
| 2 c. sugar | |

Beat the whites until stiff, adding sugar gradually and stirring it for about 7 minutes with an electric mixer—it takes longer by hand. Add blanched, ground almonds, dates and grated chocolate. Mix all the ingredients well, and pour on to a buttered baking sheet. Bake in a low oven. When ready, let it cool off and cover with paste-like icing. Needless to say—a very rich dessert—served in small squares!

## Cheese Cake

| | |
|---|---|
| 2 lb. cottage cheese | 10 eggs, separated |
| 2 c. sugar | 1 t. vanilla |
| ¼ c. flour | 1 t. cinnamon |
| 1 t. salt | ¼ c. sugar |
| 1 c. sweet cream | 1 lb. cookies or graham |
| 3 T. butter | crackers |

Pass the cheese through the sieve. Combine it with sugar, flour and salt. Beat the egg yolks well and add to cheese paste. Add sweet cream, cinnamon and vanilla. Beat egg whites and fold them in slowly. Crumble the cookies or graham crackers evenly and add sugar. Put aside some of the crumbs for the top of the cake. Butter a baking sheet, cover with a layer of crumbs and then with cheese paste and cover with crumbs again. Bake in a moderate oven for 1 hour.

## Bottomless Cheese Cake

| | |
|---|---|
| 8 c. of cottage cheese | 1 T. mashed potatoes |
| ¼ lb. sweet butter | 2 c. sugar |
| 1 t. vanilla | |

Pass the cheese through the sieve, place it in a cheese cloth or paper towel and work it as though it were dough. Beat softened butter until it is light as beaten egg white. Add the cheese, sugar, vanilla and a a spoon of mashed potatoes. Work the mixture thoroughly. Bake for 1 hour in a moderate oven. When it cools you may frost or serve plain. You should bake it in a greased angel-cake-type of pan that opens.

## Paczki

| | |
|---|---|
| ½ c. water | 6 eggs |
| ¼ c. butter melted | Fat |
| 1 c. flour | Powdered sugar |
| Dash of salt | 1 T. sugar |

Bring water to boil with the butter. Add flour gradually mixing constantly, until the butter forms a ball. Remove from stove and cool. Add salt, granulated sugar and beat in eggs one by one. Form round balls, greasing your hands in melted butter each time, and fry in hot deep fat under cover, on a low flame for about 15 minutes or until evenly browned, turning once. Drain on absorbent paper in a warm place. Cover with powdered sugar.

## Paczki II

| | |
|---|---|
| 6 c. flour | Orange peel, grated |
| 5 c. milk | ½ lb. butter |
| 2 yeast cakes | Fat |
| 12 egg yolks | 1 c. sugar |
| ¼ t. vanilla extract | Cherry preserve |

Scald 4 c. of flour with 4 c. of boiling milk stirring it constantly, so that no lumps form. When the batter cools off, fold in diluted yeast, (dilute the yeast in 1 c. of lukewarm milk). Separately mix 12 egg yolks with sugar, vanilla and grated orange peel. When the batter starts to move or grow, fold in the egg mixture and 2 more c. of flour. Add melted butter and work the dough long enough to see it bubble. Set it aside in a warm place. Cover with a towel and let it rise. When double in bulk place it on kneading board, sprinkle with flour, and roll it out to 1 inch thick. Cut out round patties, place a spoonful of cherry preserve on each patty of dough and cover again with another patty of the same size. Set aside to rise for 1 hour. Fry in deep hot fat until evenly browned. Sprinkle with powdered sugar and serve.

## Paczki III

| | |
|---|---|
| 1 c. sweet cream | 1 lb. rice flour |
| 12 egg yolks | 2 yeast cakes or granulated |
| 5 T. sweet butter | yeast |
| 6 T. sugar | Cherry preserve |
| 1 jigger apricot brandy | Fat |

Warm the cream slightly. Beat in the egg yolks and melted butter add sugar, crushed yeast, and mix together thoroughly. Fold in rice flour and add brandy. Work the batter with a spoon for 10 minutes, and when it starts to bubble, set aside to rise for approximately 1 hour or until double in bulk. Prepare small patties as in the previous recipe and fry them in deep fat.

### Filled Apple Roll

| | |
|---|---|
| 4 c. flour | Grated orange peel |
| 2 c. sugar | 1 t. vanilla extract |
| 3 eggs | 1 t. almond extract |
| 1 c. milk | 1 t. mace |
| ½ c. shortening | 1 t. salt |
| 2 yeast cakes | 5 cooking apples |

Dissolve yeast in 5 T. of lukewarm milk. Add 2 T. of sugar and let stand for a few minutes. Melt the shortening. Add 1½ c. sugar and the remaining milk. Cool. Beat the eggs well. Add salt and fold into the other mixture. Add 3 c. of flour and mix persistently with a spoon or electric beater. Let it stand and rise until double in bulk. Punch down and knead in remaining flour. Let rise again. Spread on floured board and roll to ½ inch thickness. Cover with diced apples and sugar. Roll like a jelly roll and close the edges tightly. Grease a pan and fill with apple roll. Let rise for an hour. Bake in a moderate oven for 1 hour. Sprinkle with sugar and serve.

### Babka

| | |
|---|---|
| 1 c. milk | Dash of salt |
| 4 T. milk, warm | 1 c. raisins |
| ¾ c. sugar | ½ c. butter |
| 3 c. flour | 1 c. almonds, peeled, ground |
| 12 egg yolks | ¼ c. orange peel, chopped |
| 2 yeast cakes | ½ c. lemon peel, chopped |
| 1 t. vanilla extract | Paste-like icing (see page 189) |
| ¼ t. almond extract | |

Scald the milk. Combine 1 c. flour with milk and cool. Dissolve yeast in the remaining milk. Add to the milk and flour. Beat together. Let it rise until double in bulk. Beat egg yolks with sugar until fluffy and fold into the dough. Add remaining flour and knead until elastic. Add softened butter and continue kneading. Add flavouring and chopped fruit. Punch down and let rise. Punch down again and place in a greased fluted tube pan. Let it rise for one hour. Bake in moderate oven for one hour. Spread with paste-like icing before serving.

### Baba

| | |
|---|---|
| 1 c. milk | 3 yeast cakes |
| 1 c. butter, sweet | 1 t. vanilla |
| 4 c. flour | 1 jigger cherry brandy |
| 1 c. sugar | Dash of salt |
| 12 egg yolks | |
| 1 c. raisins | |

Beat egg yolks well. Dissolve yeast in milk and combine with egg yolks. Add 2 c. flour and let stand until double in bulk. Mix again and add the remaining flour sugar, butter and flavouring. Knead until firm. Let rest again. Punch down and let rise again. Place in a greased tube mould. Let stand for another hour and bake in moderate oven for one hour. Cover with paste-like icing (see p. 189).

### Chrust or Favorki

| | |
|---|---|
| 2 c. flour | Lard |
| 2 T. sugar | Honey |
| 1 T. butter | 1 egg |
| 1 T. vinegar | ½ c. sour cream |

Mix the flour with butter, sugar, egg, vinegar and enough sour cream to work the batter into a soft dough. Place the dough on a kneading board and roll out. Cut in 2 x 4 inch strips. Cut a hole in the middle of each strip, then pass one end of the strip through it to make a knot. Fry favorki in hot lard, sprinkling it with powdered sugar when brown. Serve with honey.

### Favorki without Egg Whites

| | |
|---|---|
| 6 egg yolks | 6 T. sugar |
| 1 c. sweet cream | 1 jigger apricot brandy |
| 2 or more c. flour | |

Beat the egg yolks with sugar until light. Add sweet cream and brandy, fold in enough flour to make a firm dough. Roll it out thinly and prepare as in previous recipe.

### Poppy Seed Roll

| | |
|---|---|
| 2 c. flour | ½ c. sugar |
| 2 T. warm water | Dash of salt |
| ¼ c. milk | Dash of cinnamon |
| 2 egg yolks | 1 yeast cake |
| 3 T. butter | |

Cream butter with sugar. Beat the egg yolks. Combine eggs with butter mixture. Dissolve yeast in hot water. Mix the flour with yeast and eggs mixture, add milk gradually. Add salt and cinnamon.

Knead well together and let rise. When double in size, punch down and let rise again. Roll out until ½ inch thick and spread with poppy seed paste. Roll up, sealing the edges. Place in baking dish and let rise some more. Bake in moderate oven for 45 minutes.

## Poppy Seed Paste

| | |
|---|---|
| 1 c. poppy seed | ¼ t. vanilla extract |
| 1 c. cream | Lemon peel, ground |
| ½ c. sugar | ½ c. raisins |
| ½ c. butter | |

Scald the poppy seeds. Place in a mortar and mix with a wooden spoon. Place them in a pot with sugar and butter and simmer, mixing constantly. Boil the cream with vanilla. When the poppy seeds have lost their moisture combine with cream, mix thoroughly, add ground lemon peel and raisins and use as spread for poppy seed roll.

# COOKIES

## Butter Horns

| | |
|---|---|
| 1 c. butter | ½ c. sugar, granulated |
| 1½ c. flour | 1 t. vanilla |
| ¾ c. almonds, blanched | Powdered sugar |

Beat the softened butter with the sugar. Grind the almonds. Add them with the vanilla to the other mixture. Blend in the flour. Roll out on a floured board, and cut into cookie shapes. Bake on a cookie sheet in moderate oven until lightly browned. While still warm sprinkle with powdered sugar.

## Honey Cookies

| | |
|---|---|
| 3½ c. flour | 1 t. nutmeg |
| ½ c. honey | ½ t. cinnamon |
| 3 eggs | ¼ c. vanilla |
| ½ c. sugar | Almonds, blanched and halved |
| 1 t. baking soda | ¼ t. ginger |

Mix the honey with sugar. Add the eggs and beat well. Combine the well-sifted flour with spices and baking soda. Add the honey.

Let it set, or harden in a cool place. Roll and cut out round or heart shaped cookies. Place one almond on each cookie. Place on buttered baking sheet and bake in moderate oven for 15 minutes. To make the top shiny brush with egg white before baking. For variation use candied cherry instead of almonds.

### Makagiga

| | |
|---|---|
| 1 lb. almonds, chopped | ¾ c. butter |
| ½ c. honey | ¼ c. sugar |

Brown the sugar over a low fire until like caramel. Add honey and butter and let it cook for 20 minutes. Add nuts to the honey and cook very slowly for 10 minutes. Place waxed paper on a board. Moisten with water and drop from a wooden spoon in cookie sizes and harden in the refrigerator.

### Chocolate Cookies

| | |
|---|---|
| 8 egg yolks | ¼ c. flour |
| 1 c. sugar | ½ lb. sweet chocolate bits |
| 1 c. almonds, chopped | |

Melt the chocolate on a top of a double boiler. Beat sugar with the egg yolks. Add to the melted chocolate. Mix in the almonds and the flour. Drop from a cookie press on to a buttered baking sheet. Bake in moderate oven until lightly browned.

### Piernik

| | |
|---|---|
| 4 c. flour | ¼ t. ginger |
| 2 eggs | Salt |
| 1 c. sugar | 1 egg white |
| 1 c. honey | Powdered sugar |
| 2 t. baking soda | 1 t. vanilla |
| ¼ t. cinnamon | 1 T. water |

Beat the eggs well. Add sugar and blend in honey and vanilla. Then add the soda dissolved in 1 T. of water. Slowly stir in sifted flour, salt, cinnamon and ginger. Mix all the ingredients together well. Roll dough to a thin layer on a floured board and cut into large heart shapes. Brush with egg white and dust with powdered sugar. Bake in a moderate oven for about 15 minutes, on a greased floured baking sheet.

### Neapolitan Cookies

| | |
|---|---|
| 1 c. almonds, peeled and ground | 2 eggs |
| 1 c. butter | 4 egg yolks, hard-boiled |
| 1 c. sugar | Lemon rind |
| | 4 c. flour |

Mix ground almonds with 4 sieved, hard-boiled egg yolks. Cream butter and sugar. Add eggs, flour, grated lemon rind and finally the almond paste. Work it well into an elastic dough. Place on ice for 1 hour, then roll out and cut in cookie shapes. Bake on buttered sheet in a moderate oven.

## Coffee Bezy or Meringue

2 c. sugar
1 c. strong coffee

Whipped cream
5 egg whites

Boil sugar and coffee until it forms a firm ball when dropped in cold water. Beat the egg whites until stiff. Slowly pour the syrup on top of them, beating constantly. Cover and let stand in a cool place for 15 minutes. Place on waxed paper in little round patty shapes. Bake on a baking sheet in a slow oven for about 30 minutes. 2 meringues may be combined with whipped cream between.

## Madelaines

8 egg yolks
2 c. sugar
2 c. flour

1 jigger rum
Candied orange peel
1 c. melted butter

Beat egg yolks and sugar until light coloured. Add flour, melted butter, chopped dried orange rind and finally rum. Mix well. Butter muffin tins and fill them less than half-full with the batter. Bake in moderate oven for about 15-20 minutes.

## Little Piernik

4 c. honey
2 T. candied orange peel,
    chopped
1 t. pepper

1 jigger rum
1 t. cinnamon
1 t. ground cloves
6 c. whole wheat flour

Add the rum to the honey and warm on low flame. Remove from the flame. Add the chopped orange peel, cinnamon, cloves and pepper. Brown the flour in a pot, over a low flame for 5 minutes. Gradually pour in the honey mixture. Beat with an electric beater for 10 minutes or longer by hand, then roll out. Cut round shapes. Place on buttered sheet and bake in hot oven.

### Cup Cakes

*Filling:*

1 lb. sweet butter
2 c. sugar
2 c. flour
2 eggs

2 egg yolks
½ c. sugar
½ t. vanilla
½ c. sour cream
Bitter almonds

Beat the butter with the sugar, flour and then eggs. Knead into a dough. Half-fill greased muffin tins with part of the dough. On the side mix 2 egg yolks with sugar, vanilla and sour cream. Add a few finely chopped bitter almonds. Place this mixture on low flame until it thickens. When it cools off, pour on top of the dough in tins for filling. Cover with dough top. Seal the edges of the cakes. Place in hot oven for 30 minutes. Do not remove from the tins until they are completely cool. These cakes may be served with whipped cream.

# DRINKS, LIQUEURS AND PRESERVES

The use of wine during meals is not very common in Poland, but a glass of vodka before meal or a drink of liqueur after dinner, especially during winter is customary.

Pure Alcohol is open for sale and everyone can provide for his "needs".

## Warm Beer

4 c. beer                          1 t. cinnamon
3 cloves                           6 egg yolks
¼ c. sugar

Cook the beer with cloves and cinnamon for a few minutes. Strain. Beat the egg yolks with sugar until they become fluffy and combine gradually with the beer, beating constantly. Serve hot.

## Warm Wine

¼ c. white wine per person        Grated lemon rind
2 T. sugar per person             2 cloves per person
1 t. cinnamon per person

Cook all the ingredients, strain and serve hot.

## New Year's Wine Punch

*Juice of:*

2 c. sugar                         4 oranges
1 bottle light white wine          4 lemons
Grated rind of 4 oranges           1 c. pineapple
Grated rind of 2 lemons
1 c. sweet liquer

Mix the sugar with the orange and lemon rinds. Bring all the ingredients to boiling point. Serve very hot.

## Grog

2 c. sugar                         1 jigger of cherry brandy
1 c. strong tea                    3 c. water
Juice of 4 lemons                  Grated rind of 4 oranges

Mix the sugar with the orange rind. Cook sugar, water, tea and lemon juice. Serve very hot with 1 slice of orange in each cup. Pour in 1 jigger of brandy and serve flaming.

## Egg Punch

2 c. water                         Rind of 1 lemon
2 c. sugar                         Rind of 1 orange
8 egg yolks                        1 c. cherry brandy

Bring sugar, water and combined rind of lemon and orange to a boiling point. Strain and cool. Beat in egg yolks, add liqueur and beat on the fire until it rises. Serve very hot.

## Cherry or Plum Brandy

4 lb. cherries or plums            Alcohol
2 lb. sugar                        Pieces of lemon rind

Place the fruit in a large jar and cover with sugar and lemon rind. Cover the jar with a piece of cheese cloth and let stand for 6-8 weeks. Strain and bottle. Cover the remaining fruit with alcohol and let stand for a few months. Then pass the brandy into bottles and let the liqueur rest awaiting the worthy occasion, at least a few months . . .).

## Krupnik

| | |
|---|---|
| 3 c. alcohol | Dash of cinnamon |
| 2 c. water | 2 c. honey |
| Cloves, a few | 1 t. vanilla |
| Lemon rind | Peppercorns, a few, optional |

Warm up the honey with spices. Add water, bring to a boil, Strain. Take off the flame, add the alcohol and serve. The remaining krupnik may be bottled and served either hot or cold.

## Lemon or Orange Vodka

| | |
|---|---|
| 4 c. alcohol | Rind of 3 lemons |
| 1 lb. sugar | or 2 oranges |
| 2 c. water | |

Cut in small strips the outer skin of lemon or orange only. Place in a bottle and cover with alcohol. Let it stand for 4 days in a warm room. Make a syrup out of sugar and water and combine with the alcohol. Strain and bottle.

## Caraway Seed Vodka

| | |
|---|---|
| 3 c. alcohol | 2 lb. sugar |
| 3 c. water | ½ c. caraway seed |

Mix alcohol with caraway seed. On the side prepare a syrup out of sugar and water and combine with the alcohol. Strain and bottle. The longer the caraway vodka awaits its course the better it is.

## Apricot Vodka

| | |
|---|---|
| 1 lb. apricots | 2 c. sugar |
| 3 c. alcohol | grated lemon or orange rind |
| 3 c. water | |

Make a syrup out of 1 c. water and sugar. Place stoned apricots in the syrup and simmer for 5 minutes. Strain. Add alcohol, reserved water, orange rind and bottle. Let it stand for 6 weeks.

## Coffee Liqueur

| | |
|---|---|
| 5 c. alcohol | ½ lb. coffee (the darker roast |
| 4 lb. sugar | is better) |
| 4 c. water | |

Pour 1 c. of alcohol over the fresh coffee and let stand for a week. Prepare a syrup out of sugar and water, bring it to boil and take off the flame. Add the remaining alcohol and finally combine with the coffee. Strain and bottle. Let it stand for a few months.

### Persico Liqueur

| | |
|---|---|
| 4 c. alcohol | 4 cloves |
| 1 T. cinnamon | 2 lb. sugar |
| 4 T. almonds, bitter and ground | 2 c. water |

Pour alcohol over ground almonds and spices. Let it stand for a week. Prepare a syrup out of water and sugar. Strain the almond mixture and combine with syrup. Strain again and bottle.

### Raspberry Preserve

| | |
|---|---|
| 1 lb. large raspberries | 1 c. water |
| 2 lb. sugar | |

Prepare a syrup out of sugar and water. Bring to a boil. Add raspberries. Cook over a low flame. Cover. Let stand for a day. Place on fire again for an additional 10 minutes. Transfer into jars.

### Melon Preserve

| | |
|---|---|
| 1 melon, large | $\frac{1}{2}$ c. water |
| 3 c. sugar | 1 jigger sweet brandy |
| 1 lemon, juice | |

Clean and peel your melon. Dice. Cook in water to cover until tender or soft. Place on a colander and sprinkle with cold water. Put in a bowl and sprinkle with lemon and brandy. Let it stand for 3 hours. Prepare a syrup out of water and sugar, place in it the melon and cook for 5 minutes. Let it rest under cover for 24 hours. Cook again until transparent..Cool. Place in jars.

### Currant Preserve

| | |
|---|---|
| 4 c. cleaned currants | $\frac{1}{2}$ to 1 c. water |
| 5 c. sugar | |

Prepare syrup out of sugar and water. Bring to a boil. Add currants and cook for 15 to 20 minutes. Skim. Cool. Place in jars.

# HOLIDAY FOOD AND CUSTOMS

Christmas Eve is the most widely celebrated holiday in Poland. Keeping the fast was an important preface to the celebrations. One did not eat until after the first star rose, symbolizing the star which heralded the birth of Christ. Many Christmas rites and customs still observed today add a flair of romance and idealism to the essentially religious character of the Polish manner of keeping Christmas.

Traditionally connected with pagan thanksgiving for the coming of the Spring, the Easter celebration has retained its character of great feasting in Poland, while gaining in religious significance. Whatever appears on the table has to be blessed previously by the priest.

# CHRISTMAS

The Christmas Eve dinner in Poland was the centre of the observance. There was a custom of setting the table for more people than there were in a household in order to remember members of the family who were gone. This was done in the great houses as well as in the simplest cottages.

In the peasant huts, loaves of bread would be left on the table after dinner so that Christ might help Himself if He came during the night. Sheaves of wheat would be set out in all corners of the diningroom and bunches of wheat would be placed beneath the table cloth according to the proverb which said, "Hay in the hut and misery out of it."

An important ceremony preceded the dinner. The head of the family first divided the altar bread—oplatek—which had been prepared especially in the churches and the convents of Poland for the significant occasion. This custom symbolized the communion among family and friends.

Lighted Christmas trees were often hung from the ceiling in the country, decorated with home-made toys, nuts, apples, and candy. In the city, Christmas trees were usually placed on tables or on the floor. Gifts are given during Christmas Eve and carols are sung. In the country "travelling" boys still go from house to house with a lighted star on a stick. Images of the three kings and of cocks, traditionally honoured symbols, were also carried like banners by the carol singers who continued their journeys during the festive season, lasting in Poland until the Feast of the three kings on January 6.

The head of a household in the country would always go to the barn after dinner to give a special treat to his animals. According to Polish folklore, animals acquire human voices on Christmas Eve.

# POLISH CHRISTMAS EVE DINNER

## MENU

Clear mushroom soup with noodles

or

Clear barshch with mushroom ushka

or

Fish Soup

or

Almond Soup

Boiled carp with Polish Egg sauce or grey sauce

or

Carp in aspic

or

Carp, Jewish style

Stewed cabbage with mushrooms

Dried prunes compôte

Poppy seed roll

Apple strudel

Honey cakes

'Kutia'

Dried fruit

# EASTER LUNCHEON

Traditionally connected with pagan thanksgiving for the coming of the Spring, the Easter celebration has retained its character of great feasting in Poland, while gaining in religious significance. Whatever appears on the table has to be blessed previously by the priest.

The table, set all in white, has a center piece the traditional lamb.

In olden times, it was a broiled lamb which eventually changed into a lamb made of sugar. There are boiled and smoked ham, various kinds of Polish sausage and roast veal or a suckling pig. In keeping with the ancient tradition are the colorfully painted hard-boiled eggs, salt and bread. Cheese cakes, Easter fruit cakes, and babas fill the table. Vodkas and liqueurs add to the gaiety. Each guest upon entering the room is greeted by the host with a quartered hard-boiled egg. Sharing the egg, the host and guest express their wishes and greetings. On Easter day you may visit any friend without an invitation. Everybody who has a house has an open house.

# INTERNATIONAL "GOURMET" DISHES

Times of gluttony for its own sake have really passed. We would hardly appreciate now the banquets in which pheasant's brains or tongues of flamingos were served, or even wine with dissolved pearls .... Modern times brought with them the respect for science and with it the respect for the laws of nature, and indigestion is not acclaimed as an asset of good eating as it was during Nero's times.

In our journey through international good dishes, the idea behind was that all countries have their own "gourmet" cooking and in all countries there is good food, even if so different from our own set ways of eating.

Although it may seem very unsophisticated to some, learning about other nations' food is one way to bring us nearer to them and like them . . . After all, is it not said that the best way to a man's heart is his stomach?

# UNITED STATES

In the United States there has probably never been a general food shortage since the first winter the Pilgrims spent at Plymouth. Americans eat foods from every part of the world, cooked in every manner, and often processed to a stage where the housewife may need only to "Heat and Serve" as stated on the package. Complete dinners may be turned out of freezers or cans requiring a simple warming-up process before they are put on the table.

*Thanksgiving Dinner.* Despite the quantity of food available, too many Americans eat poor food, subsisting on the products of hurried or careless cooks. There is one day in the year, however, when every American insists upon cookery of the highest quality and quantity. It is the traditional Thanksgiving Day dinner, a custom which harks back to that first harvest of the Pilgrim Fathers. It was the day they set aside to give thanks to God for the yield of their summer's labour. It is celebrated each year on a late Thursday in November by a dinner intended to be an echo of the feast that the early settlers enjoyed with their Indian guests.

The basic and primary requirement is a turkey. Every homemaker has her own particular stuffing or basting material or manner of roasting a turkey.The following recipe is not intended to be typical. It is merely one way of roasting a Thanksgiving turkey. The

only rule that is generally accepted is that the turkey must be large
enough for every guest to have three times as much turkey as he
could eat any other day in the year.

## Roast Turkey

| | |
|---|---|
| 1 turkey, dressed and cleaned | Salt |

*Stuffing:*

| | |
|---|---|
| Sage | 1 lb. sausage meat, minced |
| Parsley, chopped | Sprinkling of poultry seasoning |
| 1 large onion | Bread-crumbs as desired |
| Salt and pepper | Stalks of celery, chopped |
| 1 egg, optional | Several apples, chopped |
| Milk or water | |

In making stuffing, the creative cook lets herself go and often cleans
her refrigerator. Using either dry bread-crumbs or small torn pieces
of moist bread as a base, she uses almost anything she likes to taste
as additional flavouring for stuffing and for the turkey itself. Although milk or water are the standard wetting agents, chicken stock
or pea soup lend delightful flavours to the mixture. An egg is a co-
hesive or binding influence in a stuffing and may be used or not,
depending upon the texture desired.

In the above, the sausage meat is browned in a frying pan until
it is crumbly and partially cooked. Onions, celery, apples are added
and browned. Remove from the fire and combine with bread and
seasonings. An unbeaten egg may be mixed into the stuffing at this
point and enough liquid to make a wet but not sloppy concoction.
If desired, the giblets may be cooked in water and when tender,
chopped and added. The water in which they are cooked makes a
good liquid agent for the stuffing.

To prepare a cleaned bird for stuffing, pat salt on to the inside of
the cavities. Now fill with the stuffing. When the bird is well packed,
secure the openings with needle and thread or skewers and twine
laced over them.

The bird will bake well and be easier to handle if the wings and
legs are bound close to the body with stout thread or string. It is
then placed in a shallow roasting pan.

There are two ways to roast a turkey in time for a noontime or
early afternoon Thanksgiving dinner. By the first, the cook rises
at dawn to prepare the turkey. She coats it with a mixture of butter
and flour and then roasts it in a moderate oven (350°), calculating
to allow 25 minutes per pound if it weighs under 12 lb. or 20 minutes
per pound if it weighs more than that. She bastes it with butter and

water every 15 minutes or as often as she remembers it during the morning hours.

By the second method she stuffs and prepares the turkey the night before Thanksgiving. Just before going to bed she coats it with salad oil and covers it closely with metal foil. She then places it in a 250° oven and goes to bed to sleep until her usual rising hour the next morning. She removes it from the oven and lets it rest until almost dinner time.

She removes the foil and browns it in a 450° oven to serve hot from the oven.

*Vegetables to accompany roast turkey*

### Mashed Potatoes

| | |
|---|---|
| Potatoes | Butter |
| Milk | Salt and pepper |
| Paprika | |

The potatoes are peeled, cut into chunks if they are large, and boiled until tender in salted water to cover or pressure cooked the recommended period of time. Drain and mash or whip with electric beaters. Add a generous chunk of butter and milk to the desired consistency, seasoning with salt and pepper and topping with a sprinkle of paprika.

### Boiled Onions

| | |
|---|---|
| Onions | Salt and pepper |
| Butter | Milk or cream |

Onions should be peeled and boiled in water to cover, starting cold, until they are easily pierced through with a dinner fork. Just before serving, drain. Add a generous lump of butter and milk or cream. Warm again and serve in small individual bowls.

### Turnips

| | |
|---|---|
| Turnips | Salt and pepper |
| Caraway seeds, several | Butter |

Peel turnips. They may either be cut in chunks for boiling, then mashed when tender, or diced for cooking and served in that style. If caraway seed is added to the cooking water some of the strong odour of turnips is eliminated. When tender, drain, salt and pepper, and top with butter.

### Squash

| | |
|---|---|
| Squash | Salt and pepper |
| Butter | Brown sugar |

A hard-shelled squash may be either baked in the shell or peeled and steamed. In baking, pieces are placed in a baking pan, inside up. They are sprinkled with salt, until tender, basting with melted butter to keep moist. When the squash is peeled and steamed the seasonings and butter are added after mashing. This, too, may be kept warm in the oven until serving time.

### Cranberry Sauce

Cranberries                                    Sugar
Water

Clean cranberries, washing and removing stems. Place in a sauce-pan with sugar and water. The proportions would be approximately $2\frac{1}{2}$ c. of cranberries to 1 c. sugar and 1 c. of water. The sugar may be increased if a sweeter sauce is desired. Cook together, until the cranberries are tender, taking care that it does not boil over. Serve cold.

### Gravy for Turkey

Turkey drippings in                            Water
   roasting pan                                Flour
Gravy concentrate

After the turkey has been removed from the roasting pan, pour off grease. Place over low flame and stir in a paste which has been made from equal parts of flour and water. When smooth, slowly add water, stirring constantly until it thickens and browns. A gravy concentrate may be added, according to instructions on the label, if desired. When ready, the gravy may be strained into a serving vessel.

### Pumpkin Pie

Crust:
   2 c. flour                                  $\frac{3}{4}$ c. shortening
   1 t. salt                                   Cold water

Mix salt with flour. Cut in shortening with 2 knives or pastry blender until pieces are pea-sized. Sprinkle in cold water until the material forms a ball. Chill. Divide in half and roll each crust into a circle the size of the pie pan. Sometimes it is easier to handle if rolled between two pieces of waxed paper. Place in 2 pans.

*Filling for 2 pies*

   2 c. cooked pumpkin                          1 c. brown sugar
   1 t. cinnamon                                $\frac{1}{2}$ t. salt
   $\frac{1}{4}$ t. ginger                      2 c. rich milk
   2 eggs, beaten

Pumpkin may be either peeled and steamed or baked in shell in a moderate oven. It should be sieved or mashed until smooth for this purpose. Stir together all the ingredients and pour into two unbaked pie shells. Bake at 425° for 10 minutes. Reduce heat to 275° and bake 30 minutes longer. In addition to these dishes, the Thanksgiving dinner includes grapefruit, fruit cup or fruit juice for the first course or sometimes a cream soup is served. A tray of relishes, including celery and carrot sticks, is passed. Hot breads or sweet rolls are usually a part of the dinner. Hot coffee and mixed nuts bring the feast to a close.—After that—bicarbonate of soda!

### Baked Beans

"Every man to his taste" is an often repeated phrase and it seems that every man has his own notion about how baked beans should taste. This is one of many.

| | |
|---|---|
| 1 lb. yellow eye-beans | 1 large onion, sliced |
| soaked overnight | 2 T. dry mustard |
| Salt and soda | Water |
| 3 slices salt pork | 1-2 c. maple syrup |

Drain beans which have soaked overnight. Cover with fresh cold water, a little salt, and boil gently under cover until skin on beans splits when blown upon. To test remove a bean or two from the pot with a spoon and blow. Keep testing until ready. Toss in several pinches of baking soda and stir. Continue cooking but take care not to overboil.

When the beans are really tender, drain in a colander. Partially dice a slice of salt pork and place in the bottom of a bean pot or casserole which has a cover. Put in a layer, about $\frac{1}{3}$ of the beans. Sprinkle with part of the dried mustard and onion slices. Put in another layer of beans and repeat until pot is full, slipping in a piece of salt pork here and there. Top with a larger piece of salt pork.

Now pour in maple syrup. The quantity is dependent upon how sweet you like your beans. The liquid should be up to the top layer of beans so water should be added to the syrup to dilute it to the desired degree and keep the beans moist during the cooking process. It may be necessary to add more liquid during the baking. A little experimentation is necessary. The size and shape of the baking dish affects the quantity of liquid needed.

Bake in a slow oven (275-300°) for at least 6 hours. Keep covered until time to brown the top. Turn up oven for a short time for this. It is strongly recommended that the real maple syrup, not cane syrup, be used for the best results.

## White Bread

| | |
|---|---|
| 2 c. milk, scalded | 5 T. vegetable shortening |
| 2 c. lukewarm water | 2 yeast cakes or packets of |
| 1 c. sugar | dried yeast |
| 3 t. salt | Butter |
| 2 eggs | 12-13 c. bread flour, unbleached |

Scald milk and melt shortening in it. Dissolve yeast in lukewarm water. Mix both these mixtures together and beat in sugar, salt and eggs. Add flour slowly, mixing thoroughly after each addition. Set bread in large bowl. Butter top and cover with a towel. Let rise until double in bulk. The rising time is dependent upon the temperature—the warmer the room the faster it rises—but usually takes about 2-3 hours. Punch dough to let fall and turn on to floured board. Knead until well blended, adding flour if necessary to make it a good working consistency. Divide into 5 loaves and place in greased and floured pans.

If you like high-rising, airy bread, cover pans and allow to rise high again. Place in 350° oven and bake. If you like a more compact bread, almost cake-like in texture, place the loaves immediately into a cold oven. Set temperature controls for 350° and let bread rise with the temperature. The bread will be done when it is browned and may be shaken free from pans easily. Brush tops with melted butter, remove from pans and cool on racks.

## Custard Pudding

| | |
|---|---|
| 4 eggs | 1 qt. milk |
| 1 c. sugar | Pinch of salt |
| 1 t. vanilla | Dash of cinnamon |
| 3 slices white bread, buttered | |

Butter a baking dish and beat 4 eggs in it. Beat in milk and sugar. Add salt, vanilla and cinnamon, mixing well. Cut three slices of buttered bread in strips and dunk these, butter side up, into the liquid. Place in a moderate (350°) oven and bake until a silver knife comes out clean when inserted in the custard. Remove from the oven and chill. Any compatible flavouring may be used here in place of the vanilla and cinnamon. Raisins or other dried fruit may be used to vary the dish. As given, the recipe is very sweet. The amount of sugar may be reduced.

### Stuffed Melon Salad

1 ripe melon
1 c. fruit juice
1 c. water
1 fruit jello

1 package cream cheese
¼ c. milk
Any fruit in season

Peel ripe melon and scoop out after cutting off end. Prepare a package of Jello (using 1 c. boiling water and 1 c. cold fruit juice, perferably pineapple juice). Put in refrigerator and when firm, slice in any fruit you have at home. Fill melon with the Jello mixture and place in a bowl so that it will not tip over. Cover with its own top. Place again in the refrigerator. When it is thoroughly set, slice lengthwise in thin pieces, and cover with cream cheese thinned with milk. Chill until ready to serve and slice.

# ENGLISH

Perhaps English people enjoy company more than food—gentle humourous company which they find in their homes, their castles, and their "pubs." Practical food is to fill rather than to admire—the gourmet goes to France or Italy. During the war, the English made incredible concoctions out of nothing rather than resort to the Black Market; and fifteen years of rationing is a long time in which to remember those subtle touches to the pallet.

Nevertheless, England was once famed for her hospitable and laden side-board, and now with the influx of travellers from abroad and the return of travellers from the continent bearing pleasant memories, English housewives are again opening their cook books to prepare their traditional dishes.

## Jugged Hare

| | |
|---|---|
| 1 hare | 1 onion, chopped |
| Butter or margarine | ¼ c. ale |
| 2 fillets of anchovy | 2 T. ground lemon rind |
| Dash of mace | Bacon or smoked lard |
| Nutmeg | 1 can mushrooms, chopped |
| Flour paste | Parsley, chopped |

"First catch your hare." Skin, clean and cut it up. Fry in shortening to a golden brown. Bone and slice. Add seasoning, chopped parsley and lemon peel. Line an oven-proof dish with bacon or lard and put in a layer of hare. Add ale. Add another layer of bacon with browned onion and mushrooms and finally drop in chopped anchovies. Cover with flour paste. Set in a pan of boiling water and cook for 2 to 3 hours. Serve hot.

## Bubble and Squeak

| | |
|---|---|
| Beef, cooked | 1 cabbage, chopped |
| 1 c. potatoes, left-overs, | Salt and pepper |
| diced and cooked | 3 T. dripping |

Cut up beef and fry in dripping. Add potatoes and fry. Chop a small cabbage, parboil it, drain and add to frying beef. Season and simmer.

## Beef Steak and Kidney Pudding

| | |
|---|---|
| 2 lb. beef steak | 1 lb. suet paste: |
| 1 t. salt and pepper | 3 c. flour, ½ lb. suet, 1 t. |
| 1 lb. ox kidneys | baking powder, salt, ¼ c. water |
| 1 T. flour | |

Chop the suet fine with a little flour. Mix it with the other dry ingredients and add enough water to make fairly stiff dough. Roll out and use at once. Cut the meat and kidneys into thin cubes 1½ inches square. Mix flour, salt and pepper together on a plate and dip each cube into the mixture. Take ¼ of the suet paste for lid. Roll out remainder to size of baking dish which must be previously well-greased. Line dish with paste, put in meat sprinkling the rest of the seasoning between layers. Leave enough space to admit water to prevent pudding from becoming dry. Fill the dish ¾ full with boiling water. Put on cover, moisten and seal edges. Tie over scalded pudding cloth. If steamed, cover with greased paper. Let water be boiling. Put in pudding and boil for 3½ hours or steam for 4.

## Leg of Lamb à la Venison

| | |
|---|---|
| 1 c. spiced vinegar | For the Marinade: |
| 1 leg of lamb | 3 c. vinegar, hot |
| 2 onions, cut | Peppercorns |
| 6 T. sour cream | 3 bay leaves |
| 6 slices bacon | Some cloves |
| Capers | 1 lemon, sliced |
| Salt and pepper | 2 onions, sliced |
| Butter | 1 carrot, sliced |
| | 1 T. sugar |

Cut all excess fat off the meat. Put it in vinegar marinade. Let it stand there for 3 days. When ready to use drain and place in a baking pan. Cover with bacon. Brown in butter with onions. Add 1 c. of spiced vinegar, capers and cook in a moderate oven basting with sour cream.

## Braised Mutton Chops

| | |
|---|---|
| 6 lamb chops | 1 celery stalk |
| 2 T. drippings | Parsley |
| 1 large onion, sliced | Salt and pepper |
| 1 carrot, sliced | 2 c. meat stock |

Brown onion, carrot and celery in dripping. When stewed, add chops and fry them on both sides. Season. Place in a baking pan, cover with fried onions and the other vegetables. Baste with gravy and meat stock and simmer under cover in moderate oven for 45 minutes.

## Lamb Tongues Boiled

| | |
|---|---|
| 6 lamb tongues | Salt |
| 2 lemons, juice | |

Place lamb tongues in salted water with lemon juice and boil until tender. Serve with a strong sauce.

## Irish Stew

| | |
|---|---|
| Neck of mutton, diced | 6 potatoes, parboiled |
| 1 T. dripping | 1 carrot |
| 2 onions, sliced | Salt and pepper |

Cut the meat into pieces two inches square. Brown in dripping, add water to cover and onions. Cover and simmer for two hours. Add more water if necessary. Cut potatoes in half, slice carrot and combine with meat. Stew for an hour. Season. Worcestershire sauce will improve the flavour, when added to the gravy.

### Stuffed Mutton

Shoulder of mutton
1 c. bread-crumbs
2 T. butter
1 egg

Parsley, chopped
Juice of one lemon
Salt and pepper
6 oysters

Have your meat boned and fill the space with a stuffing made as follows: melt butter and combine with egg, parsley and bread-crumbs. Chop your oysters and combine with the rest of the stuffing. Season, sprinkle with lemon juice. Sew up the opening and roast the shoulder, in a moderate oven, basting occasionally.

### Stuffed Calf's Liver

1 calf's liver
2 c. white sauce (see page 96)
$\frac{1}{2}$ lb. ham, chopped
Salt and pepper
$\frac{1}{2}$ c. bread-crumbs

1 onion, chopped
2 T. parsley, chopped
Bacon

Prepare stuffing by mixing ham, bread-crumbs, onion and parsley. Season and moisten with white sauce. Make a slit running along the entire length of the liver, fill with the stuffing. Secure with skewers. Cover with bacon slices, place in a baking dish and add the sauce. Bake for one hour, basting frequently.

### Kedgeree

1 c. cooked, flaked fish
  (haddock, cod, salmon, or
  halibut)
2 T. butter

1 c. rice, cooked
$\frac{1}{2}$ c. cream
2 hard-boiled eggs
Salt and pepper

Melt butter in pan, add rice, fish and sliced eggs, then fold in cream. Season. Mix well. Simmer 10 minutes and serve piping hot.

### Swordfish Steak

2 lb. swordfish
1 lemon, juice
2 T. flour
$\frac{1}{2}$ c. cream

Parsley, chopped
Salt and pepper
Butter

Sprinkle your fish with lemon and let it stand for $\frac{1}{2}$ hour. Season. Roll in flour and place in a shallow baking pan, add butter and simmer under broiler for 30 minutes or until tender. When brownish, add cream and cook for another 5 minutes.

## Angels on Horseback

| | |
|---|---|
| 12 oysters | 2 T. parsley, chopped |
| 12 slices of bacon | Lemon juice |
| 12 croutons of bread | Paprika |
| 1 onion, finely chopped | Salt |

Clean oysters. Cut bacon just large enough to roll around 1 oyster. Season with paprika and salt. Sprinkle with parsley and onion. Add a few drops of lemon juice. Roll up the bacon tightly around each oyster and fasten with a toothpick. Fry in pan or bake in oven just long enough to crisp bacon. Remove the toothpicks and serve on bread croûtons or round melba toast.

## Penny Buns

| | |
|---|---|
| 8 c. flour | 1 lb. currants |
| 1 c. sugar | ¼ t. salt |
| 2 c. warm milk | 1 t. all spice |
| 2 yeast cakes | ¼ c. butter |

Mix flour, sugar, spice and currants. Make a hole in the middle of the flour, put in the yeast and 1 c. of warm milk. Make a thin batter of surrounding flour and milk and set pan covered before fire until leven begins to ferment. Add melted butter and salt the dough. Beat well together, making rather a soft paste with the rest of the flour, using a little more warm milk if necessary. Cover with a clean cloth and let it rise once more. Shape the dough into buns and lay them on a greased baking sheet at least 3 inches apart. Let them rise now for 30 minutes. Bake in a quick oven for 15 to 20 minutes.

## Shortbread

| | |
|---|---|
| 8 c. flour | 12 almonds, blanched and |
| ¼ lb. rice flour | ground |
| 1 lb. butter | Candied orange peel, chopped |
| ¼ lb. sugar | |

Beat butter to a cream. Add sugar and beat till smooth. Gradually add flour and ground almonds. Knead till smooth. Divide into 6 pieces and roll out squares to 1 inch thick. Pinch round edges, prick well with skewer and ornament with peel. Bake in a moderately hot oven for 25 to 30 minutes.

## Orange Fritters

| | |
|---|---|
| 4-5 oranges | Frying fat |
| 2 T. warm water | 1 egg white |
| Sugar | 2 T. salad oil |
| 1 c. flour | Salt |

Remove peel and pith from oranges, divide into pieces containing two or three sections and dip in batter. To make batter sift flour and salt in basin. Add oil and water gradually. Stir until smoothly mixed and beat well. Let mixture stand 1 hour and then stir in stiffly beaten white of egg. Fry until golden brown. Drain well and dredge with sugar. Serve at once. Time 15 to 20 minutes.

## Gooseberry Fool

| | |
|---|---|
| 1 qt. green gooseberries | 1½ lb. sugar |
| 1 pt. heavy cream | 1 pt. water |

Clean gooseberries. Cook until tender with water and sugar in a jar placed in a saucepan of boiling water or a double-boiler. Rub through a sieve. Add more sugar if necessary. Whip cream stiffly and stir into preparation a few minutes before serving. Instead of whipped cream, boiled custard may be used.

## Elderberry Wine

| | |
|---|---|
| 7 lb. elderberries | 1 c. brandy |
| 3 gallons water | ¼ t. yeast |
| To each gallon of juice add | 1 lb. raisins |
|     3 lb. sugar | 2 T. ground ginger |
| 6 cloves | |

Strip berries from stalks, pour boiling water over them and let stand for 24 hours. Strain through a vegetable strainer. Measure juice and put it into a preserving pan with sugar, raisins, ginger and cloves. Boil gently for 1 hour skimming when necessary. Let liquid stand till luke-warm. Strain yeast and turn whole into a large container. Cover with cloth. Leave standing for 14 days. Stir in brandy and cover tightly. After 6 months draw off, bottle, cork and store.

### Plum Pudding Cake for Christmas Tea

| | |
|---|---|
| 2 c. of chopped suet | 1 c. sour milk |
| 3 c. currants | 1 c. flour |
| 2 c. dates | 1 t. salt |
| ¼ lb. candied orange peel | 2 t. mashed cloves |
| 4 T. molasses | ½ c. candied cherries |
| ½ c. bread-crumbs | ½ c. candied pineapple |
| 2 t. cinnamon | 1 c. sherry |
| 3 c. raisins | ¼ lb. candied lemon peel |
| 2 c. walnuts, chopped | 2 t. baking powder |
| 2 c. sugar | 4 eggs |

Chop fruit and nuts. Combine suet with mixture. Mix baking powder, spices, sugar and salt. Beat eggs well. Mix with molasses and sour milk. Combine everything. Pour into buttered and floured bowl ¾ full. Be sure mould cover fits well. Steam 8 hours. Serve with brandy butter.

### Brandy Butter

| | |
|---|---|
| ½ c. butter | 1 egg, separated |
| 1 c. powdered sugar | Brandy to flavour |
| 1 pinch salt | |

Cream butter and sugar till light and fluffy. Add egg yolk, salt and brandy. Beat egg white till stiff and mix in. Serve with plum pudding.

# ITALIAN

One cannot go wrong in describing the Italian cuisine as that of "spaghetti" . . . in fact the Italians have over three hundred and sixty ways to prepare their daily pastasciutta, in addition to their famous "risotto" or "polenta." Olive oil is the basic fat used, veal the most common meat, tomatoes and lettuce the most popular vegetables, local wine and cheese are usual with meals and fruit rather than cake a preferred dessert, especially if followed by a warm "demitasse" or "espresso." The Italians know how to get the most pleasure out of their daily existence and certainly food is not considered in Italy only as a necessity of life. Although they are not as sophisticated as the French, they like to eat heartily and their meals represent an important part of their family and social life.

## Minestrone alla Fiorentina

| | |
|---|---|
| ¼ lb. boiled ham | 1 ham bone |
| 2 c. kidney beans, cooked | 2 T. tomato paste |
| 3 carrots | Handful of peas |
| 3 celery stalks | Handful of string beans |
| 8 T. olive oil | Grated cheese |
| 1 large onion, chopped | Salt and pepper |
| 1 quarter, red cabbage | Croutons of dark bread |
| 2 cloves, garlic | 2 qt. water |
| Rosemary | Thyme |

Sauté chopped onion in some of the oil. Add sliced ham. Simmer for a moment. Add chopped cabbage and all the cut up vegetables. Mix a few times. Add tomtato paste and stew until the vegetables begin to be tender, then add water and cooked beans. Cook on slow flame for 1 hour. On the side prepare rosemary thyme and garlic and fry them in oil, until the garlic becomes golden brown, then pour this mixture in the minestrone. Serve with grated cheese and with croutons of dark bread. Rice or noodles may be substituted for croutons.

## Minestrone alla Genovese

| | |
|---|---|
| Water | Salt and pepper |
| 4 potatoes, cubed | 3 T. basil sauce: |
| Cabbage, a piece | Handful of fresh basil, handful |
| 1 c. kidney beans, soaked | of fresh parsley, 3 sections |
| 1 lb. peas | garlic, 4 T. olive oil, 5T. |
| ½ lb. string beans | grated cheese, 1 T. pignoli |
| ¼ lb. zucchini or squash | pine nuts |
| 2 T. olive oil | |
| ¼ lb. maccaroni | |

Cook the kidney beans in an ample amount of water. When almost tender add all the vegetables, cleaned and cut in pieces. Add seasoning and oil and cook for 2 hours. At the end add macaroni and the basil sauce. You can prepare your basil sauce a day to two in advance and keep under refrigeration. Chop basil and parsley fine. add garlic and nuts and chop together again. Place in a bowl, add oil and grated cheese. Mix well. It is a delicious sauce for spaghetti, or seasoning for any vegetable soup.

## Lasagne Neapolitan Style

| | |
|---|---|
| 1½ lb. lasagne | Salt and pepper |
| 1 lb. cottage cheese (ricotta) | Grated cheese |
| 2 eggs | 3 c. tomato sauce (see page 99) |
| ¼ lb. pork sausage | ¼ lb. of mozzarella or any |
| ½ lb. pork, cooked and chopped | melting cheese |

Cook the lasagne in a large amount of salted water. When not quite done, drain the water and pass in cold water. Take a large baking dish, grease it well and line with the lasagne. Prepare the cottage cheese by mixing it with well-beaten eggs, grated cheese and salt and pepper. Simmer the tomato sauce with the meat. Cover the lasagne with a layer of cottage cheese, then alternate between the cheese layer, a layer of tomato sauce ending with the lasagne layer. Cover the top with the melting grated cheese and then place in a moderate oven for 30 minutes. If you like your lasagne to have a touch of colour, place a few spoons of tomato sauce on the top.

## Gnocchi

| | |
|---|---|
| 4 lb. potatoes | Tomato sauce (optional) |
| 1 lb. flour | Cheese, grated (optional) |
| 2 eggs | Salt |

Cook clean, unpeeled potatoes, until soft, Peel them. Pass through the strainer. Place the flour on a board, add the mashed potatoes, salt and eggs. Knead well together. Cut a small piece of dough. Roll out with your hands until 1 inch thick. Cut strips 1½ inches long with a knife. With your finger shape each piece around so that they are thinner in the middle, forming a canoe-like shape. Drop them into rapidly boiling, salted water. Let them float, and boil a few moments. Drain. Serve with tomato sauce or melted butter and grated cheese.

## Gnocchi di Semolino

| | |
|---|---|
| 1 qt. milk | Salt |
| ¼ lb. cream of wheat | 6 T. grated cheese |
| 2 egg yolks | ¼ lb. butter |

Bring the milk to the boil. Gradually mix in cream of wheat. Add salt. Cook for 15 minutes, mixing constantly with a wooden spoon. Add eggs and a piece of butter. Spread the cream of wheat on a large, wet surface, like a kneading board or a marble top, until about 1 inch thick. Let it cool off completely. Cut with a knife into 1 inch squares. Place in a baking dish, previously greased. Sprinkle with grated cheese and cover with butter. Put in the oven for 15 minutes and serve.

## Torta di Polenta

| | |
|---|---|
| 1 lb. corn meal | 5 slices bacon |
| ¼ lb. melting cheese | 6 c. water |
| Butter | Salt and pepper |

Bring water to the boil. Mix in corn meal. Add salt, and pepper. Let it cook for 15 minutes mixing all along with a wooden spoon. When ready, turn into a square baking dish. Let cool. When cold, cut 1 inch thick slices with a sharp knife, and on top of each square, place a slice of any melting cheese and top with slices of bacon. Put in a well greased baking dish and place in a hot oven for 15 minutes.

### Risotto alla Milanese

| | |
|---|---|
| 1 lb. rice | 1 chunk of bone marrow |
| 1 onion, chopped | Salt and pepper |
| Dash of saffron | Cheese, grated |
| 4 c. meat stock | 3 T. butter |

Cut the bone marrow into pieces and place in a large pot, where you plan to cook your risotto. Add a chopped onion and a spoonful of butter. Simmer slowly until golden brown. Drop in the rice, mixing with a wooden spoon. Let the rice soak in the butter. On the side bring to a boil meat stock. Add part of it to the rice. Let it cook, adding the broth gradually, when needed. Season. Add saffron, butter and grated cheese. Do not over cook. Serve with grated cheese sprinkled over it.

### Ravioli

| | |
|---|---|
| 3 c. flour | Salt and pepper |
| 3 eggs | |

*Filling:*

| | |
|---|---|
| 2 eggs | 3 T. olive oil |
| Parsley, chopped | 2 c. tomato sauce |
| 2 T. red wine | 1 c. boiled beef, minced |
| 1 onion, chopped | 1 c. cooked spinach |
| ¼ c. water | ¼ lb. pork sausage |

Place flour on a kneading board in a mountain fashion. Hollow out centre and fold in the eggs, and salt. Start mixing with a fork adding oil and water. Knead well together, and set aside. Prepare your filling by browning the onion, with chopped spinach and chopped meat and sausage meat. Let cool. Add all the remaining ingredients and mix. Season. Divide the dough and roll out very thin. Place spoonfuls of filling on the dough 2 inches apart. Cover it with the second dough sheet and press together between the filling. Cut the ravioli with a pastry wheel. Drop the ravioli into rapidly boiling salted water. Cook until they float. Drain off the water. Place in a serving dish and top with tomato sauce and grated cheese.

### Uccellini Scappati

| | |
|---|---|
| 1 lb. veal cutlets, lightly pounded | Sage |
| ¼ lb. ham, boiled | Butter |
| 6 slices bacon | Salt and pepper |

Cut the pounded cutlets in long strips. Place in each strip a piece of ham, sage (fresh preferably) and seasoning. Roll up each piece of meat with its filling, cover it with bacon secure with a tooth pick and fry on a slow fire in butter. Serve with rice.

## Scaloppine al Marsala

| | |
|---|---|
| 1 lb. veal cutlets | Salt and pepper |
| lightly pounded | 1 lemon, juice |
| 3 T. butter | 1 lb. mushrooms, browned in butter |
| 3 T. olive oil | Garlic, 2-3 sections |
| Bay leaf | 3 T. Marsala |

Fry the meat in a mixture of butter and olive oil. and bay leaf and garlic. Season, add Marsala. Put on a platter. Warm up the remaining juice in the frying pan and add it to the meat. Sprinkle with a few drops of lemon juice. Brown the whole mushrooms in butter and serve with meat.

## Veal Scaloppini alla Cacciatora

| | |
|---|---|
| 1 lb. veal cutlets, pounded | 3 T. flour |
| 2 T. parsley, chopped | 1 can mushrooms |
| 4 T. olive oil | 3 T. grated cheese |
| 2 sections of garlic, juice | 1 can of tomatoes |
| Salt and pepper | Rosemary |

Sprinkle the meat with flour. Heat the oil, add garlic. Add meat and brown on both sides. Add mushrooms and tomatoes. Cover. Simmer together for 10 minutes. Add seasoning and grated cheese, sprinkle with parsley and serve.

## Cima alla Genovese

| | |
|---|---|
| 1 lb. skirt steak | 1 egg |
| ¼ lb. pork | ¼ lb. peas |
| 4 slices of bread | 1 T. gelatine |
| 4 slices of bacon | Olive oil |
| Marjoram | Butter |
| Salt and pepper | 3 cloves of garlic |
| ¼ c. milk | 1 onion, chopped |
| 3 T. grated cheese | |

Take a skirt steak and with a very sharp knife, make a cut in the middle, forming a pocket-like opening, where you will place the filling. Brown a chopped onion in oil, add garlic and simmer it with onion. On the side, soak the bread in milk, and pass it with the pork meat and bacon through a mincer. Add salt and pepper, marjoram, grated cheese, and egg. Add the peas to this meat and seasoning mixture. Fill the meat pocket with this mixture and sew it up with a thick needle. Cook the "cima" in boiling water for a couple of hours. Reserve the stock and cool the meat. Place in the refrigerator. When very cold, cut in slices and serve with gelatine, which you have prepared with the meat stock.

## Vitello Tonnato

| | |
|---|---|
| Veal roast (2-3 lb.) | Rosemary, salt and pepper |
| Juice of 1 lemon | ¼ c. vinegar |
| 1 can tuna fish | Capers |
| 5 fillets of anchovy | Parsley |
| 3 T. oil | |

Boil the veal in water with seasoning for 2 hours. Change to another pot in which you have put ½ c. of vinegar and ½ c. of the meat broth. Cover the pot, and simmer under cover for 15 minutes. Cool off. On the side prepare a mixture of: finely chopped anchovies with tuna fish, oil and lemon juice. Add ½ c. of the meat stock to this sauce. Slice the meat, cover with tuna fish sauce and garnish with capers and parsley. Serve with salad.

## Stuffed Zucchini

| | |
|---|---|
| 1 lb. zucchini | 3 eggs |
| 5 slices of white bread | Salt and pepper |
| 4 T. grated cheese | 1 c. milk |
| 1 onion, chopped | 2 slices of Canadian bacon |
| 2 sections garlic, chopped | |

Clean the zucchini, cut off the ends. Parboil in salted water for 10 minutes. Drain. Split lengthwise, and scoop out the pulp. Soak the bread in milk. Squeeze dry. Chop the zucchini pulp fine. Combine with chopped bread, onion, garlic and chopped bacon. Add eggs. Season to taste. Fill the zucchini. Top with grated cheese and place in a moderate oven for 15 minutes.

## Carciofi alla Giudea

| | |
|---|---|
| 6 artichokes | Oil |
| Salt and pepper | Juice of 1 lemon |

Clean the artichokes. Remove all the outer leaves. Put in water with lemon and soak. Cut them lengthwise and fry in deep olive oil. Season and serve when soft and tender.

## Zuppa Inglese

| | |
|---|---|
| ½ lb. sponge cake | 4 T. flour |
| Rum | 2 c. milk |
| 3 eggs, separated | Orange peel, candied |
| ½ c. granulated sugar | 1 pint heavy cream, whipped |
| 4 T. powdered sugar | |

Cut the sponge cake in thin slices. Place the slices in a round platter and sprinkle with rum. On the side prepare the cream filling by beating the egg yolks with granulated sugar, adding flour and milk, and cooking the cream over a very slow fire. Let it boil once. Cool. Beat the egg-whites until stiff, add powdered sugar and combine with the cream. Cover the first layer of the cake with the cream, then alternate cake layer, cream filling. Top with whipped cream. Keep in refrigerator until very cold.

### Zabaglione

| | |
|---|---|
| 1 egg yolk per person | 1 T. sugar per egg |
| 2 T. marsala or white wine per egg | Dash of lemon rind |
| | Drop of sweet liqueur |

Beat the eggs with sugar in a double boiler. When white and fluffy, add wine, and lemon rind. Liqueur is optional. Place on a low flame, mixing constantly with a wooden spoon. Take off the fire at the point of boiling. Serve immediately.

Genova

# FRENCH

The French cuisine is that of studied detail and sophistication. So much has been written about it, that in most countries many words pertaining to cooking and eating have been borrowed from the French language. A valuable characteristic of a French menu is the stress given to a balanced composition—quality and variety rather than bulk. In spite of the rather feeble French café-filtre, one usually leaves the table still awake and full of energy.

239

### Potage à l'Oignon

| | |
|---|---|
| 4 onions | Fried or toasted bread |
| 4 T. butter or margarine | 5 c. meat stock |
| Garlic | Salt and pepper |
| 5 T. cheese, grated | |

Peel and slice the onions. Fry them gently in butter until golden-brown. Pour the meat stock over the onions and simmer together for 15 minutes. On the side prepare the toast. Rub it with garlic and fry in butter for a moment, just on one side. Place the bread in individual serving bowls. Serve the soup very hot and sprinkle generously with grated cheese.

### Vichyssoise

| | |
|---|---|
| 1 large onion, chopped | 3 large potatoes, cubed |
| 2 stalks celery, chopped | 4 c. meat stock |
| 4 T. butter | 2 c. cream |
| Fresh dill | Parsley |
| Chives | |

Cook the onions in butter until golden brown. Add celery and simmer for a few minutes. Add potatoes and broth. Cook until the potatoes are soft. Pass through a strainer. Season. Just before serving, add cream and chopped dill, parsley and chives.

### Consommé Talleyrand

| | |
|---|---|
| 3 truffles, grated | 4 c. consommé |
| 3 T. white wine, dry | 2 T. cream of wheat |

Mix the truffles with wine. Let them stand for 30 minutes. Bring the consommé to the boil, add the cream of wheat, cook for 3 minutes and pour it over the truffle mixture.

### Bouillabaise

| | |
|---|---|
| Lobster | 2 carrots, sliced |
| Crab meat | 2 celery stalks |
| ¼ lb. salmon | 1 c. white wine |
| ½ lb. eel | Saffron |
| ¼ lb. cod | Water to cover |
| 4 T. olive oil | Toasted bread |
| 3 sections garlic | 2 potatoes, cubed |
| 3 tomatoes, sliced | Parsley |
| Salt and pepper | |

Cook the vegetables in water for 5 minutes. On the side, season the fish, cover with oil and wine, let stand for 10 minutes. Place the fish in vegetable stock and boil rapidly for 10 minutes. Take the lobster out, extract all the lobster meat, and put it back in the soup. Toast the bread, rub it with garlic. Serve the bouillabaise with toasted bread.

## Coquilles St. Jacques

| | |
|---|---|
| 1 lb. scallops | ¼ c. wine, white |
| ¼ lb. mushrooms | Bread-crumbs |
| Olive oil | Salt and pepper |
| 1 T. parsley, chopped | Cheese, grated |
| 2 sections garlic | 1 onion, chopped |

Brown the onion in oil, add mushrooms and simmer on a low fire. Season scallops, add squeezed garlic. Roll scallops in bread-crumbs, and simmer them with the onion, for a while. Add wine and grated cheese. Serve, garnished with parsley.

## Morue en Brandade

| | |
|---|---|
| 1 lb. salt cod | Garlic |
| 2 onions, chopped | Parsley, chopped |
| 6 T. olive oil | Sage |
| 1 c. sour cream | Bread, toasted |
| Juice of 1 lemon | Salt and pepper |

Soak fish for 24 hours, changing water several times. Cook in ample amount of water for 10 minutes. Sauté garlic and onion in 2 T. of oil, add the fish and simmer for 3 minutes. Mash the fish thoroughly with a fork. Season and mix in lemon juice. Rub the toasted bread with garlic and fry it in oil. When ready lay it on a hot platter and top it with mashed cod fish. Sprinkle with parsley.

## Gigot á la Provençale

| | |
|---|---|
| 5-6 lb. leg of lamb | 1 c. white wine |
| ¼ lb. bacon | Salt and pepper |
| 3 sections garlic | Carrots |
| Thyme | Onions |
| Parsley, chopped | 2 eggs |
| 1 c. milk | 4 slices of bread |

Bone your leg of lamb. Soak the bread in milk and squeeze dry. Mix with chopped bacon (smoked lard would taste even better . . .). Season, add herbs, chopped garlic and eggs. Stuff the roast and sew up the cavity with a heavy thread. Place in a moderate oven with onions and carrots. Add wine and some water. Baste occasionally. In 2 hours your leg of lamb should be tender. Serve with French-fries and eggplant.

## Poulet sauté Bordelaise

| | |
|---|---|
| 1 frying chicken, cut | 2 sections of garlic |
| 3 slices bacon | 1 T. chopped dill |
| Butter | Salt and pepper |
| 2 onions, chopped | Juice of 1 lemon |
| Flour | Hearts of artichokes, sautéd |
| 1 glass of white wine | 3 tomatoes |

Dredge chicken with flour. Brown the onion lightly in butter and chopped bacon. Add the chicken and fry on both sides. Add artichokes, cut in quarters and sliced tomatoes. Season. Add wine.

Simmer under cover for 30 minutes. Add lemon. Sprinkle with dill, or if not, with parsley. Serve with baked potatoes.

### Lapin au Champagne

| | |
|---|---|
| 1 rabbit, cut in pieces | 2 onions, chopped |
| 3 slices of bacon | Parsley |
| 4 T. butter | 1 c. champagne |
| Salt and pepper | Bay leaf |
| Rosemary | |

Brown the bacon and onion lightly in butter. Add rabbit and seasoning. Heat for a moment. Add champagne and a drop of water if necessary. Simmer under cover. Baste and turn occasionally. Serve with mashed potatoes.

### Canard aux Olives

| | |
|---|---|
| 1 duck | Thyme |
| Flour | Parsley |
| Bacon, 3 slices | Sage |
| 2 c. meat stock | 15 green olives |
| Salt and pepper | Butter or margarine |

Dredge the duck in flour and brown it in bacon fat and butter until golden brown. Remove the duck, keeping it in a warm oven, while you prepare the sauce. Stir into fat 2 T. of flour, or enough to make a thick sauce. Mix with a wooden spoon until brown. Add boiling stock gradually and all the seasoning. Replace the duck, and cook under cover until soft and tender. Add olives 15 minutes before serving, and arrange the olives around the duck when you do serve. Garnish with parsley.

### Laitue au Jus

| | |
|---|---|
| 2 large lettuces | 1 onion, chopped |
| Butter | Parsley, chopped |
| Flour | Chives, chopped |
| Salt and pepper | 4 c. vegetable stock |

Wash the lettuce well and cook in boiling stock (reserve on the side 1 c. of stock) until soft (about 15 minutes). Drain. Melt butter, stir in a little flour. mix well, stir in the remaining stock, mixing constantly. Season, adding chopped onion and parsley. Replace the lettuce and simmer for 20 minutes. Serve with boiled meat or roasts. You may sprinkle it with chopped chives, if you wish to have this additional flavour.

### Les Champignons en Blanc

| | |
|---|---|
| 1 lb. large mushrooms | 3 T. grated cheese |
| Butter | Grated horseradish, fresh |
| Salt and pepper | 1 c. white sauce (see page 96) |

Clean your mushrooms. Put them in a greased baking dish. Season. Add some butter and place in moderate oven for 15 minutes.

Sprinkle with horseradish and cover with white sauce. Top with grated cheese and replace in the oven for an additional 10 to 15 minutes.

### Mousse de Chocolat

| | |
|---|---|
| 1 lb. unsweetened chocolate | 2 c. heavy cream |
| 2 T. corn syrup | 3 T. powdered sugar |
| ¼ t. vanilla | |

Grate the chocolate, melt in a double-boiler, stirring constantly. Add syrup and mix some more. Take off the flame when starting to boil. Pass through the vegetable strainer. Cool. Add vanilla and sugar if desired. Add gradually and slowly well beaten heavy cream. Place in a pudding mould and put in the refrigerator for 6 hours.

### Pudding Diplomate

| | |
|---|---|
| Lady fingers | Raisins |
| Candied fruit | Strawberry or cherry jam |
| 2 c. vanilla pudding | Whipped cream |
| Cherry brandy | Butter or margarine |
| Cherry or strawberry syrup | |

Take a pudding mould and grease it. At the bottom place some candied fruit. Alternate layer of lady fingers (moisten them with liqueur, diluted with fruit syrup and vanilla pudding). Add a few drops of cherry brandy to your pudding. Over each layer of lady fingers place some raisins which have previously been soaked in brandy. You may also add a little jam over each layer of lady fingers. Place a piece of greased wax paper over the pudding and press firmly. Place the pudding in the refrigerator for 6 to 8 hours. Before serving turn it over, (if difficult, dip it in warm water for a moment). Decorate with Whipped cream.

# SPANISH

Spanish cooking although not highly original itself, has influenced many countries of the New World. It often combines some elements of Italian cooking, such as its use of oil and generous seasoning with some elements of French cuisine, such as frequent use of garlic, stewed tomatoes etc. The whole is blended with local characteristics of the Iberian peasantry.

### Sopa de Ajo

| | |
|---|---|
| 4 c. water | 6 garlic cloves, crushed |
| 5 T. olive oil | 2 hard-boiled eggs, sliced |
| 3 slices of bread | 1 T. parsley, chopped |
| Salt and pepper | |

Slowly brown the garlic in 2 T. of oil. Add boiling water and season. Cook 5 minutes. Rub the toasted bread with garlic and fry in oil. Place pieces of fried bread in individual soup bowls. Pour the soup on top of the bread, sprinkle with parsley and garnish with egg.

### Sopa de Castanas

| | |
|---|---|
| 1 lb. chestnuts | ½ c. cream |
| Salt and pepper | 2 T. butter |
| 7 c. of water | Croutons |

Make a slit in each chestnut with a sharp knife. Place in boiling water and cook for 15 minutes. Drain. Take off the 2 skins and put in a pot with 7 c. of water and seasoning. Cook until tender, Sieve, return to the pot, warm again and then add cream and butter. Serve with croutons.

### Sopa de Almendras

| | |
|---|---|
| 6 oz. almonds, blanched | 4 c. meat stock |
| and peeled | 1 T. chopped smoked lard |
| Dash of cayenne | Salt |
| Marjoram | |

Pass the almonds through a mincer (reserve ¼ of the almonds for garnishing). Simmer almonds in stock for 20 minutes, adding all the seasoning. At last sprinkle the remaining shredded almonds on top of the soup and serve hot.

### Paella alla Valenciana

| | |
|---|---|
| 2 breasts of chicken | 2 c. rice |
| ¼ lb. pork sausage | 4 cloves garlic |
| ½ lb. scallops | crushed |
| ½ lb. oysters | Salt and pepper |
| 1 lb. shrimps | 4 fresh tomatoes |
| ¼ lb. green peas | 4 c. water |
| 2 red peppers | ¼ c. oil |
| Saffron | 1 bay leaf |
| ¼ lb. lima beans | |

Place oil in a deep casserole. Add sliced sausage and brown it lightly. Add chicken and simmer for 15 minutes. Place scallops and oysters in the pot. Season. Add garlic. Simmer for 10 minutes. Add all the vegetables, sliced and cooked and peeled shrimps. Take the chicken out and bone. Return it to the casserole. Add rice and water and cook until rice is done. Add saffron and serve.

## Cocido Español

| | |
|---|---|
| 2 cans chick peas | Cinnamon |
| ¼ lb. corn beef | 1 can lima beans |
| ¼ lb. smoked bacon | 5 large beets, cooked |
| ¼ lb. pork sausage | 3 carrots, sliced |
| 1 pig tail | 6 potatoes |
| 1 chicken, cut | ¼ lb. veal |
| 1 onion | ¼ lb. ham, cooked |
| 2 cloves garlic | Saffron |
| Salt and pepper | |

Place all the meat in water and bring to the boil. Lower the flame and simmer slowly for 3 hours. Add chick peas and all the other vegetables. Season. Let your vegetables become tender. Cool and cut the meat in pieces. Just before serving, add saffron and cinnamon.

## Tortilla de Salmon

| | |
|---|---|
| 1 c. salmon, fresh or canned | 3 eggs |
| Salt and paprika | 1 t. parsley, chopped |
| 1 t. chives, chopped | 2 T. olive oil |

Pass the salmon through a mincer. Add beaten eggs and seasoning. Sprinkle with parsley and chives and form oblong shaped pancakes with a spoon. Fry in oil. Serve very hot with green salad.

## Anquilas

| | |
|---|---|
| 1 large eel | Juice of 1 lemon |
| 3 cloves garlic, crushed | 1 egg |
| 3 T. olive oil | 1 c. almonds, blanched and |
| Parsley, chopped | peeled |
| Dash of cinnamon | 3 T. vinegar |
| Salt and pepper | Saffron |

Place the cleaned eel in water and vinegar and boil for 10 minutes. Reserve 1 c. of the eel broth. Drain fish and bone it. Cut in pieces. On the side fry the garlic. Mix in all the spices and seasoning. Add eel and the c. of fish broth. Simmer for a few minutes or until the eel is tender, but not over-cooked. Add almonds, cut lengthwise and the lemon juice. Remove from fire and add the beaten egg. Serve hot with boiled potatoes.

## Huevos con Ajo

| | |
|---|---|
| ¼ c. almonds, blanched and peeled | ¼ t. cinnamon |
| 2 cloves garlic | ½ c. water |
| 1 slice of bread | ¼ t. saffron |
| 1 t. caraway seed | 5 eggs |
| Salt and pepper | 4 T. olive oil |

Fry garlic, small pieces of bread and almonds in oil. Remove from fire and pass through vegetable strainer. Return to pan, adding water and all seasoning. Take off the fire and add beaten eggs, one spoon at a time, while stirring. Return to the flame and cook slowly until the desired consistency is obtained.

## Rinones al Jerez

| | |
|---|---|
| 1 lb. veal kidneys | 3 T. olive oil |
| 1 large onion, chopped | 1 c. sherry |
| Salt and pepper | Sage |

Brown onion in oil. Wash the kidneys well and cut them in pieces, add to onion. Add seasoning and finally sherry. Simmer 10 minutes. Serve with boiled rice.

## Esparrago de modo Andalusia

| | |
|---|---|
| 1 lb. asparagus | 2 T. vinegar |
| 2 cloves garlic | 5 eggs |
| Salt and pepper | Paprika |
| Dash of nutmeg | Olive oil |
| 2 red peppers | |

Cook asparagus in boiling water. Fry slices of peppers with garlic until soft. Add seasoning. Drain the asparagus. Place on a hot platter, cover with pepper sauce. Poach the eggs and top the asparagus with them. Sprinkle with paprika.

## Torrijas de Almendras

| | |
|---|---|
| 1 c. almonds, blanched and peeled | ½ t. vanilla |
| 5 egg yolks | Dash of nutmeg |
| ¼ c. flour | ½ c. sugar |
| Butter | Raspberry syrup |

Grind almonds to a paste and mix with vanilla and nutmeg. Add sugar and egg yolks. Then slowly work in a small amount of flour to make a soft dough. Fry in butter, dropping small balls by spoonfuls. Serve with fruit syrup.

### Peras di Mallorca

8 small pears, preserved
2 envelopes of gelatine
1 c. cold water
3 c. boiling water

Juice of 2 lemons
4 egg whites, stiffly beaten
1 c. cherry brandy
1 c. sugar

Dissolve the gelatine in cold water. Add boiling water. Cool slightly. Stir in sugar, lemon juice and finally egg whites. When completely cooled, add brandy. Slice canned pears lengthwise. Place some of the mixture in a wet pudding mould and place in the freezing compartment of the refrigerator. When it is set, add a layer of pears, then liquefied jelly and repeat the procedure, alternating the layers of pears with jelly, until the mould is full, ending with the jelly. Chill. This delicious dessert may be served with whipped cream.

### Natilla

| | |
|---|---|
| 5 egg yolks | Dash of salt and nutmeg |
| 2 T. sugar per egg | ½ t. vanilla |
| 4 c. milk | ½ c. brown sugar |
| 3 T. rum | 4 T. flour |

Mix granulated sugar, flour, salt, nutmeg and vanilla. Add egg yolks one by one. Pour milk gradually and scald the mixture in the top of a double boiler. Stir constantly until thick. Pour custard into a pudding mould. When cold top with brown sugar. Place the mould in the broiler and let the brown sugar form a glaze. Place in the refrigerator and serve after a few hours. You may decorate your caramel pudding with whipped cream and candied cherries.

# GERMAN

German cooking is substantial, in many ways reflecting the general characteristics of this nation and its people. Rather simple flavours are usually preferred and contrasts such as salt and sugar. A large glass of its famous beers is a fortunate adjunct to its heavier dishes.

### Aal Suppe

| | |
|---|---|
| 1 large eel, cleaned | Parsley, chopped |
| 3 T. butter | 1 qt. bock beer |
| Bay leaf | 2 c. light white wine |
| Thyme | 3 slices rye bread, chopped |
| Sage | Salt and pepper |

Clean and wash eel well. Cut in pieces. Place in a pot with all the remaining ingredients except the butter. Simmer for 20 minutes. Add butter and serve with boiled potatoes.

### Marrow Soup

| | |
|---|---|
| 2 lb. shine bone | Salt and pepper |
| 8 c. water | Flour |
| 2 large onions, sliced | Noodles |
| Celery, 3 stalks | 3 carrots, sliced |
| 2 potatoes, cubed | |

Place the shin bone with all the vegetables in a pot with water. Cook until tender. Take off the meat and reserve. Also set aside 2 c. of broth. Remove the marrow from the bone and add to the stock. Pass through a vegetable strainer. Cut the reserved meat in small pieces, and heat it in the set-aside broth. Thicken this meat broth with some flour and add to the strained marrow soup. Serve with wide egg-noodles. If desired, you may use some chopped dill, and quartered hard-boiled eggs for garnishing the marrow soup.

### Pig's Feet

| | |
|---|---|
| 3 pig's feet | Lemon, sliced |
| 1 bay leaf | A few whole cloves |
| 2 cloves garlic | 5 T. salad oil |
| 1 large onion | 2 T. bread-crumbs |
| Peppercorns | 3 T. vinegar |
| Salt | 3 T. prepared mustard |
| 4 c. water | |

Split pigs feet in halves. Put in a pot with vinegar, lemon, bay leaf, peppercorn, salt, cloves, squeezed garlic and onion. Cover with water and cook until tender. Drain. Place in a baking dish, sprinkle with crumbs and oil and broil for ½ hour. Serve with horseradish and boiled potatoes.

### Sauerbraten

| | |
|---|---|
| 3-4 lb. chuck beef | Sage |
| 3 cloves garlic | Thyme |
| 2 large onions | Rosemary |
| 2 c. wine vinegar | 1 T. sugar |
| 1 lemon, sliced | Salt and pepper |
| 5 c. water | |

With a sharp, pointed knife prepare slits in your roast, and insert pieces of garlic and spices. Rub with salt and pepper and place in an earthenware bowl. Bring to a boil water, slices of lemon, vinegar and pour it over the meat (top the meat with slices of onion). Cover and let stand for 2 days. Cook in the oven, under cover for 2 hours. Add the sugar to the meat sauce. Serve with boiled potatoes.

## Gebackenes Kalbshirn

| | |
|---|---|
| 2 calf's brains | Salt and pepper |
| Carrot, sliced | 1 egg |
| Onion, chopped | 3 T. milk |
| Bay leaf | Flour |
| Butter | 3 c. meat stock |
| 2 lemons | Sage |
| Peppercorns | |

Wash brains well. Place in cold water for a few hours. Place in pot with meat stock, vinegar, all the vegetables and seasoning. Cook under cover for 20 minutes. Remove from stock. Cool. Dip in egg and milk, and dredge in flour. Top with butter and place in a hot oven for 15 minutes. Sprinkle with the juice of 1 lemon and serve with quartered lemon pieces.

## Bratwurst and Sauerkraut

| | |
|---|---|
| 1 lb. beef sausage | Salt and pepper to taste |
| ½ lb. sauerkraut | 1 T. sugar |
| ¼ lb. mushrooms | 1 c. brown sauce (see below) |
| 2 T. butter | |

Broil the sausage. Place the sauerkraut in an oven proof dish. Add sausage. Slice mushrooms and sauté lightly with onion. Top the sausage and sauerkraut. Sprinkle with sugar. Cover with brown sauce, and put in the oven for 15 minutes.

## Brown Sauce

| | |
|---|---|
| 1 c meat stock | Parsley, chopped |
| 4 T. bone marrow | Thyme |
| 1 onion, chopped | Sage |
| 2 T. flour | 1 c. white wine |
| 1 section garlic | Salt and pepper |

Melt marrow bone. Brown onion, add flour, stir constantly until browned. Add hot meat stock gradually and mix. Add herbs and seasoning, and finally wine. Simmer together for a few moments.

## Sweet and Sour Red Cabbage

| | |
|---|---|
| Red Cabbage | ½ c. water |
| 1 large onion | Salt and pepper |
| 4 slices of bacon | Thyme |
| 3 apples, sliced | 3 tomatoes, cut |
| ½ c. vinegar | 2 T. sugar |

Shred the cabbage. Brown the onion in bacon fat. Add the cabbage, tomatoes and apples. Cover and simmer for 15 minutes. Add water when necessary. Season and cook until tender. Add vinegar and sugar. Serve with boiled potatoes.

## Rice with Raisins

| | |
|---|---|
| 2 c. rice | Salt |
| 2 onions, finely chopped | Butter |
| ½ c. raisins | Paprika |
| 6 c. vegetable stock | |

Sauté onion in butter. Stir rice into it, and let it absorb all the fat. Add hot stock. Cook under cover. Add seasoning and raisins and simmer until the stock is absorbed.

## Rhamkuchen

| | |
|---|---|
| 1 lb. cottage cheese | Lemon rind |
| ½ c. sugar | Vanilla |
| 3 eggs, separated | 1 T. powdered sugar |
| 1 c. sour cream | 1 t. lemon juice |
| 2 c. rolled zwieback crumbs | 4 T. butter |
| 3 T. sugar | |

Blend the crumbs with soft butter and sugar. Press the crumbs to a pie sheet. Place in a hot oven for 10 minutes. On the side mix the cheese with sugar, lemon and vanilla. Add beaten egg yolks and mix well. Beat the egg whites stiff and fold slowly to the cheese mixture. Put the cheese on top of the crumb base and bake in a moderate oven for 1 hour. Mix the sour cream with powdered sugar. Spread on top of the cake 10 minutes before removing from the oven.

## Apfel Strudel

| *Dough:* | *Filling:* |
|---|---|
| 2 c. flour | ½ c. bread-crumbs |
| 2 eggs | 4 T. margarine |
| 1 T. lard | 5 sour apples |
| Dash of salt | ½ c. sugar |
| ½ c. water | ½ c. raisins |
| 3 T. butter | Cinnamon, optional |

Mix flour with eggs, lard, salt and water. Knead until firm. Let it stand for 30 minutes. Roll out very thinly and brush with melted butter. On the side prepare the filling. Brown the crumbs in butter.

Cool. Peel and slice apples. Sprinkle them over the dough. Drop the raisins evenly over the crumbs. Cover with evenly spread apples. Add sugar and cinnamon. Roll up and place on a greased baking dish. Brush with an egg yolk or butter and bake in a hot oven for 30 minutes. Sprinkle with sugar and serve either hot or cold.

# DANISH

Danish cuisine is a combination of health and aesthetics: importance is paid to the caloric value of food and to the way it is served. A table set for the evening meal in Denmark is so pleasant to the eye, that everybody's appetite is sharpened. After all, we have learned too that the eye and the mind are important in helping the functions that would seem purely physiological. . . .

### Leverpostej

| | |
|---|---|
| ½ lb. calf's liver | ½ lb. pork liver |
| ¼ lb. lard | 1 onion |
| 6 boned herrings | 1 t. sugar |
| ¼ t. ginger | Salt and pepper |
| 1 c. heavy cream | 3 eggs |
| 2 T. corn starch | |

Pass liver, onion, lard and herring through a mincer at least 4 times. Mix the liver mixture, with all the spices. Add cream, eggs and cornstarch. Place in a greased pudding mould, and cook in a moderate oven for 1 hour.

### Kaernemaelkssuppe

| | |
|---|---|
| 4 c. buttermilk | 3 T. butter |
| 3 T. flour | 4 T. raisins, optional |
| ½ c. sugar | 2 eggs, beaten |

Heat the butter, mix in flour gradually. Add buttermilk slowly, mixing constantly. Bring to the boil on a low flame, stirring constantly. Remove from the fire, then mix the sugar with the beaten eggs and add to the soup. Serve immediately. The soup is delicious with the raisins. You may serve it with blackberry preserve or whipped cream.

### Kaernemaelksoldskaal

| | |
|---|---|
| 4 c. buttermilk | ½ t. vanilla, optional |
| ½ c. sugar | Juice of 1 lemon |
| 1 c. heavy cream, whipped | |

Mix butter milk with lemon juice and sugar to taste. Place in the refrigerator and cool. Top with whipped cream and serve with dry cookies. Mind you—it is a soup and not a dessert!

### Korvelsuppe

| | |
|---|---|
| 6 c. meat stock | ¼ lb. cabbage leaves |
| 2 T. margarine | Salt |
| 2 T. flour | 1 poached egg per person |
| ¼ lb. carrots | |

Cook the carrots in meat stock and then remove. Heat the margarine, add flour and mix constantly while diluting with warm meat stock. Slice carrots and return to thickened stock with cabbage leaves which have been chopped very fine. Salt to taste. A poached egg may be served in each bowl if desired.

### Kryddersild

| | |
|---|---|
| 2 lb. fresh herrings | ½ lb. sugar |
| 4 c. vinegar | ¼ lb. salt |
| Handful of peppercorns | 12 bay leaves |

Clean the herring and place in a large container with vinegar. Leave until the skin loosens and the herring become white. (This is at least

2 days). Crush the peppercorns. Remove the herring from vinegar. Place in another container in alternating layers of herring and spices. The longer it marinates before serving the better it tastes.

### *Torskerogn*

1 lb. cod's roe                    Butter or margarine
Lemon                              Salt and pepper

Wrap the roe in a piece of cheese cloth. Place in salted boiling water and cook for 20 minutes. Drain. Cool. When cold, slice and fry in butter. Serve with slices of lemon and boiled potatoes.

### *Fiskerand*

1½ lb. fillet of cod               Bread-crumbs
2 T. flour                         1 egg
2 T. margarine                     ¼ c. milk
Salt and pepper

Pass the cod fillets through a grinder twice or more. Add flour and seasoning. Pour milk in gradually, while mixing. Add a beaten egg. Grease a pudding mould and sprinkle it with bread-crumbs. Fill with the fish mixture. Place the mould in a larger pot of boiling water. Place in a moderate oven for 45 minutes. Serve with spinach and mushrooms.

### *Frikadeller*

¼ lb. beef                         3 T. margarine
¼ lb. pork                         1 onion, optional
3 T. flour                         ¼ c. milk
¼ c. water                         Salt and pepper

Pass the meat, together with an onion, through a mincer, two or more times. Add seasoning. Mix in milk and water and beat with an electric mixer for 5 minutes. Form balls with a T. and fry in margarine. Serve with potatoes.

### *Forloren And*

1 lb. pork steak, cut              Salt and pepper
12 prunes                          ¼ c. boiling water
¼ lb. apples                       4 T. margarine
1 t. sugar

Soak prunes overnight. Take out the stones. Pound pork steak, rub with margarine. Sprinkle with a mixture of salt, pepper and sugar. Place the prunes on top of steaks together with pieces of apple. Roll the steaks up and tie them with heavy thread. Fry them. When brown and crisp, add water and simmer under cover for 45 minutes. Use the meat juice for gravy.

### Rodgrod med Flode

| | |
|---|---|
| 1 lb. black currant | 1 c. cream |
| and raspberries | ½ c. almonds, blanched and |
| 2 c. water | peeled |
| ¼ lb. sugar | 3 T. corn starch |

Clean the fruit. Boil to a pulp in water. Strain. Add sugar and corn-starch. Mix cornstarch with a few spoons of juice first and then add to the rest. Pour into a bowl. Top with almonds and serve with cream on the side.

### Aeblekage

| | |
|---|---|
| 1½ lb. cooking apples | Raspberry jam |
| ¼ c. sugar | ½ c. water |
| 1 c. bread-crumbs | 4 T. margarine |
| 1 c. heavy cream | |

Clean, peel and core the apples. Boil to a pulp in water with half of the sugar. Mix bread-crumbs with the remaining sugar and fry in margarine until golden brown and crispy. Remove from fire and stir while cooking. When cold place in a bowl, alternating layers of bread-crumbs with apples and jam. Before serving, cover with whipped cream and decorate with spots of raspberry jam.

### Kromandstaerte

| | |
|---|---|
| 4 T. rum | |
| ½ lb. almonds, blanched | ½ lb. potatoes, cold boiled, |
| peeled and ground | grated |
| ¼ lb. butter | ¾ lb. sugar |
| 3 eggs, separated | Paste-like icing (see page 188) |

Do not overcook the potatoes as you have to have them firm enough for grating when cold. Whip the butter, add sugar and egg yolks, one by one, while mixing. Add potatoes, ground almonds and at last fold in gently the stiffly beaten egg-whites. Place in a greased baking dish which has been sprinkled with bread-crumbs, and bake in a moderate oven for 1 hour. Cool. Before serving cover with a rum glaze and decorate with maraschino cherries.

# ARMENIAN

Armenian cooking dates far in the past. It has inherited some of the Byzantine culinary traditions with its emphasis on vegetables, mutton and oil. The use of rice came to the Armenian kitchen from Persia with the Turks, and Armenian cooking itself later influenced the kitchens of other countries in the Balkans.

## Stuffed Leaves—Dolmas

| | |
|---|---|
| 1 c. rice, uncooked | 1 t. cinnamon |
| ½ c. parsley, chopped | Salt and pepper |
| 4 onions, chopped | Grape leaves (buy at Greek |
| 2 c. peanut oil | store) |
| ¼ c. raisins | 1 c. meat stock |
| ½ can tomato paste | 1 c. water |
| 1 t. allspice | |

If you cannot find the grape leaves, cabbage or lettuce leaves may be used as substitutes. Pour the oil into a large, shallow pan. Add onions chopped fine, and brown them. Add water and rice, and simmer over a slow fire for 15 minutes. Add all the seasonings including raisins and tomato paste and continue to cook for an additional 5 minutes. Cool. When the mixture is lukewarm, fill the grape leaves, putting 1 t. of mixture in each leaf. Roll up. Cover the bottom of a frying pan with grape, cabbage or lettuce leaves. Place the stuffed leaves, side by side in a pan. Sprinkle with broth and cover. Simmer for 1 hour. Dolmas may be served hot or cold.

## Artichokes Armenian Style

| | |
|---|---|
| 5 artichokes | 2 cloves garlic |
| 1 onion, chopped | 2 T. chopped parsley |
| Juice of 2 lemons | ½ c. olive oil |
| 1 T. sugar (brown is best) | Dash of nutmeg |
| 1 c. water | Salt and pepper |

Clean the artichokes, cut off the outer leaves and the tops. Place oil in a large pot. Let garlic simmer for two minutes. Add artichokes, onions, sugar, lemon juice, parsley and seasonings. Stew without water under cover, for 5 minutes. Add water, cover tightly, and simmer for 1 hour. Serve hot as a vegetable, or cold as appetizer.

## Piaz-Fasula ab Piaz

| | |
|---|---|
| 2 onions, chopped | Salt and pepper |
| ¼ lb. kidney beans, cooked | ¼ c. parsley, chopped |
| Juice of 1 lemon | |

Slice onions, cover with salt and let stand for 6 hours. Rinse with cold water and drain dry. Combine with chopped parsley. Add lemon and seasoning and mix with cooked kidney beans.

## Beurek

| | |
|---|---|
| 1 lb. cheese (mild) grated | ½ package or 3 oz. cream cheese |
| Paklava sheets (bought) | 2 eggs |
| 1 egg yolk | ¼ c. parsley, chopped |

Buy paklava sheets in any Greek or Armenian grocery store. Cut them in half. Prepare the cheese mixture, by combining all the ingredients and mixing well together, reserving on the side only the egg yolk. Place the paklava sheets on a baking sheet, spread the cut paklava sheet with the cheese mixture, cover with another paklava sheet. Cut into 2 inch squares. Brush the egg yolk on top of the little squares and bake in a moderately warm oven until lightly brown.

## Herissah

| | |
|---|---|
| 1 large fowl, cut up | 2½ c. barley, soaked overnight |
| Water | Butter |
| Salt and pepper | |

Boil the chicken in water to cover. Add salt and pepper. When very well done, take out the chicken, reserving the broth on the side. Bone the chicken and cut the meat into small pieces. Replace the chicken meat in the broth. Add barley and cook until the barley is well done, adding water if necessary. Stir often with a wooden spoon. When ready serve in individual bowls with a spoonful of butter in each bowl.

## Pilaff

| | |
|---|---|
| 1 lb. rice | ¼ lb. butter |
| 6 c. of beef or lamb broth | Salt and pepper |

Melt butter, add rice. Let rice absorb the butter and fry it for one minute. Add warm broth and seasoning. Stir well. Place on a moderate flame and stew under cover for 25 minutes.

## Shish Kebab

| | |
|---|---|
| 5 lb. lamb, cubed 1½ inch squares | 1 c. sherry or white wine |
| 5 large onions | Rosemary |
| Oregano | 1 c. olive oil |
| | Salt and pepper |

Marinate the meat with sliced onions, seasoning, and sherry in oil, preferably overnight. Place on skewers and broil on charcoal until crisp. If you cannot produce any open fire or a charcoal stove your broiler may serve almost the same purpose. Serve with rice pilaff.

## Harput Kufte

*Soup Stock:*

1 lb. ground meat, beef or lamb
1 c. cracked wheat
Salt and pepper
Dash of nutmeg

Beef bones
½ c. parsley, chopped
2 onions, chopped
1 can tomato paste
Salt and pepper

Mix the meat with seasoning and cracked wheat. Knead for a few minutes until the mixture is elastic. Make into balls. On the side prepare a stock by boiling beef bones with seasoning. After 1 hour of boiling add onions, parsley and tomato paste. Simmer for 25 minutes. Drop the meat balls into rapidly boiling soup. When the balls are ready they rise to the surface. The kufte are better when served in their own broth but they may be served dry.

## Misov Sempoog

1 lb. stewing lamb
1 large eggplant
3 large onions, sliced
2 c. water

Paprika
1 can tomatoes
4 T. olive oil
Salt and pepper

Brown the meat in oil. Add sliced onions, and braise with meat until tender. Cube the eggplant, and add to the meat. Stew under cover. When the eggplant seem softened add tomatoes, water and seasoning and place in a moderate oven for 45 minutes.

## Stuffed Peppers

8 peppers
1 lb. chopped lamb
2 large onions, chopped
2 T. tomato paste
½ c. rice, cooked
2 T. parsley, chopped

Dash of chili powder
Salt and pepper
2 T. fresh mint, chopped
2 T. olive oil
1 c. meat stock

Scoop out the seeds from the peppers. Mix all the ingredients for the filling. Fill the peppers and place in a baking pan. Sprinkle with olive oil. Cover the bottom of the pan with broth. Place in a moderate oven for 1 hour.

## Patlijan Hunkar

1 lb. lamb, cubed in 1 inch
    squares
2 large eggplants
1 large onion, chopped
2 T. tomato paste
½ c. rice, cooked
2 T. olive oil

Salt and pepper
2 cloves garlic, pressed
1 c. water
1 c. milk
2 T. flour
2 T. butter
½ c. grated cheese

Brown meat in oil, then add onions and fry together until lightly brown. Add tomato paste, garlic, water and the seasoning. Cook under cover for approximately 1 hour. On the side broil the eggplants over an open fire. When soft, let it cool then peel off the skin, and pass through a sieve. Separately prepare a cheese sauce by melting butter with flour, and mixing with warm milk and grated cheese. Season to taste and add mashed eggplant. Simmer together for a moment and serve with lamb fricasse.

### Imam Bayeld

| | |
|---|---|
| 2 eggplants, quartered | 1 c. olive oil |
| 3 large onions, sliced | 1 c. water |
| 2 peppers, chopped | ¼ c. parsley |
| 1 can tomatoes, drained | Salt and pepper |

Let the quartered eggplant rest in salt for 2 to 3 hours. Squeeze out the water. Wash. Make an opening in each quarter and stuff. Prepare the stuffing in the following manner: sauté the sliced onion in oil. When golden brown, add parsley, peppers, tomatoes and seasoning and simmer together for 10 minutes. Place the stuffed eggplant in a baking dish, add water to cover the bottom of the pan and bake in a moderate oven for 45 minutes.

### Armenian Zucchini

| | |
|---|---|
| 1 lb. chopped lamb | 1 T. tomato paste |
| 7 large zucchini (1½ lb. each) | 4 T. olive oil |
| 2 large onions, chopped | 1 egg |
| 3 T. parsley | Salt and pepper, paprika |
| | 1 c. broth |

Brown the onions in oil. Add meat and brown together. Add parsley, tomato paste, seasoning, well-beaten egg, while mixing vigorously. On the side clean the zucchini and cut off the ends. Slice them lengthwise, place a layer of zucchini in a baking dish, alternating with the meat mixture, until all the ingredients have been used. Pour the broth over and bake for 1 hour. Serve with rice.

### Ekmek Khadayiff

| | |
|---|---|
| 10 slices of Zwieback | 2 T. raisins (soaked in |
| 3 c. water | sweet wine) |
| Juice of 2 lemons | Whipped cream |
| 2 c. honey | 3 T. chopped blanched almonds |
| 2 T. chopped pine nuts (pignoli) | |

Pour hot water and lemon juice over Zwieback. When soft, place in a round oven-proof serving dish. Sprinkle with raisins, chopped nuts and cover with honey. Place in the oven (400°) and bake for 45 minutes. Serve with whipped cream.

## Paklava

Paklava sheets (bought)
1½ c. water
Juice of 2 lemons

1 lb. sweet butter, melted
2 c. sugar

Cook the sugar, lemon juice and water together until a consistency of honey is reached. Bake the ready-made paklava sheets in a hot oven, covering them with melted butter every 5 minutes or so, for approximately 20 minutes. When ready, pour the syrup around the edges and between cut pastry and on top. Do not let it stand long. Serve as soon as ready.

# CHINESE AND JAPANESE DISHES

Nowhere as much as in the Far Eastern countries does the art of cooking suggest some inner cultural trends and long traditions. Whoever has eaten a Chinese or Japanese meal can easily guess the patient care and the discriminating refinement spent in the preparation of its several courses. A very old civilization and gentle wisdom may be sensed through the varied and colourful menus of a Chinese or Japanese dinner.

## Egg Foo Yung

| | |
|---|---|
| ¼ c. bacon, chopped | 1 T. cornstarch |
| 1 large onion, chopped | 2 T. water juice from bean |
| ¼ c. cooked meat, chopped | sprouts |
| 6 eggs, well beaten | 5 T. corn oil |
| ¼ c. celery, chopped | 2 T. Soya sauce |
| 1 c. bean sprouts | 2 t. sugar |

Fry for one minute, in oil, celery and onion. Add soya sauce and sugar and simmer for a moment. Add the meat and simmer for 5 minutes. On the side prepare well beaten eggs and fry them in hot oil in a shallow skillet, on both sides, folding in the meat and vegetables. Prepare a sauce with the reserved bean sprout water and corn starch, and cook it in the skillet, in which the onions were fried. Serve together with the Egg Foo Yung.

## Yuen Tsi

| | |
|---|---|
| 1 onion | ¼ c. soya bean sauce |
| 1 carrot | 2 green peppers |
| 5 radishes | Salt and pepper |
| 1 lb. raw pork roast (fat) | Water |
| ¼ c. rice flour | 1 c. spinach, chopped |

Chop the onion, carrot, peppers and radishes and stew with the meat adding water gradually. Remove the meat and cut up fine. Mix with spinach and rice flour. Season, adding soya sauce. With a spoon form balls and drop them into boiling soup in which the meat has been cooked. Simmer for 5 minutes.

## Fried Rice

| | |
|---|---|
| 2 c. long grain rice | 2 green peppers |
| 5-6 lb. pork tenderloin | 4 eggs, beaten |
| Peanut oil | 3 large onions |
| ¼ c. soya bean sauce | |

Cook the rice in cold, salted water until just tender. Drain and dry in a warm oven. Cut pork into small pieces and brown rapidly in oil. Remove the meat. Cut onion and peppers into oil and simmer under cover until tender. Remove and mix together with the meat. Add some more oil to the skillet and cook beaten eggs. When firm add to the meat mixture. Warm up rice in the skillet (adding more oil if necessary). Mix the meat and rice, add soya sauce and serve immediately.

## Har-Chow-Fon

| | |
|---|---|
| 1 lb. raw shrimps | 4 c. boiled rice |
| 2 large onions, cut | 1 T. sugar |
| 1 can mushrooms | 5 T. soya sauce |
| 3 eggs | 4 T. peanut oil |
| Salt and pepper | |

Cook beaten eggs in oil until firm. Shred. Set aside. Shell the shrimps.

Simmer them with onion and mushroom for 5 minutes. Add cooked rice and shredded eggs. Mix in soya and sugar and serve hot.

### Roast Spare Ribs

| | |
|---|---|
| 2 lb. pork spare ribs | 1 c. chicken broth |
| 3 T. soya bean sauce | 3 T. honey |
| 3 T. brown sugar | Salt and pepper |

Marinate the spare ribs in the mixture of soya, honey, sugar and seasoning for an hour. Remove from this sauce and place on a rack in a large pan in a moderate oven for 2 hours. Baste with chicken broth. Serve with boiled rice.

### Chicken Wings and Red Sauce

| | |
|---|---|
| 2 T. cornstarch | 2 c. chicken broth |
| 4 T. peanut oil | $\frac{1}{2}$ c. scallions |
| 2 cloves garlic | 1 c. tomato sauce |
| Salt and pepper | 4 T. soya sauce |
| 2 T. cornstarch | 2 lbs. chicken wings |

Cook garlic in oil. Season the chicken wings and fry in oil on both sides over a high flame. Add chicken broth and simmer under cover until tender. Add tomato sauce and scallions. Mix thoroughly. Finally add soya sauce and cornstarch while stirring. When sauce thickens serve with rice.

### Loh Pai Kwut

| | |
|---|---|
| 2 lb. pork shoulder, boned | *Sweet Sour Sauce:* |
| 2 c. water | 4 T. sugar |
| Salt and pepper | 4 T. cornstarch |
| 4 T. soya bean sauce | 4 T. wine vinegar |
| | $\frac{1}{2}$ c. pineapple juice |
| | 1 can pineapple chunks |
| | Meat stock from pork |

Cube meat. Put in a pot, add water to cover. Season and sprinkle with soya sauce. Bring to a rapid boil. Simmer for 1 hour. Set aside meat broth. Prepare the sweet and sour sauce by blending pineapple juice with sugar and vinegar. Slowly mix in cornstarch and gradually add meat broth. Heat until sauce thickens. Add pineapple and meat. Serve hot with rice.

### Moo-Goo-Ngow

| | |
|---|---|
| 1 lb. beef steak, cut in long pieces | 2 T. soya sauce |
| 1 large onion, cut | 3 T. cornstarch |
| 4 T. peanut oil | 1 c. meat stock |
| Salt and pepper | 1 lb. large mushrooms |
| Garlic | Water |

Fry garlic in oil. When brown remove it. Add meat and onion. Season and brown. Add meat stock and mushrooms. Cook under cover for 10 minutes. Dilute cornstarch with soya and some water to make a thin paste. Mix into the boiling meat, stirring constantly until it thickens. Serve at once with boiled rice.

### *Don-Far-Tong*

| | |
|---|---|
| 5 c. chicken broth | Salt and pepper |
| 4 celery stalks, chopped | Soya bean sauce |
| 1 onion, chopped | 1 c. watercress or spinach |
| 3 eggs | |

Cook celery and onion in chicken broth just for a minute. Stir in beaten eggs and season. Add soya bean sauce and finally watercress and bring to the boil together, serving piping hot.

## Almond Cakes

2 c. flour
½ c. sugar
1 t. baking powder
¼ c. lard
2 eggs

2 T. water
1 t. almond extract
1 egg white
Blanched almonds

Sift together all the dry ingredients. Mix in softened lard. Beat in the eggs one by one. Add water and almond extract. Knead well together. Roll out not too thin, cut with a glass. Press almonds in centre of each cookie. Place on a cookie sheet. Brush with egg white and bake in a moderate oven for 30 minutes or until light brown.

## Walnut Pudding

2 c. walnuts
1 c. brown sugar

3 c. water
1 c. rice flour

Grind the nuts several times. Boil 2 c. of water and then add the nuts and cook for 20 minutes. Cool and pass through a vegetable strainer. Mix with sugar, rice flour and the remaining water. Put in the top of a double boiler and cook for 5 minutes mixing constantly Serve immediately.

## Benne Cookies

¾ c. butter
1 c. brown sugar
1 c. flour

½ c. benne
2 eggs
¼ t. baking powder

Cream until smooth, butter, (sweet preferably), with sugar and mix in eggs one by one. When smooth add flour and baking powder. Finally add toasted benne. Grease a baking sheet and cover with wax paper. Drop the dough with a spoon on the wax paper and bake in a moderate oven for about 10 minutes.

## Japanese Dishes

### Cucumber with Lobster

4 cucumbers
1 can lobster meat
2 T. soya sauce
2 T. vinegar

1 t. sugar
Salt and pepper
Scallions, optional

Slice cucumber fine. Set aside with salt. Drain all the water, combine with chopped lobster meat and add dressing. Prepare dressing by mixing soya sauce with vinegar and sugar. Sliced scallions are optional.

## *Tempora*

| | |
|---|---|
| 2 lb. shrimps | Water |
| 3 T. flour | 2 lb. carrots, sliced lengthwise |
| 3 eggs | Salt and pepper |
| 2 T. vinegar | 4 c. corn oil |
| 3 T. soya sauce | |

Clean and shell the shrimps. Make batter out of flour and eggs, add water, vinegar and Soya sauce to make a thin batter. Cut very thin strips out of carrots. Season shrimps and carrots. Heat your oil. In preparing tempora the difficulty lies certainly in attaining the right temperature of oil. You can test your oil with a drop of the batter— it should float just below the surface of the boiling oil, if it falls down it means that the oil is too cold, if it stays on the surface you will soon realize that it is too warm as it will turn black. . . . When you have attained the right temperature of oil, the rest of the task will be easy, you just fry the shrimps and carrots, after having rolled them in batter. Serve hot or cold.

## *Sukiiaki*

| | |
|---|---|
| 2 lb. beef, cut in strips | 1 lb. bean cake, diced |
| 6 large onions, sliced | 1 lb. Chinese mushrooms |
| 2 lb. Chinese cabbage, diced | 1 lb. bird nests |
| 3 bunches scallions, cut | Soya sauce |
| Oil | Sugar |
| Salt | Rice |

Buy all your supplies in a Japanese or Chinese grocery. Slice the meat in 1½ x 4 inch strips. Soak the mushrooms in water. Simmer onions and scallions in oil, under cover. Drain mushrooms, cook with onions, also under cover. Add cabbage and meat. Season with Soya sauce and sugar to taste. Mix in bean cake. On the side cook bird nests in salted water, when soft, drain and combine with the meat. The whole procedure of preparation of sukiiaki should take place before the actual cooking. Sukiiaki should be prepared at the dinner table on a hot plate, if you want to follow the Japanese customs closely, or in the kitchen, but you should allow the minimum cooking time. Instead of bread, serve pressed sea weeds. The sea weeds are eaten sprinkled with Soya sauce. If you want to serve wine with your Japanese dinner, Saki, mind you, not chilled, but warmed up, would be appropriate. Your rice should be well done, and served in separate bowls.

### *Curry for 12—Philippine East Indian Style*

| | |
|---|---|
| 2 chickens, boiled and boned | ¼ c. flour |
| 2 lb. lobster | 4-6 t. curry powder |
| 2 lb. shrimp | Onion salt |
| ¼ lb. butter | Thyme |
| ½ pt. coffee cream | Paprika |
| 3 lb. apples | 4-6 t. salt |
| 1 bunch celery | Pepper |
| 2 lb. onions | Worcestershire sauce |
| Milk of one fresh coconut | Dry mustard |
| 2 lb. mushrooms | ½ c. white wine |

Cut celery, onions and apples and cook slowly in butter with mushrooms until slightly soft. In another pan make a sauce by skimming fat from chicken stock, adding flour and chicken stock, lobster stock, wine, and seasonings. Let stand at least several hours before re-heating and adding fish and meat, add cream just before serving so that flavours may be blended. Serve over steamed rice.

### *Suggested Condiments*

| | |
|---|---|
| Ginger | Sliced bananas |
| Coconut freshly grated | Chutney |
| French fried onions | Papaya |
| Peanuts | Mango |

# ALPHABETICAL CONTENTS
# OF CHAPTERS

## APPETIZERS

## APPETIZERS—*continued*

# SOUPS

# MEAT

## HOT SAUCES

## COLD SAUCES

## SWEET SAUCES

## DAIRY DISHES

# MUSHROOMS

# VEGETABLES

# SALADS

# DESSERTS

## COOKIES

## DRINKS, LIQUEURS AND PRESERVES

# BREAD

# MISCELLANEOUS

# INDEX

# POLISH COOKBOOKS FROM HIPPOCRENE

**The Polish Country Kitchen Cookbook**
*Sophie Hodorowicz Knab*
From top-selling author Sophie Hodorowicz Knab comes a new book that combines recipes for favorite Polish foods with the history and cultural traditions that created them. Arranged according to the cycle of seasons, this cookbook explores life in the Polish countryside through the year. *The Polish Country Kitchen Cookbook* gives its readers priceless historical information such as the type of utensils used in Poland at the turn of the century, the meaning behind the Pascal butter lamb, and many other insightful answers to common questions asked by descendants of Polish immigrants.

The over 100 easy-to-follow recipes are all adapted for the modern North American kitchen. Lovely illustrations and pearls of practical wisdom ("Household Hints") from the old Polish kitchen marvelously complement this book.
*307 pages • 6 x 9 • b&w photographs and illustrations • $24.95hc • 0-7818-0882-0 • (25)*

**Polish Heritage Cookery, Illustrated Edition**
*Robert and Maria Strybel*
Over 2,200 authentic recipes!
Entire chapters on dumplings, potato dishes, sausage-making, babkas and more!
American weights and measures
Modern shortcuts and substitutes for health-conscious dining
Each recipe indexed in English and Polish

"An encyclopedia of Polish cookery and a wonderful thing to have!" —Julia Child, *Good Morning America*

"Polish Heritage Cookery is the best [Polish} cookbook printed in English on the market. It is well-organized, informative, interlaced with historical background on Polish foods and eating habits, with easy-to-follow recipes readily prepared in American kitchens and, above all, its fun to read."

—*Polish American Cultural Network*
*915 pages • 6 x 9 • 16 pages color photographs • over 2,200 recipes •$39.95hc • 0-7818-0558-9 • W • (658)*

## Poland's Gourmet Cuisine

*Bernard Lussiana and Mary Pininska*
*Photography by Jaroslaw Madejski*

Here is Poland's cuisine as you've never seen it before! Bernard Lussiana, Executive Chef of Warsaw's celebrated Hotel Bristol, has taken traditional Polish dishes, like pierogi, golabki and flaki, and re-interpreted them in fresh, sophisticated and delicious new ways. Inspired by the beauty and spirit of the nation's lakes, rivers and plains, Lussiana takes bold new culinary initiatives with Poland's wealth of indigenous ingredients like buckwheat, poppyseeds, carp, pike, beetroot, suckling pig, wild boar, horseradish and dill, creating not only new dishes, but paving the way for a new era in Polish culinary history. Among the 52 recipes included are such exquisite offerings as "Delicate stew of perch fillet, chanterelles and ceps flavored with marjoram," "Barley consommé served with quenelles of smoked game," "Pan-fried fillet of lamb served with a juice of fresh coriander and saffron kasza," and "Iced parfait flavored with zbozowa coffee."

Along with stunning, full-color food photographs of every recipe, are captivating photographs of the beautiful Polish countryside, and fragments of some of Poland's most evocative poetry. The recipes are provided in a step-by-step format and all adapted for the North American kitchen. A mingling of the senses—visual, artistic, literary, sensual and culinary—this book unfolds to reveal a dream of Poland rarely glimpsed.

*143 pages • 9¼ x 11¼ • color photographs throughout • $35.00hc • 0-7818-0790-5 • (98)*

**The Best of Polish Cooking, Expanded Edition**
*Karen West*
*Now updated with a new chapter on Light Polish Fare!*
"Ethnic cuisine at its best."—*The Midwest Book Review*
First published in 1983, this classic resource for Polish cuisine
has been a favorite with home chefs for many years. The new
edition includes a chapter on Light Polish Fare with ingenious
tips for reducing fat, calories and cholesterol, without compro-
mising the flavor of fine Polish cuisine. Fragrant herbal rubs
and vinegars add panache without calories. Alternatives and
conversion tables for butter, sour cream and milk will help
readers lighten other recipes as well.

In an easy-to-use menu format, the author arranges comple-
mentary and harmonious foods together—all organized in sea-
sonal cycles. Inside are recipes for Braised Spring Lamb with
Cabbage, Frosty Artichoke Salad, Apple Raisin Cake, and
Hunter's Stew. The new Light Polish Fare chapter includes
low-fat recipes for treats like Roasted Garlic and Mushroom
Soup and Twelve-Fruit Brandied Compote.
*248 pages • 5½ x 8¼ • $9.95pb • 0-7818-0826-X • (274)*

**A Treasury of Polish Cuisine:**
**Traditional Recipes in Polish and English**
*Maria de Gorgey*
Polish cuisine is noted for its hearty and satisfying offerings,
and this charming bilingual cookbook brings the best of tradi-
tional Polish cooking to your table—with recipes in Polish
and English! Among the chapters included are Soups and
Appetizers, Main Courses, Desserts, and 2 special holiday
chapters—one devoted to "Wigilia," the festive Polish
Christmas Eve Dinner, and one devoted to "Wielkanoc," the
Polish Easter Luncheon.
*148 pages • 5 x 7 • 0-7818-0738-7 • $11.95hc • (151)*

**Old Polish Traditions in the Kitchen and at the Table**
A cookbook and history of Polish culinary customs. Short
essays cover subjects like Polish hospitality, holiday traditions, even the exalted status of the mushroom. The recipes
are traditional family fare.
*304 pages • 6 x 9 • 0-7818-0488-4 • $11.95pb • (546)*

**The Art of Lithuanian Cooking**
Maria Gieysztor de Gorgey
This volume of over 150 authentic Lithuanian recipes includes
such classic favorites as Fresh Cucumber Soup, Lithuanian
Meat Pockets, Hunter's Stew, Potato Zeppelins, as well as del-
icacies like Homemade Honey Liqueur and Easter Gypsy
Cake. The author's introduction and easy step-by-step instructions ensure that even novice cooks can create authentic, delicious Lithuanian recipes.
*230 pages • 5½ x 8½ • 0-7818-0899-5 • $12.95hc • (100)*

---

All prices subject to change without prior notice. **To purchase
Hippocrene Books** contact your local bookstore, visit
www.hippocrenebooks.com, call (718) 454-2366, or write to:
HIPPOCRENE BOOKS, 171 Madison Avenue, New York,
NY 10016. Please enclose check or money order, adding
$5.00 shipping (UPS) for the first book and $.50 for each
additional book.

Printed in the USA
CPSIA information can be obtained
at www.ICGtesting.com
JSHW012019140824
68134JS00033B/2782